Movies

on

Trial

ALSO BY ANTHONY CHASE

Law and History

Movies
on
Trial

The Legal System
on the Silver Screen

Anthony Chase

The New Press
New York

Published in the United States by The New Press, New York, 2002
Distributed by W. W. Norton & Company, Inc., New York

LIBRARY OF CONGRESS CATALOGING-IN-PUBLICATION DATA

Chase, Anthony, 1948–
    Movies on trial : the legal system on the silver screen / Anthony Chase.
    p.   cm.
    ISBN 1-56584-700-8 (hc.)
    1. Justice, Administration of, in motion pictures.   2. Lawyers in motion
pictures.   I. Title.

PN1995.9.J8 C49 2002
791.43'655—dc21

2001052219

The New Press was established in 1990 as a not-for-profit alternative to the large,
commercial publishing houses currently dominating the book publishing industry.
The New Press operates in the public interest rather than for private gain,
and is committed to publishing, in innovative ways, works of educational, cultural,
and community value that are often deemed insufficiently profitable.

The New Press
450 West 41st Street, 6th floor
New York, NY 10036

www.thenewpress.com

Printed in the United States of America

2   4   6   8   10   9   7   5   3   1

TO CHRISTOPHER

Contents

Acknowledgments

I WOULD LIKE to take this opportunity to express my appreciation to all those over the years who have encouraged my interest in motion pictures and supported my film writing: organizers of the Faunce House foreign film program at Brown University, Ellen Whitman at *Rosebud*, Russell Campbell at *The Velvet Light Trap*, the editors of the *Daily Cardinal* in Madison; and to (more recently) Rick Abel, Milner Ball, Max Bloomfield, Jim Elkins, and antiquarian bookseller par excellence, Rob Hittel. I would also like to thank my students and colleagues at NSU Law Center in south Florida, especially including professors resident in the notorious West Wing (Cathy Arcabascio, Kathy Cerminara, Mike Dale, Mike Flynn, and Joel Mintz). Marc Galanter and Susan Silbey kindly provided me with a chance to present some of my ideas on tort films to a panel at the 1999 annual meeting of the Law & Society Association in Chicago, Illinois. Above all, however, I would like to thank Sarah Fan of The New Press for her intellect, common sense, aesthetic sensibility, and wit. Every writer should be so fortunate in finding an editor. And the skillful production editing of Maury Botton and copy editing of Andrew Frisardi are much appreciated.

I would also like to acknowledge a few publications which helped lead the way to this book. An earlier version of chapter two, section six, appeared in 4 *Left History* 71 (1996), and a similar trial run for some of the material in chapter three, section four, appeared as part of the "Film & the Law Symposium" in 22 *Oklahoma City University Law Review* 167 (1997). An initial though different version of chapter four was in the 1999 *Law Review of Michigan State University-Detroit College of Law* 945 (1999), and of chapter five in 24 *Legal Studies Forum* 559 (2000). An earlier version of chapter six, section five, was in 24 *Legal Studies Forum* 269 (2000), and some of the ideas in chapter seven, section four, were introduced to readers in 9 *Cardozo Studies in Law & Literature* 107 (1997). Every effort has been made to attribute the source of any quotation used in this book, both initially in the text itself and subsequently in the bibliographic notes at the end. I have frequently located helpful commentaries or filmographic information on particular films at the Internet Movie Database (www.imdb.com) to which I refer those who wish to read the full text of reviews upon which I have relied, or in fact, anyone interested in doing comprehensive film research.

Introduction

ALONG WITH FILMMAKERS like D. W. Griffith and F. W. Murnau, Charlie Chaplin and Abel Gance, John Ford and Akira Kurosawa, Orson Welles and Roberto Rossellini, French new wave director Jean-Luc Godard has left an important mark on the historical development of motion pictures. In an interview with the editors of *Cahiers du Cinema* granted by the avant-garde critic-turned-director shortly after the release of *La Chinoise* (1967), Godard recounted an amusing anecdote. He had been reading an article in a film magazine and said to himself that the article's author should write something about Ingmar Bergman's striking but difficult film, *Persona* (1966). The guy would be just terrific, thought Godard. The only problem, he told his interviewers, was that the article he had been reading was *supposed to be about* Persona!

Godard is not the only reader of film books and essays to discover that a promising critical text somehow never managed to get around to actually talking about the movies it was supposed to address. Someday someone will figure out why so many film scholars and theorists are able to successfully write so little about *film*.

For the time being, however, rest assured that in *Movies on Trial*, movies are in the book, not just in the title. Films themselves are discussed here, and there are a lot of them. Many of the motion pictures readers expect to be here *are* here. But there are also a number of films included which one might not necessarily anticipate: *The General, Revolution, Johnny Tremain, Shakedown, Fight Club, Silkwood, The Rise to Power of Louis XIV, Three Kings, Heart of Glass,* and *Wall Street,* just to name a few. Some films included may be unexpected because they are less well known or perhaps because they are used primarily to help define the boundary lines which separate film genres. And some unlikely pictures have a particularly important "legal scene" or point to make about law, even though law is not their main subject.

The surprises are mostly a consequence of how I define the legal genre itself. Although "trial films" may represent for many the backbone of the legal movie genre, they hardly exhaust it. Since I focus on this issue in the text, I will not explore it further here. But it should be stated up front that this book defines law as a moral and political system, not just a regime of rules. Analysis therefore covers not just trial films but the entire legal system on the silver screen. Just as law is more than litigation, legal movies are more than courtroom drama.

In one sense, however, this book remains rather traditional in approach—as lawyers, law professors, and their students would surely attest. I have used as a structuring device the legal curriculum or professional taxonomy employed by attorneys in practice. With the exception of opening and closing chapters, our discussion of legal films is organized around independent doctrinal areas common to legal work: constitutional law, criminal law, tort law, international law, and comparative law, with a nod to the law of property. Organizational schemes like this one, points out Stanford Law School professor Thomas C. Grey, when employed "in elementary pedagogy and in indexing legal materials, seem relatively trivial." Nevertheless, Grey says, such categorical schemes "channel the attention of those who use them, structuring experience into the focal and the peripheral" and, Grey continues, with respect to law, this "classical ordering [has been left] to half-survive in the backs of lawyers' minds and the front of the law school curriculum, where it can shape our thinking through its unspoken judgments. . . ." Fidelity to this classical ordering scheme, even in a book about film, no doubt betrays the author's own intellectual predisposition if not professional prejudice.

The first chapter confronts two issues head on. The first: Where do films tell us (or show us) that law is to be found? However tricky applying rules to facts may be, you cannot apply a rule until you find one. The second: How does cinema—a powerfully visual form of art—unmask or reveal the true relationship between law and justice, between equality and the legal system? The inability of law embodied entirely in legal language to actually picture justice turns out to have real consequences for the relationship between law in the books and law on the screen. This initial chapter is designed to make the case for a cinematic jurisprudence—a way of looking at law through the lens of the camera that projects an alternative view of legality, one every bit as likely to undermine ruling ideas about fairness and formal legal equality as it is to reinforce them.

The second through sixth chapters, as indicated above, deal with relatively independent areas of legal doctrine and experience. The second chapter, for example, addresses some of the constitutional foundations of the American legal system. Given the shortage of movies dealing with constitution-making and interpretation—or even films showing appellate courts deciding dramatic constitutional issues—an historical approach is taken to films of America in revolution and to the "government of laws and not men" on behalf of which liberal revolutions are fought. My emphasis upon historical movies in this chapter (*America, Revolution, The Patriot, Johnny Tremain*, Disney's *Ben & Me*) also reflects the influence on an American civic faith in constitutionalism exerted by historical background images—what Frances FitzGerald once called "white noise." Other approaches to the problematic subcategory of constitutional cinema are sketched as well.

The third and fourth chapters deal with what are perhaps the two most visible departments of American law, at least as it is portrayed on the silver screen: criminal law and the civil law of tort. "Tort" is often defined simply as liability for non-criminal wrongs, so these two chapters belong back to back. The criminal law chapter organizes the field into crime control films, due process films, a third (and emerging) category which attempts to get beyond the familiar juxtaposition of prosecution and defense—public safety versus rights of the criminally accused—and, finally, legal conspiracy thrillers. Not surprisingly, *Dirty Harry, True Believer, The Gingerbread Man, Touch of Evil, Traffic, All the President's Men, The Pelican Brief,* and *Extreme Measures* are among the films considered.

While the criminal law chapter centers upon a dialectical tension existing between due process and crime control movies, the civil law (torts) chapter is shaped by a contrast between what I call the "master discourse of tort cinema" (*The Verdict, A Civil Action, Philadelphia, The Rainmaker*) and more recent efforts to develop or transcend that discourse (*The Sweet Hereafter, Civil Action, Erin Brockovich*).

The fifth chapter initiates a discussion of international law cinema. Crucial notions within international legal theory and practice (sovereignty, idealism, consensus) are explored through an examination of *A Man For All Seasons, The Rise to Power of Louis XIV, Wilson, Three Kings*—even *X-Men* and *Enemy at the Gates* are worked into the discussion. A detour is taken into the parallel field of international relations cinema in order to see what might be borrowed for use in constructing both the international legal genre and its critique.

The sixth chapter is devoted to comparative law and politics on film. While every national legal system can be studied in terms of specific doctrinal fields (for example: criminal, tort, property, contract, constitutional law, or their equivalents in different legal cultures), a full range of national legal systems can be set side by side and a single doctrinal level may be traced horizontally across this array of state legal structures: criminal law in common law and civil law countries, the law of agreements (contract) in industrial and agricultural societies, property law in Africa, Europe, and Asia, and so forth. This ambitious chapter focuses on European constitutionalism and looks closely at the legal and political reflection of modern German history in film (*Heart of Glass, Judgment at Nuremberg, The Marriage of Maria Braun*). A brief look at films of historical reconstruction made by Italian director Roberto Rossellini (*The Rise to Power of Louis XIV, Italy: Year One*) prefaces this chapter while anticipating the discussion of "realism" (or realist film criticism) in the concluding chapter.

The seventh chapter ties together, in a systematic way, many themes implicit in the previous chapters. While this is, to be sure, the book's predominantly "theoretical" chapter, it sticks closely to analysis of particular movies and does not stray into abstraction for its own sake. This concluding chapter explores, in sequence, issues relating to the relationship between popular and elite art, social theory and cultural production, the definition and parameters of cinema's legal genre, and the peculiar attraction of "realism" to both enthusiasts and skeptics in the small world of writing about law and lawyers on film. Thus the chapters which open and close this book are modestly theoretical bookends supporting the more discreetly doctrinal and down-to-earth chapters in between.

This is not the first book titled *Movies on Trial*. In 1936, the Macmillan Company in New York published *The Movies on Trial: The Views and Opinions of Outstanding Personalities Anent Screen Entertainment Past and Present*. The book was compiled and edited by William J. Perlman of the Cinema Research Bureau in Hollywood, California and reflected the social and cultural values and concerns of its day, the tensions and fears of a world in turmoil. From within the universe of that particular historical moment, *Movies on Trial* sought to referee the debate raging over what had become the nation's most popular art: motion pictures. According to the book's editor, seventy million Americans went to the movies every week. Civic and religious leaders, "alarmed by the films' exploitation of indecency," called upon Americans to boycott motion pictures until, writes Perlman, "the screen had been made safe for the 'family.'" Facing the greatest crisis in their history (which, at that point, spanned all of about eight years) talking pictures were under attack from "the pulpit, from the rostrum, from the floors of [legislative] chambers" and, Perlman continues, across the land "accusers pointed menacing fingers at Hollywood."

They still do.

In late July 2001, a brutally hot summer dragged on in the nation's capital. Jack Valenti, President and CEO of the Motion Picture Association of America, went to Washington to testify before the U.S. Senate Governmental Affairs Committee on behalf of film industry self-regulation. Valenti, himself an architect of the industry's movie-rating system, stated that while there "will always be disagreements about the rating of a specific film," industry self-regulation was far more desirable than heavy-handed governmental interference or, worse, control. If there are "errors in some ratings," Valenti told the senators, "it is a matter of a judgment call, not an exile of integrity." He added, with a rhetorical flourish, that those who apply the rating system to movies are condemned, just like "social scientists [and] Wall Street forecasters," to suffer the hazards of subjectivity, using an evaluation process unavoidably "barren of Euclidian precision."

If Perlman's *Movies on Trial* was, in part, a response to the introduction of a National Censorship Bill during the New Deal Congress, Valenti's testimony before a Senate Committee was partially a response to the Media Marketing Accountability Act of 2001—legislation which, if adopted into law, would require the Federal Trade Commission to "specify a set of guidelines for movie ratings and marketing, and be empowered to levy heavy fines against producers whose rated films violate broad, subjective guidelines." Better to leave subjectivity in the nimble hands of business (and professional movie raters) than in the hands of a ham-fisted Big Brother. The proposed film industry regulatory legislation, said Valenti—sounding like he had just come from the premiere of *Jurassic Park III*—"treads heavily on the spine of the U.S. Constitution." Valenti may well have seen some of the films which Depression-era proponents of moral rearmament, including a few contributors to *Movies on Trial*, feared were corrupting America's children. Who knows how some of those movies may have shaped Valenti's fragile early moral development?

Of course, much is different today. American social institutions and the free-market economy seem less open to criticism—or at least there seems to be much less of it than there was in the 1930s. As legal historian Maxwell Bloomfield reminds us, during the turbulent Depression decade, even a lawyer and civil libertarian like Morris L. Ernst could call for reconsideration of "our present wasteful theory of checks and balances." New Deal–era social experimentation and ideological diversity were eventually replaced, by century's end, with a sense of political exhaustion, if not complacency. If contrary to popular retrospection, fascism's defeat in the Second World War was never a foregone conclusion (as Mark Mazower persuasively argues in *Dark Continent: Europe's Twentieth Century*), then communism's disappearing act certainly provided a late-century surprise. "What remains of Marxism, 'the unsurpassable philosophy of our time' [Sartre]?" asked Cornelius Castoriadis in 1990. "Upon what map, with what magnifying glass, will one now discover the 'new continent of historical materialism,' in what antique shop will one purchase the scissors to make the 'epistemological break' [Althusser]?"

But if much has changed, culture wars over the movies continue unabated. This *Movies on Trial*—published almost seventy years after Perlman's—is, in part, a contribution to that contest, to the ongoing debate about the nature and impact of motion pictures as a public art form. Specifically, this book puts movies on trials (and movies about all aspects of the legal system) *on trial*, entering many verdicts along the way, even when such judgments inescapably share the kind of subjectivity attributed by Jack Valenti to social scientists, Wall Street forecasters, and movie appraisers. My book shares with Perlman's a central focus on how motion pictures fit into our history, our politics, and especially here, our legal values and assumptions.

Six weeks after his testimony before the Senate committee debating new regulations for Hollywood, Jack Valenti contacted the major studio heads to warn them of new threats to the motion picture industry. This time, however, the threats came not from legislators, government bureaucrats, or charismatic Christian preachers and their politically conservative television audience. On the contrary, it was not Washington's attack on Hollywood but rather a terrorist assault on Washington (and New York) which caused U.S. Attorney General John Ashcroft to personally warn Valenti of the looming danger: The FBI believed major movie studios in Los Angeles could become the next terrorist target.

In August 2001, Ronald Brownstein reported in *Premiere: The Internet Movie Magazine* that the American motion picture industry had not had to endure such sharp public criticism since the days of HUAC investigations and the Hollywood blacklist. Only a month later, Paul Bond could write in *The Hollywood Reporter* that movie-industry insiders believed terrorist threats relayed by the attorney general were directed against "a major film studio because American values and culture—anathema to fundamentalist Islamic terrorists—are distributed throughout the world via Hollywood movies." So was Hollywood anti-American, a cultural fifth column, or an authentic representative of national life and character?

One of the best films of 2001, John Herzfeld's remorselessly violent and cruel *15 Minutes,* was generally greeted by movie critics with disdain. Reviewers typically claimed Herzfeld had unwisely pushed his satiric portrait of America over the edge. Or they claimed the picture misfired because of its message, both heavy-handed and trite: the power of mass media and the celebrity industry dangerously jeopardize a fragile legal system, and even our basic notions of civility. Andy Warhol's line about everyone's right to fifteen minutes of fame was clever when *he* said it, implied the critics, but not any more—pop art is over.

However, Herzfeld's scenarios may not seem so exaggerated when compared with Attorney General John Ashcroft's testimony before Congress in late 2001 in defense of employing special military tribunals to prosecute terrorists: "When we come upon those responsible in Afghanistan," Ashcroft asked legislators, "are we supposed to read them Miranda rights, hire a flamboyant defense lawyer, bring them back to the United States, [and] create a new cable network of Osama TV?" Ashcroft's political soul mates might well censor films like *15 Minutes* (if Jack Valenti would only let them), and yet the nightmare scenario Aschcroft wanted Congress to take seriously is virtually indistinguishable from the best sequences in Herzfeld's not-so-surreal motion picture.

Whether or not recruited for service in the culture wars, the movies continue to stimulate animated discussion. One of the most popular approaches to thinking and writing about film is called the auteur theory. It is based, argues Raymond Durgnat, on the "assumption that most films can be interpreted in terms of their directors' artistic personality just as intensively as a novel can be interpreted in terms of its authors'." The auteur theory is fun and frequently quite useful in interpreting motion pictures, especially if they can be understood as an expression of a particular director's visual style and moral or political perspective over an entire career in filmmaking. But the reason I generally refer to films in this book, at least the first time each is mentioned, in immediate association with their director's name is less because of any commitment on my part to the principles of auteur theory than because doing so provides a handy literary device for generating variety in the way films are referred to in the text; it is a descriptive handle which helps avoid repetition.

Durgnat suggests that the auteur theory is "obviously true" with regard to directors like Carl Dreyer and Robert Bresson. The real argument, he claims, is over American directors making pictures within the studio system. Much of the controversy, according to Durgnat, "has centered on the question of how far, if at all, such an approach is relevant or adequate to Hollywood directors." In this book Hugh Hudson and Don Siegel, Sidney Lumet and Steven Soderbergh, Alan J. Pakula and Stanley Kramer, are treated as authors of their films in the same way as Orson Welles and Jean Renoir, Werner Herzog and Rainer Fassbinder. But they are thus regarded for the sake of convenience rather than on behalf of an iron discipline imposed by the rules of auteur theory.

Finally, I would like to underscore the most important thing about this book: It tries to think through the cultural and political issues that law has always raised everywhere, here in terms of a particular visual culture: the independent discourse and perspective of motion pictures. One of the first issues we track, for example, is how and why our most familiar symbol of justice became blindfolded in popular representation about four or five centuries ago. In 1987, law professors Dennis Curtis and Judith Resnik published an article in the *Yale Law Journal* titled "Images of Justice." They do a marvelous job of tracing the iconographic history of Justitia and even include, in passing, one sentence about the procedural "blindfolding" of juries—a bit of legal history from which I extract rather a lot in this book.

But what is so disconcerting about the Curtis and Resnik essay is its conclusion. The authors ask whether we still have a need or use today for images of justice. "Abstraction has shown us what kind of painting and sculpture can be created when the need for representation is fulfilled by other media," they observe. One way of responding to this situation is to simply dismiss the idea that justice—or our conception of what justice means—can still, in part, be visually constructed. "One might be tempted to claim that iconography is dead. . . ."

Immediately refusing this temptation, they assert on the contrary that "sovereigns continue to have use for the deployment of images." Curtis and Resnik illustrate this key notion by devoting several paragraphs to the Statue of Liberty, the American flag, the Great Seal, and Smokey Bear. The flag in particular continues to have enormous symbolic significance and carries a powerful ideological payload. But what happened to the "other media" to which Curtis and Resnik refer as having already monopolized, at the expense of painting and sculpture, our need for representations of law and its main aim?

"The idea of justice," the professors contend, "exists not only on the pages of books, but also, on a deeper level, in present-day psyches." So how, exactly, are these shared images of justice produced and consumed? What source of visual imagery, it must be asked, rules the psyche as completely as cinema?

Movies oddly seem almost invisible to the pioneering authors of "Images of Justice." That will not be the case here.

Chapter 1

Legal Visibility:
Finding and Looking at Law

MOST AMERICAN JUDGES wear traditional black robes. British barristers still wear wigs. The law is long on etiquette. Form and process are so frequently linked in the construction of legal meaning that the phrase "procedural formality" rolls off the tongue. Examples are easy to identify. Consider Howard Hawks's Western masterpiece, *El Dorado* (1966). Holed up inside the local jail, just as in *Rio Bravo* (1959), and gesturing toward the character played by a youthful James Caan, John Wayne says, "Mississippi, you and I'll have a look around." Arthur Hunnicutt interjects, "If'n you're gonna do that, here's a couple of badges. Raise your right hand," he says, adding, "I forget the words but you better say 'I do.'" Wayne and Caan say in unison, designated hands raised: "I do." Hunnicutt smiles, making it official: "Now you're deputies." The words of the oath did not really matter; it was the procedural formality of "swearing in" that made possible the deputization of these two itinerant gunslingers.

Law is replete with such procedural formalities. The Supreme Court of the United States, for instance, has carefully outlined a handful of exceptions to the warrant requirement in search-and-seizure law. Police officers are expected to testify at trial that in the event they engaged in a warrantless search they did so in accordance with one of the constitutionally mandated exceptions to the general rule. Thus Los Angeles police detective Philip Vannatter, testifying in a pretrial suppression hearing in the O. J. Simpson homicide case, stated that he and his fellow officers did not initially regard O. J. Simpson as a suspect in the case.

The reason, according to Vannatter, that the LAPD conducted an early-morning search of Simpson's Rockingham estate, without having first obtained a lawful search warrant, was to arrange for disposition of Simpson's children and make sure there was no danger to anyone in the estate. These were constitutionally permissible reasons. What would not have been a legitimate reason for the search, or so the officers feared, was that they suspected Mr. Simpson in the Nicole Brown Simpson / Ron Goldman murders and wanted to obtain any evidence against him that might exist before he had an opportunity to destroy it.

In fact, mystery novelist and attorney Scott Turow famously remarked at the time of the Simpson case that if Detective Vannatter and his colleagues on the force did *not* suspect O. J. Simpson, given the circumstances and his history of wife battering, they should have been fired. Almost all commentators on the trial felt that Vannatter was, in fact, trying to fit the search into one of the recognized exceptions to the warrant requirement and thus—however predictably, routinely, and, according to some, harmlessly—was lying under oath. Was this one of the first missteps by police, and by the prosecutors who put such witnesses on the stand, knowing what their testimony would be, that eventually led to Simpson's acquittal? In any event, being sworn in (even without the deputy's oath in *El Dorado*), and finding an exception to the warrant requirement (even when the facts at Rockingham stubbornly resist), is all that counts. Presiding at the Simpson preliminary hearing, Judge Kennedy-Powell admitted into evidence everything the officers obtained from their warrantless search of the Rockingham estate. And so did Judge Lance Ito at trial.

At times, one of the legal system's greatest interlocutors, novelist Charles Dickens, appeared to regard the whole of law as one appalling, Behemoth-like, procedural formality. The procedure/substance dichotomy looms large in legal interpretation. But there is an even more significant, if less familiar, opposition with which we will be concerned in this initial chapter of *Movies on Trial*—one even more basic. It is impossible to talk about the meaning of law's image until the law itself can be seen. Thus a central concern, right at the beginning, must be with the relationship between visibility and invisibility. How, exactly, do we see the law?

Unwritten Law

Figuring out exactly where the law can be found, in any legal system, is no easy matter. The fact is well illustrated by the famous trial of William Penn in London in 1670. According to U.S. Supreme Court Justice William O. Douglas, writing in the case of *Illinois vs. Allen* (1970), Penn was charged with inciting a riot when all he had done, in fact, was preach a sermon on Grace Church Street. Demanding to know under what law he had been indicted, Penn was told the charge against him was grounded in the common law. Penn is said to have inquired, "Where is that common law?" It was suggested, in reply, that this was a silly question since the common law, in essence, was constituted by all the decisions rendered to that date by English courts. Penn would not give up. He wanted to know why, if the law "be common, it should be so hard to produce." This sort of clever banter continued for a while until the court lost its patience and a judge instructed Penn that he was an impertinent fellow if he thought he would teach the court what the law was, adding, "It is 'Lex non scripta,' that which many have studied thirty or forty years to know, and would you have me tell you in a moment?"

Perhaps a moment was not enough time but Penn did indeed have a right to know under exactly what law he was being prosecuted, a right shared by criminal defendants in common-law jurisdictions and of sufficient import to lead eventually to the abolition of "common-law crimes" in England and the United States. Consequently, no individual can today be prosecuted without there being a clear statement of law, embodied in a statute, in advance of the purported unlawful conduct, under which the defendant is to be charged. Individuals may be tried by courts but under laws written by legislators, elected by the people. The criminal jurisdiction of judges, independent of legislatures, was thus sharply curtailed.

But for the whole of the common law separate from the specific rules under which criminal prosecutions are brought, Penn's query remains. Where is the common law? Where do we find the law judges have made, including those sitting on all the courts of record in the common-law world in the additional three hundred years since Penn spoke up? And even with regard to "written" or statutory law more generally, we still have to know where it is before we can take a look at it. First-year law students certainly wish to learn, as quickly as possible, where the law is. An introductory course titled "Legal Research and Writing," or something along those lines, is uniformly required of novitiate law students in the United States. And with the same intensity as these legal rookies, if for a different reason, the hapless and frustrated litigant, a modern-day refugee from the pages of Dickens, waiting patiently by the reference desk of a downtown law library, hat in hand, is also hoping for the inside story: where is the law?

The short answer to their question can be conveyed with a number, some letters, another number, and a parenthesis. It is not what they expect but it *is* the answer. Consider for example, the tale of William Penn, as related by Justice Douglas. It is found in a published report of the Supreme Court's decision in the *Allen* case, mentioned above. We could call it the *Illinois* case but there are a lot more cases with the word Illinois in the title than the word Allen, so *Allen* is better. It narrows the field a little. But not enough. Who would want to try to look through all the common-law cases ever decided with the name Allen in the title? The specific case in which Douglas wrote the opinion on which we have relied for the Penn story has a *citation* that makes it possible for us to quickly put our hands on that specific case report. The citation for Justice Douglas's account of the trial of William Penn is *Illinois vs. Allen*, 397 US 337, 353–55 (1970). Translated, the citation means the case we are looking for is in a series of bound volumes called the *United States Reports* ("US," for short). We have to determine where these volumes are kept in the law library (usually near the entrance) and then locate volume 397. In that volume, we turn to page 337, where we find the first page of the official report of *Illinois vs. Allen*, a case decided by the U.S. Supreme Court in 1970 (as revealed initially by the year indicated, at the end of the citation, in parentheses). If we turn to pages 353–55, we will find the two or three pages within the *Allen* case where Douglas talks about Penn.

There are lots of other points that could be made here. There is more than one report of the *Allen* case in most law libraries. That means the case has more than one citation and is found in more than one set of books in the library. The year in the citation tells us something interesting but not exactly where to find the case, because most years the Supreme Court has produced too many decisions for them to be reported in just one volume. Thus the volume number remains crucial. That is why it comes first in the citation. Perhaps most important of all is the pending disintegration not only of the citation system I am describing here but of the actual incarnation, so to speak, of law in the books to which the system refers. This apocalyptic demise (of the books themselves, at any rate) can be put in the form of a fairy tale.

Once upon a time there was no law, though it is hard to imagine. Skipping ahead, as in the sequence in Stanley Kubrick's *2001: A Space Odyssey* (1968), where what goes up as a bone comes down as a space ship, there comes a time when the American Revolution generates a country, constitution, courts, cases, case reporters, and law libraries regularly used by American lawyers—libraries, that is, which contain mostly bound volumes of American law reports, state and federal. Access to that law is radically simplified by the West Company, a private corporation that devises the system by which all citizens, though mostly lawyers in practice, are able to gain entry to the universe of these materials of public record. With the help of their legal-writing instructors, brightly color-coded brochures published by the West Company, and by each other, first-year law students learn this obsessively logical yet aesthetically irresistible system, a secret sister to minimalist art, by which the materials of law are organized. Once they know it, they stop thinking about it, period, let alone as a system actually devised at some point in time by a living person. As with so much else, like bicycle riding or using your head to deflect a soccer ball into a net, once it becomes second nature it is difficult for law students and lawyers to imagine that this could possibly constitute specialized knowledge.

At a certain point during this tale's unfolding, Alan M. Turing and the folks at Bletchley Park, Buckinghamshire, build a real computer.

The machine is then downsized, information becomes digitized, and law goes online. The books themselves, too bulky even to store randomly in boxes, are burned or given to prison libraries, and law goes straight from the legislatures, courts, and administrative agencies into the computer, without passing "Go" or collecting $200, and without ever being put into "hard copy." Or so the story almost certainly turns out in the end. But for a brief and intoxicating interlude, late in the tale, the one (Westlaw) system—like a magical figure from Greek mythology, with one head but two bodies, one edition of the law in the library and another in cyberspace—exists in suspended animation.

In an episode of television's venerable legal series *Law and Order*, broadcast during the 2001 season, the district attorney is buried beneath a pile of law books—bound volumes of appellate case reports—on her desk. One of her assistants—a youthful, vigorous, well-trained prosecuting attorney—comes into the office and gently informs her boss, "You know you can get anything you want on the computer off Westlaw." The district attorney smiles considerately but declines the suggestion. "No," she says, "I like working with the books." Even in law, it is hard to teach an old dog new tricks.

This contradictory situation, the same law existing simultaneously on the computer and in the books, cannot last indefinitely. So cherish the moment. Remember that the public library on Nantucket Island still employs a card-catalogue system. Visit your local law library, especially during the "withdrawn book" sale. Save a few leatherbound law books for old time's sake. Talk about unwritten law.

Right and Wrong

So in the warm autumn glow of the story's unwinding, we consider images of the law being looked at, as written, in actual books, unceremoniously dumped from a dusty barrel, for example, in the first reel of John Ford's *Young Mr. Lincoln* (1939). A family is passing through New Salem, Illinois, in 1832, aboard a covered wagon, and stops off at the local country store to pick up supplies. Unfortunately, they have no money. But that is no problem for the gangly proprietor greeting them from the establishment's front porch: young Abe Lincoln.

He says they can send him what they owe somewhere down the

road. The whole operation is run on credit anyway, admits Abe, apparently not much of a businessman. The hard-bitten pioneer moving his family out west, standing in the dirt road alongside his buckboard, suggests that they *do* have something in the back that might be of some value: a barrel of old books that belonged to his grandpappy. "Books?" says Henry Fonda, playing Lincoln, a kind of wonder spreading across his face. "You folks go on in the store and help yourself," says Abe, "I'll go back and get the barrel." He gingerly swings down the barrel in back and opens it, removing the volume on top. "Blackstone's *Commentaries*," says Abe, reverentially. "That's law. Law!" The kindly pioneer wife, holding back her two young sons, leaning out of the wagon exclaims, "I knew that book was about somethin'. Hardly a thumb mark on it either. Reckon you can read it, sir?" Abe reveals a modest self-confidence: "I expect I can make head or tails out of it if I set my mind to it. . . . Law."

Ford cuts to a shot of Fonda, long legs outstretched, leisurely reading a book beneath a spreading oak by the river. Abe reads aloud, the leather volume open in the middle: "Law: The rights of persons and the rights of things. The right to life, reputation, and liberty. Rights to acquire and hold property. Wrongs are violations of those rights. By jing, that's all there is to it: right and wrong. Maybe I ought to begin to take this up serious." In two quick scenes, Ford has told us a lot about Lincoln and about the kind of lawyer (and leader) he will become.

First, he is not your "cash on the barrelhead" type of up-and-coming entrepreneurial capitalist, one of the stock characters of 1830s America, commonplace in both fact and fiction. Lincoln sets his sights higher. Plus he is a fair man, possessed of a deep insight, for whom the human touch comes absolutely naturally. And he is, fundamentally, *the* American lawyer, self-taught, Blackstone all the way, for whom reputation and liberty are almost religious principles. And his law, like gospel, is simple and obvious, with nothing tricky about it—crystal clear, like the opposition between right and wrong. In the criminal trial at the heart of *Young Mr. Lincoln*, Abe will put that notion of simple justice to good use defending two young men accused of a murder they did not commit.

Paul Biegler (James Stewart) and his alcoholic law partner, Parnell, played by the garrulous Arthur O'Connell, in Otto Preminger's

Anatomy of a Murder (1959), are, like Lincoln, criminal-defense attorneys engaged in a high-stakes homicide case. Their Korean War–
veteran client, Lieutenant Manion (Ben Gazzara), shot a bartender
who may or may not have raped Manion's wife (Lee Remick). The
problem is that, like Lincoln, Manion knows the difference between
right and wrong, even though he shot and killed Barney Quill. How
can he be found not guilty by reason of (temporary) insanity if he
knew perfectly well that what he was doing was wrong—even if
(according to a psychiatric expert witness) he was in the grip of an
irresistible impulse at the time he pulled the trigger?

The answer, at least in this film, is found in a law book; not in
Blackstone but in the report of an actual, nineteenth-century Michigan Supreme Court case, *State vs. Durfee*. Working at fever pitch in
the courthouse law library, the legal team played by Stewart and
O'Connell are searching for some precedent for the legal argument
that an irresistible impulse, by itself, is enough to make out a successful criminal defense for Manion. Preminger's first shot in this sequence, panning up from Parnell buried in books piled high on a long
library table, along with an open coffee thermos and crumpled pages
from a legal pad, all the way to Biegler, high above in the mezzanine
or balcony stacks, standing on a wooden stool, his head bumping
against the ceiling, gives the viewer a feeling for the physicality of
old-fashioned legal research, a kind of looking for the law that someday may be completely unrecognizable, a pantomime of lost art or
unknown ritual.

First, it takes that many books and that much physical space to
house the law that lawyers need in one place. Second, without sophisticated computer search mechanisms, which today turn up *Durfee* in
a couple of minutes (so long as you remember your Westlaw or Lexis
password), the process of legal research involves a lot of moving
around—both laterally and up and down—pulling reporters, getting
the fine print into a ray of light from window or lamp, piling up books
with cases that are close but not quite . . . and then they find it,
simultaneously.

Parnell calls out to Biegler, his voice trembling, pencil hand raised.
Preminger tracks up to the mezzanine: "Hey, listen to this, Parn," says
Biegler. Back down to Parnell: "Never mind that. Just find . . . *People
vs. Durfee*, 62 Michigan 486, year 1886." Back up to Biegler: "Yeah,

that's it, I have it right here in the ALR," stepping down from the chair and hanging over the ornate metal bannister as if he wants to reach down to touch his partner, "Listen, the right and wrong test, though condemned as being unscientific by most of the states . . ." And thus Biegler reads out to his partner the very language from the *American Law Reports* that Parnell has located in a different reporter system, indicating that in 1886 the Michigan State Supreme Court had embraced the irresistible-impulse test, the very rule these two lawyers need to secure their client's acquittal. Biegler later proudly presents the volume of the Michigan reports containing *Durfee* to the trial judge, in his chambers, the correct page of the reporter marked with a handmade lure for fly fishing, a hobby that jurist and defense counsel happen to share.

In a way, the lure matters almost as much as the *Durfee* citation because it symbolizes the subtle camaraderie that has been developing between Biegler and the judge (played by attorney Joseph Welch) who controls every aspect of the trial. Biegler's adversary, the elegant prosecutor from Lansing (George C. Scott) says that "the people" are hooked by *Durfee* and by Biegler in more ways than one. After the judge instructs the jury to ignore a comment made by Biegler, Lt. Manion asks his attorney how they can ignore something they have already heard. "They can't," whispers Biegler. In Preminger's motion picture, the judge is played by a real lawyer, the *Durfee* case is real, even the trial tactics are real.

The film's nascent legal realism, however, stands knee-high to its fact-skepticism, as Jerome Frank might put it. *Anatomy of a Murder* makes it quite clear that facts are not always black and white; it is never easy to know for sure who is telling the truth, and trial courts can only do their best to try to fashion a version of justice. Perhaps Lt. Manion beat up his wife, after all. Maybe he knew exactly what he was doing when he shot Barney Quill. And what about Mrs. Manion, anyway? "Chilling, ironic, and skeptical," says Geoff Andrew in the *TimeOut Film Guide*; *Anatomy of a Murder* is "far less confident in the law than most courtroom dramas, which makes one suspect that it was this probing cynicism rather than the 'daring' use of words that caused controversy at the time of release."

Perhaps even less confident in the law is the portrait of the legal system painted by British director John Boorman in his film *The*

General (1998), which is about the life and times of Dublin gangster and Irish folk hero Martin Cahill. On trial for larceny, Cahill has one of his low-life crew stand up in the courtroom gallery and denounce him as a murderer and drug dealer, and then flee the environs. Cahill disowns knowledge of the outburst and his counsel immediately rises to ask for a mistrial, based upon possible jury prejudice against the defendant. A stern judge, wise to the gambit, gives Cahill a cold stare and says, "Members of the jury: this is a cynical ruse and I direct you to disregard what was said. Are you taking up study of the law, Mr. Cahill?"

Boorman cuts immediately from courtroom to darkness, with a man sliding down a rope into the frame. The man has a light attached to a band around his head, like that of a coal miner, a glow that picks up a small sign on the wall that reads, "Law Library." The next shot is from the floor area upward, to a balcony very much like the one in *Anatomy of a Murder*, with the same imposing wall of aging books, same iron grillwork and bannister—only instead of Paul Biegler it is Martin Cahill wearing a leather jacket, poking through the stacks. He finds just what he is looking for, slides out a tattered volume, and opens it to the page on which is printed the Larceny Act of 1916. With the bright circle of light from Cahill's headlamp illuminating the page, the definition of larceny literally fills the entire wide screen and Boorman cuts to a huge close-up of Cahill's gloved finger tracing just the words "person in fear of being . . ." Cahill's finger taps the line, as if he is nodding his head—he got what he came for.

The next shot is of the same gloved hand, now outstretched across the mouth of a sleeping woman, who awakes in terror to find a pistol in her face. Cahill uncovers her mouth but continues to hold the gun on her, and explains he has been doing a bit of reading and has learned that if she, a cashier during the robbery for which he is being prosecuted, was not in fear of her life when Cahill and his mates took the money from her, then he cannot be convicted. He promises her that if she says in court that she was in fear of her life, then he will have to make sure that she has reason to be afraid. He asks her if she has got the message and, shaking, she replies that she has.

Cahill and company then proceed to pull off another lucrative heist. Back in court on the earlier theft charge, the woman Cahill threatened—changed from pajamas into smart suit—calmly tells the prosecutor that she was not afraid of being shot, not really, since she has had a gun pointed at her more than once. She sounds as if she is getting bored with stickups. Pressing his witness, the prosecutor asks her if it was not, as it surely must have been, a terrifying experience. She glances at Cahill sitting across from the witness box, pauses, and replies, "Well, I wouldn't say that." The defense counsel rises, patiently reads out section 23 of the Larceny Act of 1916 to the members of the jury, asks the judge for, and gets a directed verdict of acquittal. Boorman cuts from shots of disgruntled prosecutors and police in court to the young rowdies in the street, cheering and slapping Cahill on the back as he rides off on his motorcycle, a free man.

Boorman, himself purportedly one of the victims of a Cahill burglary, presents the freebooter as an extremely complex character, a man as capable of brutality and pettiness as of loyalty and courage. An antiauthoritarian outcast, Cahill is at the same time a very traditional, even old-fashioned man—an embodiment, perhaps, as *Salon* contributing writer Charles Taylor puts it, of Ireland's "sentimental and black-humored hard-luck soul." One worries, however, that for Martin Cahill, like Ford's Lincoln, all there is to the law, by jing, is right and wrong. For Cahill, at any rate, the cops and the establishment are wrong, your friends are right, and the law books are a useful guide to the tactics of intimidation and how to jimmy the system. "What do you stand for," Cahill is finally asked by someone from the old neighborhood, "thievin' and killin' and scarin' people to death?"

Blind Justice

Law in the books is often contrasted with law in action, and we know that law is more than what is printed on the pages of Blackstone or the Michigan Supreme Court reports or the volume containing the British Larceny Act. But John Ford, Otto Preminger, and John Boorman have done a better job, in the three films discussed above, *showing* us the law than did the court that dismissed William Penn's impassioned request to know, exactly, where the law was. Whoever saw *The General* in a movie theater with a large screen probably witnessed (in the scene where Cahill locates the definition of larceny) as grand a legal visualization, in terms of sheer size, as any outside the edicts published as wall posters in Mao's China or Tokugawa Japan. Only, perhaps, in Orwell's *1984*, do the agitprop legal banners and projected political slogans come any bigger.

Why, when it comes to what the law looks like, did the judges who sought to prosecute William Penn for causing riot have so little to show? Why, for them, was law not only blind, but very nearly invisible? "Allegorical images of justice, historians of iconography tell us," according to political philosopher and Frankfurt School of Social Research biographer Martin Jay, "did not always cover the eyes of the goddess Justitia." And therein lies a fact of considerable interest for what we have to say here about law's visibility.

Jay employs a story about Justitia's blinding as a way of raising crucial jurisprudential questions about the nature of justice and the relationship between substance and procedure. After reprising the iconographic history of justice and its representation in a range of artistic forms, Jay describes how by the middle of the sixteenth century the blindfolding of justice, at least in Europe, had become commonplace. The blindfold, Jay reports, "was transformed into a positive emblem of impartiality and equality before the law."

Morris L. Cohen, perhaps the only individual ever to serve as librarian of both Harvard and Yale law-school libraries, provides support for Jay's iconographic account. In *Law: The Art of Justice*, Cohen points out that the feminine figure of justice has a long and important history in the development of Western law. In Ambrogio Lorenzetti's *Allegory of Good Government* (1338–40), one of the panels in a fresco at the town hall of Siena, Italy, reproduced in Cohen's book, the figure of Justice sitting on her throne appears with familiar measuring scales and, significantly, is not blindfolded. An illuminated fifteenth-century Spanish manuscript, reproduced by Cohen, shows Justice wearing a crown, sitting on a table, and holding a sword. Again, she is without blindfold.

Perhaps most familiarly, Cohen reproduces and discusses Raphael's *Justitia* (1510) from one of the frescoes at the Vatican. While Cohen is quick to point out that Raphael's figure of Justice is more modern than Lorenzetti's, and also appears more graceful and gentle, it is clear that her vision is equally unobstructed. How remarkably, then, do we come upon the figure of Justice—brass scales held high but dramatically casting a shadow that falls directly across her eyes—painted in the eighteenth century by Sir Joshua Reynolds, a picture appropriately reproduced facing the title page of the classic law-school textbook *Procedure*, edited by professors Robert Cover, Owen Fiss, and Judith Resnick.

Blind justice and impartiality may go hand in hand, but Martin Jay is at pains to question whether *not* making distinctions is always a good thing, even legally. He concedes that equality before the law may have been "required by the new urban, secular, bourgeois culture of the early modern period, which left behind the personalism of private, feudal justice." But it did not represent, in Jay's view, an unalloyed triumph for fairness and justice. Consider some of the changes presaged by the blindfolding of justice: "The law was now to be presented entirely in language and justice dispensed only through language rather than appearing in images, which might overwhelm through dazzlement."

There is quite a literature on this capacity for the visual image to overwhelm through dazzlement and, especially, on what might be called the fear of pictures. David Freedberg, for example, uses a particular painting—Poussin's *The Worship of the Golden Calf* (c. 1636)—to illustrate his argument about the power of images. Freedberg claims that putting works of art in museums may represent an effort to neutralize their emotional impact. Placing visual images at arm's length and calling them "art" is a product of the same kind of anxiety that can result in the actual destruction of dangerous art. Politicians may try to close museums for more deeply felt reasons than the simple desire to win elections. While finding much of value in Freedberg's critique, Anne Hollander thinks that there is more to aesthetic appreciation than merely an anxiously defensive move in the direction of detachment. But she does acknowledge the importance of Freedberg's theories of iconoclasm, observing that "the thought that God might be properly accessible to everyone only if contained in some comprehensible vessel . . . and that the container of holiness might rightly fuse with holiness itself and be the just recipient of worship, was frightening."

Here we can connect Jay's analysis of law's blinding with Freedberg's and Hollander's critique of iconoclasm and the fear of images. Jay says that the blindfolding of justice prevented judgment from being swayed by visual recognition. Thus, not only would a blindfolded justice move cautiously, avoiding the errant step, but she would be less tempted by favoritism or personal vengeance. So far, so good. Relying, however, on Frankfurt School philosophers Horkheimer and Adorno, and also, more significantly, on gender theorists, Jay points out some of the baggage that comes with presenting law entirely in language and dispensing justice only through language.

A blindfolded, impartial, procedural justice may fall far short of "real" or substantive justice. Jay cites the debate over affirmative action in the United States to support his case. Beyond his position here, it should be acknowledged that a justice of language, rather than of images, can be far more successful in drawing a veil across that which cannot be shown: the fundamental dichotomy between legal equality and class inequality, the illusion fostered by an idealized fairness in societies of radically disparate access to social and economic power. It is odd that Jay does not drive this point home more forcefully, considering that it was a common observation made by Neumann, Marcuse, and other Frankfurt School critics.

Franz Neumann's teacher at the London School of Economics, British socialist Harold J. Laski, argued that outside the narrow circle of property owners, the individual on whose behalf legal equality is proclaimed necessarily remains a bloodless abstraction. Anatole France said it too: the law in its majesty prohibits the rich as well as the poor from sleeping beneath the bridges of Paris. But Daumier *showed* it—witness the power of the image, especially when unmasking hypocrisy.

Barbara Maria Stafford writes: "Contemporary iconoclasm, like early modern versions, rests on the puritanical myth of an authentic or innocent epistemological origin. Clinging to the Rousseauean fantasy of a supposedly blotless, and largely imageless, print ecology ignores not only contrary evidence from the past but the real virtues of colorful, heterogenous, and mutable icons, whether on or off screen." So we can argue that the blindfolding of justice, one of Stafford's "early modern versions" of iconoclasm, rests on a puritanical myth of epistemological innocence, or neutrality, is canonized (again, according to Martin Jay) by political philosophers like John Rawls, challenged by feminists like Carol Gilligan, and ends up producing a one-sided jurisprudence that at best misses the point. Disembodiment, disembeddedness, decontextualization: these are the three words that Jay, at his pithiest, uses to describe the vertigo generated by a system of blind justice.

We will return to Jay's critique, especially to his reference to "disembodiment," when we confront the U.S. Supreme Court's transformation of the American corporation into a constitutionally recognized person, an individual well inside Laski's narrow circle of privilege. But first we need to ask whether Jay's compelling, if admittedly tentative, outline description of the blindfolding of Justitia constitutes something that transcends an essentially anecdotal iconography, something that parallels the early history of legal institutions themselves.

Trial by Jury

In *The Palladium of Justice*, his heralded investigation into the origins of trial by jury, legal historian Leonard W. Levy, like Justice William O. Douglas in the *Allen* case, gives special focus to the trial of William Penn in 1670. Again, Douglas regarded the case as significant in terms of its contribution to the development of an accused's right to know precisely what he was charged with as well as the defendant's right to confront those making the accusation. Levy, instead, emphasizes the Penn trial's importance in signaling the power and authority that juries had managed to acquire by the end of the seventeenth century. Refusing to budge in the face of appalling intimidation by the judges in the case, the Penn jury persisted in their not-guilty verdicts and were not only fined as a result, but were initially jailed. While the trial judges found Penn's jurors as impertinent as the defendant himself, the jury could not be cowed. "The king could dismiss judges and discipline lawyers," Levy concludes, "but jurors were impregnable."

That was by the end of the seventeenth century. The jury itself had emerged gradually from the inquest proceeding, a Norman contribution, approximately four hundred years earlier. Another name for the inquest procedure was *recognitio*, which simply meant the proceeding involved a statement of fact or finding of truth by a body of men, summoned for that purpose, who answered under oath and whose word could be trusted precisely because they were from the neighborhood where the matter being tried had taken place and would thus have firsthand knowledge about it. There was no distinction between jurors and witnesses: the jury was actually made up of those individuals whose testimony could best be relied upon to settle affairs conclusively.

Levy describes the gradual process by which witnesses were distinguished from jurors and indicates that one method of punishing jurors who swore falsely, the "attaint," fell into disuse by the sixteenth century because it was unnecessary in a system where jurors no longer gave sworn testimony. Witnesses who lied, on the other hand, would be vulnerable to prosecution for perjury, but jurors increasingly only decided cases. Maximus Lesser, writing at the end of the nineteenth century, in his classic account of the historical development of the jury system, like Levy a century later, also describes a gradual process by which the separation in function between jurors and witnesses was accomplished in English common-law courts.

Sir James Fitzjames Stephen, one of the sharpest intellects in the field of common-law jurisprudence and the best-known historian of English criminal law, describes a homicide case from the reign of Henry III in which, although jurors were the witnesses whose evidence decided the case, their testimony was supplemented by that of other, independent witnesses. The rules for the exclusion of evidence at trial and for challenging jurors remained the same. Nevertheless, like Levy, Stephen indicates that the "attaint," whose decline signified the separation of witness from juror, was hardly known by the end of the sixteenth century and was formally abolished, by statute, in 1825.

Finally, attorney (and coeditor of the still much praised *Encyclopedia of the Social Sciences*) William Seagle wrote that the specifically English contribution to the development of trial by jury was to convert a practice of local accusation into a system of trial by facts known to the members of the neighborhood. "The jury," says Seagle, with considerable import for our present inquiry, "which in its origin was a royal inquisition by which men of the neighborhood were compelled to give answer under oath *on the basis of their own knowledge* to questions propounded by royal officials, was slowly transformed until by the fifteenth century it was a mode of trial in which the jurors resolved disputed issues of fact *on the basis of testimony which they heard for the first time in court.*"

Not without reason did Seagle italicize the two separate portions of his commentary on the transformation of the jury. The very thing that had initially qualified one to be on a jury, intimate personal knowledge of the matter in question, eventually would come to disqualify one from serving on a jury in the same matter. In the beginning, jurors doubled as witnesses and so it was crucial that they knew what they were talking about. But once the jury's role became that of disinterested trier of fact, based upon testimony presented by witnesses whose veracity the jury would have to assess as part of its deliberations, then it was essential the jury be as impartial as possible.

The point here is simple yet telling. Martin Jay argues that by the middle of the sixteenth century the iconographic blindfolding of justice had become commonplace. By the fifteenth century, says Seagle, the separation of witness and juror roles within the legal process had been made secure, and certainly by the end of the sixteenth century, assert Levy and Stephen, the foundation of the modern jury system had been laid. Equality before the law and impartiality of justice, signified for Jay by the blindfolding of justice, is mirrored in the impartiality and disinterestedness represented by the transformation, during the same historical period, of the trial jury itself.

"The method of judicial precedent," Seagle adds, "which, apart from trial by jury is perhaps the chief technical glory of the common law, is supposed to reflect its . . . predilection for leaving the law as far as possible an unwritten maze of precedent rather than embodying it in neat and systematic codes or even in authoritative textbooks written by learned jurists." Thus the infinite frustration of Harvard law students on the first day of classes in 1871 when a new professor, Christopher Columbus Langdell, introduced them to study of law by the case method, utilizing case books whose case reports had their headnotes removed, depriving the students of even a bare bones summary of the court's findings. Thus the equivalent frustration, two hundred years earlier, of defendant William Penn, when told that the common law was *lex non scripta*, something that many had studied thirty or forty years to know, and could not be conveyed to the unlearned in the blink of an eye.

Seagle's pairing of the method of legal reasoning by judicial precedent with the method of legal decision making through trial by jury is intriguing. Just as the transformation of the jury from something all knowing and *all seeing* into something indifferent and blind (thus unprejudiced and impartial) mirrors the blindfolding of Justitia, Seagle's comments are mirrored by Martin Jay's description of changes flowing in the wake of law's own iconoclastic movement. The law was now to be presented entirely in language, and with the image of justice banished, law would become disembedded and decontextualized. The unwritten maze of precedent would become, for Dickens and Kafka, a labyrinth of bureaucratized madness and violence. Last but not least, every American law student would be required to discover for himself or herself, with varying degrees of surprise and shock, the simple but inescapable fact revealed over and over each time a law-school textbook was opened for the first time: no pictures.

Early-American Labyrinth

"You're twisting my words," the witness complains. But the hapless individual on the stand testifying defenseless against a withering cross-examination is not the first to lodge this complaint. In a letter to Spencer Roane in 1819, no less an authority than Thomas Jefferson complained that judicial supremacy would permit unelected judges to "twist and shape" the constitution into any form they pleased. A year later, in a letter to Thomas Ritchie, Jefferson referred to the judiciary as a "subtle corps of sappers and miners constantly working under ground to undermine the fabric of our confederated republic." The law—disembodied, expressed exclusively through language, an unwritten maze of precedent, uncontrolled and unaccountable—clearly did not please Jefferson.

In a letter published in 1819—the same year that Jefferson wrote to Spencer Roane, but originally circulated during the first decade after the ratification of the United States Constitution—antifederalist Benjamin Austin, writing under the pen name Honestus, attacked the notion that the legal profession constituted a necessary order in a republic. While confining his criticism to lawyers guilty of malpractice, he nevertheless provided a damning portrait of the legal system. Austin demanded to know by what authority the men of law should be permitted to complicate legal procedure inordinately, employ the art of delay, render intricate the most basic legal propositions, and confound those who sought only legal advice and counsel. In Austin's view, about 90 percent of legal disputes could be resolved by utilizing panels of referees. Moreover, Austin proposed that courtroom trials, in which lawyers were able to collect larger fees through procedural delays, could be dramatically improved simply by removing the lawyers. Judges and juries would be left to their own devices under this scheme. "Is it not a disgrace to a free republic," Austin inquired of his readers, "that citizens should dread appealing to the laws of their country?"

Austin was an opponent of federalism; Robert Rantoul wrote as a radical or Jacksonian democrat. A law graduate of Harvard University and himself a member of the bar, Rantoul would eventually serve five years as a U.S. attorney for Massachusetts and be elected to fill the U.S. Senate seat vacated by Daniel Webster. But in his Fourth of July *Oration at Scituate*, 1836, Rantoul echoed the suspicion of common law and preference for codification expressed by the greatest continental philosopher of the time, G. W. F. Hegel. Both Hegel and Rantoul argued that common law, or judge-made law, the kind of law William Penn had been told could not possibly be explained to him in a moment, was rather dangerous, at least when compared with statutory law, legal rules enacted and promulgated by the legislature. In his *Philosophy of Right*, for example, Hegel claimed that common law was no more than unwritten law (the *lex non scripta* vigorously defended by William Penn's interlocutors), buried in a maze of judicial reports, and was thus capable of transforming mere judges into legislators, that is, those who govern. Hegel was an early critic of "government by judiciary."

Though common-law judges were, in theory, bound by precedent, Hegel argued that prior law was itself the product of judges interpreting unwritten, or nonstatutory, rules. The judges themselves became "repositories of the unwritten law," and were empowered to determine whether previous decisions coincided with that unwritten law. The United States Constitution is, of course, a written constitution. Nevertheless, it's rather short and, more significantly, it is written, for the most part, in such general terms that its *interpretation* is no more limited in the hands of what Robert Rantoul called a "thorough-bred lawyer" than would be its application to concrete cases by those Hegel referred to as legal practitioners of a "monstrous confusion."

What was at the bottom of Rantoul's and Hegel's hostility to common law and common lawyers? Two further letters written by Thomas Jefferson may help illuminate a shadowed aspect of the relation between common law and democratic revolution in the nineteenth century. Writing to Edmund Randolph in 1799, Jefferson assailed the notion that common law should be utilized by the new federal courts of the United States. The Bank Law, the Alien and Sedition Acts, and a host of other Federalist horrors were timid and of no consequence compared to the "audacious barefaced and sweeping pretention to a system of law for the United States without the adoption of their legislature, and so infinitely beyond their power to adopt." Two months later, Jefferson wrote to Charles Pinckney, providing what today might be regarded as the scenario for an Oliver Stone film: "In short, it would seem that changes in the principles of our government are to be pushed, until they accomplish a monarchy peaceably, or force a resistance, which with the aid of an army may end in monarchy." Jefferson could sense a coup d'etat coming and, like Oliver Stone in Dallas, did not have far to seek for its authors.

Jefferson's anxiety resembled that of Rantoul, Hegel, and many early skeptics of the common law. "No man can tell what the Common Law is," asserted Rantoul, "therefore it is not law. . . . [A] rule which is unknown can govern no man's conduct." Because the common people, the democracy, had no independent means of access to the common law—seen, on this view, as little more than an antiquarian mystery—political reaction would find in the common law and its judicial interpreters tools of great precision in giving the law a conservative cast and even, perhaps, weapons with which to strike boldly against popular government. Common law versus statute, judges versus legislators, lawyers versus the people: the battle lines could not have been more sharply drawn.

But why would lawyers and judges necessarily wish to use the common law's extraordinary flexibility to turn back the historical clock? To be sure, Rantoul, for example, argued that the discretion, even arbitrariness, built into common-law adjudication threatened the authority of democratically accountable legislatures, which, in his view, spoke with the voice of the people. But the common law also embodied values that "came down from the dark ages." Rantoul regarded the common law as static and unchanging, wedded to rules and principles from the deep past. Such defects in the common law had "existed from time immemorial" and, for Rantoul, within the common law "precedents are everything: the spirit of the age is nothing."

Had not Hegel and Rantoul argued that judges applied an unwritten law and thereby managed to escape the obligation of following precedent? As Rantoul, in his crypto-legal realist mode, put it: the "judge makes law by extorting from precedents something which they do not contain." If the law was whatever the judges, employing this essentially linguistic art, said it was, why were common-law judges any more locked into the past than any other kind of judge? In fact, why not much less? The remnants of ancient legislation might well be of little practical use in Rantoul's world, the nineteenth-century American equivalent of Martin Jay's new, urban, secular, bourgeois (and increasingly capitalist) Europe. But if the common law could embody whatever set of values an elite order of lawyers might wish to impose, why would the law have to remain frozen in time? Why, indeed, if the mandarins of the legal order felt it was in their interest for it to change?

The critics of the common law were right to see in its infinitely shifting sands a legal Mojave or Sahara, wherein the stranded litigant should abandon all hope of finding some remote oasis of binding precedent and fixed rule, a shimmering pool of predictability and legal certainty. But that did not somehow place law and lawyers outside of time—or of history.

In Chancery

While neither was a lawyer nor devoted his writing primarily to the subject of law, Alexis de Tocqueville and Charles Dickens were two of the nineteenth century's most important legal commentators. De Tocqueville, like Rantoul, viewed lawyers as a social elite; he is famous for his characterization of the American legal profession as the new nation's natural "aristocracy." What differentiates de Tocqueville, however, is his positive celebration of this separation of lawyers from the people. The distance from the popular mass and its political passions that had bothered critics like Rantoul became, for de Tocqueville, the very reason why lawyers could be trusted. In his most famous work, *Democracy in America*, first published in the 1830s, de

Tocqueville suggested that the sentiments and habits of the aristocracy could be found in the characters of American attorneys.

According to de Tocqueville, lawyers "participate in the same instinctive love of order and formalities; and they entertain the same repugnance to the actions of the multitude, and the same secret contempt for government of the people." While rejecting Rantoul's disdain for the legal profession, de Tocqueville nevertheless shared the view that common lawyers were an obstacle to social change. American lawyers, de Tocqueville asserted, were not only opposed to the revolutionary spirit but, further, such men revealed a "superstitious attachment to what is old" and routinely exhibited an "habitual procrastination."

De Tocqueville had yet to learn the fundamental lesson of social history that is at the heart of one of Italy's greatest modern novels, Giuseppe Tomasi di Lampedusa's *The Leopard*. "Unless we ourselves take a hand now," says Lampedusa's youthful Tancredi, "they'll foist a republic on us. If we want things to stay as they are, things will have to change. D'you understand?" De Tocqueville appears not to have understood this principle, at least not when he wrote *Democracy in America*. Like Robert Rantoul, he underestimated the potential of common law and common lawyers to contribute to a process of political and economic transformation, if for no other reason than to preserve an existing order of society and its relations of production.

After the revolutionary struggles that gripped Europe in 1848, de Tocqueville amended his views somewhat and acknowledged that not only would the constitutional structure of society undergo modification, but that it had already done so in quite fundamental ways—as was certainly true of the common law in the United States. As legal historians Willard Hurst and Morton Horwitz have argued, and as I have tried to demonstrate in considerable detail in *Law and History*, transformation of the rules of contract, property, and tort, along with much of the rest of the fabric of American law, was a crucial factor in the rise of a laissez-faire capitalist political economy in the United States. Historian Gordon Wood acknowledges that most historians now believe this transformation largely occurred in the United States between the Revolution and the Civil War.

It is sufficient to observe, however, the way in which a number of early legal commentators, including both critics and proponents of the common law, underestimated the capacity of common law (and common lawyers) to revise the entire body of doctrinal law over time to reflect new historical realities. Not everyone made this mistake. Had not Edmund Burke saluted Lord Mansfield, made chief justice of the King's Bench in 1756, for his ability to conform "our jurisprudence to the growth of our commerce and of our empire"? Common-law courts, and the new system of federal courts when tasked with constitutional interpretation, would perform the same function of conforming the law to American commerce and culture, empire and expectations.

Apparent ignorance of this transformative principle at the heart of the common-law process—a principle sometimes actually referred to as the *genius* of the common law—permitted Rantoul, as well as de Tocqueville prior to 1848, to overestimate the rigidity (from Rantoul's perspective) or the stability (from de Tocqueville's) of the legal system. In the United States, the common law and its practitioners demonstrated an ability to provide the system with a veneer of consistency and continuity, only barely concealing an instrumental commitment to change, indeed radical social and economic change, when required.

But what these early observers of the American legal scene got right was that a common-law system routinely channeled the politics of law into a politics of language. Another one of de Tocqueville's most famous comments, frequently quoted even today, is that all great social and political issues in the United States eventually are transformed into legal questions. What that also means, of course, is that great moral and political dilemmas are eventually seen as problems of language, the kind of language lawyers use not just to try cases but to argue in their briefs and in the appellate courts—the kind of language you need a *Black's Law Dictionary* to decipher. In America, the lives and sacred fortunes of the people would ultimately turn on—of all things—words.

The American system of government, the Revolution notwithstanding, was derived from that of Britain, and the common law was the same the world over. Historian Eric Hobsbawm says there was a time when every English schoolboy learned that the sun never set on British territory or British trade. Eventually, Hobsbawm adds, that sun went down below the horizon. But it has yet to set on the common law, and likely never will. So it is not surprising that in the middle of the nineteenth century one of Britain's great public novelists should write a book about how the legal system dominated, with dreadful consequences, the lives of English men and women. In *Bleak House*, Dickens created a powerful and enduring portrait of the kind of injustice and legal delay that he believed cast a plague upon the nation.

The fog rising from the wretched courts of London and the mists surrounding the judicial process ultimately prove impenetrable for Dickens's hapless and brutalized characters. Chancery and Parliament, according to Dickens scholar Steven Connor, are presented as "diseased excrescences upon human life," the kind of parasitism associated with "malign proliferation, exhibited alike in disease and finance." Chancery in *Bleak House*, like the Circumlocution Office in *Little Dorrit*, represents the solid embodiment of a system so cruel and impersonal that it eventually drags down into miasma and ruin nearly everyone it touches.

Whether it is the legal system, as in *Bleak House*, the factory system in *Hard Times*, or the financial system in *Our Mutual Friend*, systems are damaging because they "draw the self away from immediate experience" and subject the individual, now lost, to "infinite mazes of delay and confusion." But even beyond the impersonality and indifference of systems, Connor locates at the heart of *Bleak House* Dickens's appreciation of the relation between language and negation. After demonstrating the way that language itself is turned against character after character in the novel, Connor finally arrives at Jo, the pathetic sweep. Jo "resembles Krook, in being illiterate," says Connor, "but is more profoundly 'outside' language than Krook is, unable as he is to make anything of the 'unintelligible mess' of 'all that unaccountable reading and writing.'"

Of the diverse characters who populate Dickens's *Bleak House*, Jo is most appallingly victimized by language. But here is the point: *everyone* in Bleak House is a *legal* illiterate, a victim of legal language—except, of course, the lawyers, the grim masters in Chancery. We need only briefly retrieve Martin Jay's comment that Justitia blindfolded meant, above all, that the law would now be presented entirely in language and justice dispensed only through language. Only those who knew the language of law would be able to dispense truth and participate in justice.

Clearly, it can be argued that confining legal meaning to legal language removed the law from public perception and thus from the public realm. Writing specifically about *Bleak House*, historian Peter Hoffer claims that Dickens provides us with a great social canvas, a portrait of the civil side of legal affairs unmatched in literature. Whether one's personal copy of *Bleak House* happens to be "illustrated," we know what Hoffer means. Dickens was able to visualize justice, hence injustice. Without images, iconoclasm run rampant, could language ever do justice to what we expect from the law?

Constitution and Magic Lantern

Leland Stanford was a nineteenth-century railroad magnate who helped give meaning to the appellation "robber baron." Eric Hobsbawm indicates that Stanford, along with other California venture capitalists, men who represented the highest echelons of money and power, managed without embarrassment to charge several times the real cost of building Pacific Coast railroad systems. But Stanford was not only interested in making money. Actively involved in politics, he served as California's governor, represented the state in the U.S. Senate, and earlier lobbied President Lincoln on behalf of Stephen J. Field's nomination to the U.S. Supreme Court. He was also, of course, an important benefactor of higher education (having founded Stanford University in Palo Alto) and engaged generally in the funding of elite, private institutions.

It is perhaps less well known that Stanford was a horse breeder—a fairly typical avocation for a rich westerner. According to a much repeated story, to help Stanford settle a bet on whether all four of a trotting horse's hoofs were ever completely off the ground simultaneously, Eadweard Muybridge was retained to engage in a number of photographic experiments. These first efforts, carried out at Sacramento in 1872, utilized a series of trip wires to capture a succession of images of the famous racehorse Occident in motion. More rigorous experiments conducted at Palo Alto later in the decade produced an amazing set of sequential images, mostly of horses, which later appeared in Muybridge's groundbreaking *Attitudes of Animals in Motion* (1881). But Muybridge had already developed a moving-picture projector, the zoopraxiscope, and demonstrated its use in Stanford's home by the time his first classic book of serial photographic images was published.

In his history of the documentary film, Erik Barnouw reports that by 1880 Muybridge "had learned to project sequences of his photos with an adaptation of the magic lantern, and thus to present a galloping horse on a screen." Although, as film theorists David Bordwell and Kristin Thompson point out, the kind of glass-plate film used by Muybridge was impractical for the future development of genuinely moving pictures, Barnouw nevertheless credits Muybridge with showing us how photography could open our eyes to an available but previously unperceived world.

While expressing the same reservation as Bordwell and Thompson, German media theoretician Friedrich A. Kittler still contends that had they only "been copied onto celluloid and rolled into a reel, Muybridge's glass plates could have anticipated Edison's kinetoscope, the peephole precursor to the Lumières' cinematic projection." Perhaps most dramatically, art historian Jonathan Crary argues there is a direct relationship between the technological advance represented by Stanford's railroads, as a form of capitalist modernization that sharply reduced the time and cost of *movement*, and the kind of "renovation of perception and information" represented by Stanford and Muybridge's photographic experiments. Moving images made it possible for visuality to "coincide with the speeds and temporalities" of both telecommunications (e.g., the telegraph) and an acceleration in the flow of circulating capital itself.

Only a few years after the photographic experiments Muybridge conducted with financing from Leland Stanford, the U.S. Supreme Court also became directly involved with Stanford and his railroads. In a pair of decisions arising from San Mateo and Santa Clara counties in California, the Supreme Court had to decide whether Stanford's railroads should be protected from some forms of state regulation by the Constitution of the United States. While *San Mateo County vs. Southern Pacific Railroad Co.* (1886) was pending before the Court, Stanford hosted a dinner at Chamberlain's Restaurant in Washington, D.C., to which he invited the top railroad attorneys. Among the guests was Roscoe Conkling, who had argued to the Supreme Court that one of the purposes behind the Constitution's Fourteenth Amendment was to protect corporations like Stanford's Southern Pacific from governmental regulation. It is not surprising that Conkling would attend such a gala banquet thrown by a prized client. What is extraordinary, however, is that the dinner was also attended by none other than Supreme Court justice Stephen J. Field.

Justice Field's brother, attorney David Dudley Field, who had corrupted judges while representing crooks like Jim Fiske and Jay Gould, had played a critical role two decades before in Abraham Lincoln's nomination as the Republic Party's candidate for the presidency. So it came as no surprise when Lincoln, once in office, named Stanford's friend Stephen J. Field to the nation's highest bench. And it was Field, alone among the justices of the Supreme Court, who showed up at Stanford's dinner party for the big guns of the railroads' corporate bar. The *San Francisco Chronicle* even charged that no other justices had been invited because it was taken for granted they would have felt ethically obliged not to attend.

Santa Clara County vs. Southern Pacific Railroad Co., the companion to the *San Mateo* case and handled by the Court at the same time, involved the question of whether corporations should be protected as "persons" within the meaning of the Fourteenth Amendment, and it was chosen by the Supreme Court as the vehicle for its decision. Interestingly enough, although the Court *did* interpret the Fourteenth Amendment as including corporations within the meaning of the word "persons," it did not explain the ruling. Constitutional treatise writers Nowak and Rotunda indicate that the Court decided the issue without discussion. Historian Robert McCloskey states that in *Santa Clara*, the Court "conceded, rather offhandedly, that corporations were 'persons' within the meaning of the Amendment," and that concession, within a decade, was "seen to be of epic importance and of incalculable value to the business community."

Law professor J. M. Balkin has argued that the decision in *Santa Clara* meant corporations had rights courts were bound to enforce and that courts did so vigorously during a period of rapid capitalist expansion. A century after the case came before the Supreme Court, Chief Justice William Rehnquist admitted that in *Santa Clara* the Court had decided the key issue without argument or discussion. Although legal historian Morton Horwitz believes inclusion of corporations within the Fourteenth Amendment developed gradually, over time, and was not fully accomplished until around 1910, he too observes that the Court's opinion in *Santa Clara* appears to be remarkably brief and without either elaboration or citation of legal precedent. Law professor Eben Moglen says the status of railroad corporations as "persons" within the meaning of the Fourteenth Amendment was hammered out in the cases that flowed in the wake of *Santa Clara*. Yet no effort was made by the members of the high court to square their decision pertaining to corporate personality with either the original intent of the Constitution or of the drafters of the Fourteenth Amendment itself.

Directed by Kathleen Hughes and Tom Casciato, and hosted by Bill Moyers, the documentary film *Free Speech for Sale* (2000) was nationally broadcast in the United States during public television's viewer pledge week. In the film, Moyers asks New York University professor and constitutional law expert Burt Neuborne why the courts allow huge companies to influence politics in ways the Constitution never intended. "You could do a Ph.D. thesis in the law on the strange way we treat corporations," replies Neuborne, "sometimes as though they were human beings and sometimes as though they were not." Neuborne, a former national legal director of the American Civil Liberties Union, goes on to explain that the Supreme Court has ruled that "corporations are going to be treated as though they are a human being and they are going to be given the same rights to speak that human beings are given."

Is it too much to suggest that the William Penn who in 1670 wanted to know exactly where in the law his indictment was, in truth, founded would also have liked to know, were he still around two hundred years later, just where it was written that corporations were persons within the constitutional sense and thus entitled to many of the same rights and liberties to which flesh-and-blood human beings are entitled before the law?

"Disembodiment" was one of the charges leveled by Martin Jay at legal iconoclasm, the blindfolding of Justitia. But just as a blind justice could produce a disembodied law, causing that which is real to melt into thin air, the same legal process, turned on its head, could produce embodiment, causing that which was imaginary or pure spirit to take on human form. Substituting language for images permitted the visible to be rendered invisible and simultaneously allowed something abstract, like the corporate entity, to be made concrete, as real as anything gets. The former process (the visible made invisible) allowed injustice and social inequality—like formal segregation and the "separate but equal" doctrine in American race relations—to be ignored or tolerated. But the latter (making the abstract into something concrete) provided the legal framework for American economic transformation. Corporate incarnation, in American legal history, is inescapably a product of equality before the law—not just formal equality between the strong and the weak, rich and poor, but also between the real and the unreal.

So this jurisprudence of the blindfold could, almost like Dr. Frankenstein, make a human being—or at least a legal person—out of one of Leland Stanford's railroad corporations. At the same moment, however, that the Supreme Court was deciding the *Santa Clara* case in Stanford's favor, Stanford's photographer was inventing a process that ultimately could threaten to remove Justitia's blindfold and let in the light. Motion pictures, invented late in the nineteenth century, threaten to undo the sixteenth-century process of blindfolding justice by making visible that which covering Justitia's eyes had rendered invisible.

A camcorder captures a moving image of Los Angeles police officers beating Rodney King into the pavement. This visualization of crime, by itself, will not decide the case, but it is more than a thumb on the scales. It shows what previously could not be shown. The police officers' defense counsel begin by trying to "uninvent" the movies, step by step. They take away the sound. They break the projected videotape down into a series of separate still pictures, mounted on posters in the courtroom, like Muybridge's sequential images of human movement—"Stanford University's fencers, discus throwers, and wrestlers," says Friedrich Kittler. But in federal court, the government puts the images back together, shows them as a moving picture, in real time, with sound, even "enhances" the video to assist the jury. Separate from the trials themselves, the court of public opinion renders a verdict, based upon the televised video. *Seeing* is believing.

Martin Jay's view of Justitia blindfolded remains nuanced and ambivalent. As indicated before, he acknowledges the real benefits of legal equality. Perhaps, he concludes, it was not altogether without reason that vision was denied to symbols of justice, "in the name of impartiality and the banishment of monsters." An editor as well as keen student of the work of German-emigré lawyer Franz Neumann, one of thousands of political refugees from Nazi Europe who found a safe haven in the United States, Martin Jay would be quick to agree with Neumann's warning against discarding juridical liberties and procedural protections simply because of their purely formal, that is, "negative" character.

Negative rights say only what government cannot do, not what it *should* do. "Congress shall make no law . . ." begins the Bill of Rights. It does not say that Congress *will* guarantee that everyone has a right to food or housing or a job, however important such rights may be in the real world. But negative rights remain crucial within a free society. Jay cites the "prohibition of laws referring to specific people with proper names, famously banned in the United States Constitution as 'bills of attainder.'"

A constitutional companion to the prohibition of bills of attainder, the ban on ex-post-facto laws provides another example of a purely procedural yet essential safeguard of liberty, as well as a subject on which Franz Neumann wrote with great insight. General rules—such as the one prohibiting prosecution for offenses that did not yet exist in law when the "criminal" conduct occurred—constitute a significant barrier against the development of totalitarian power. *The Special Section* (1975), a film directed by Constantine Costa-Gavras, brilliantly illustrates the way the Vichy regime in France during World War II deployed ex-post-facto law to buttress the legal practice of authoritarianism. General principles of law, equality before the law, impartiality—the hallmarks of blind justice—cannot be taken lightly.

But they also cannot be uniformly relied upon to reveal the big picture. Jay argues that what is needed, following Adorno's critique, is a jurisprudence that can "temper the rigor of conceptual subsumption," the subordination of individual case to abstract rule, "with a sensitivity to particularity." The popular art of motion pictures may be one of the most effective instruments ever invented for providing just that sensitivity to particularity in law. The practice of law itself, asserts Barbara Maria Stafford, "has become increasingly cinematic. Trials are now routinely shaped by reliance on so-called demonstrative evidence in the form of videos. The filming of everything from dramatized mugshots to 'a day in the life' of a victim, to the reenactment of crime" underscores the way new modes of visualization are constantly transforming the way we see the law.

Perhaps no technical apparatus can do more to unblindfold justice than the movie camera. It is certainly ironic that the ultimate development in legal abstraction, the embodiment of the corporation as a person with rights, should have taken place in such close connection to the invention of the magic lantern. In revealing law's truth, cinema claims a special authority simply because, as everyone knows, a picture is worth a thousand words. And as Jean-Luc Godard said: "Film is truth at 24 frames per second."

Chapter 2

Constitutional Foundation:
Revolution and the Rule of Law

BLIND JUSTICE, FORMAL juridical equality, legalism, "a government of laws and not men"—all are attempts to put into words the concept of the rule of law. There is no single idea more central to American legal culture; the rule of law, for better or worse, is historically inseparable from liberal constitutionalism. Liberal constitutionalism, it is important to add right away, is not the same thing as capitalism. Pointing to Nazi Germany and contemporary China, historian Stanley Hoffman reminds us that capitalism is clearly compatible with a wide range of political regimes. But an equally wide variety of governments have not employed the rule of law as their fundamental norm or principle of justification; only liberal constitutional regimes have sought to use an essentially jurisprudential concept to provide the system with moral and political legitimacy.

Rule-of-law regimes remain problematic. The same Franz Neumann who, as we saw in our discussion of justice blindfolded, warned against discarding procedural guarantees simply because of their purely formal, negative character, also reminds us that even where there is a government of laws and not men, it is nevertheless men and women who rule. Subordination of political process to legal regulation and constitutional limitation is no guarantee that power will not corrupt. In the frequently cited conclusion to his book *Whigs and Hunters*, Edward Thompson contends that justice in capitalist societies must always remain in some part sham. Even during the age of democratic revolutions, Hegel warned that concentrations of private wealth necessarily threaten the political order of constitutional regimes. The relationship between the rule of law and liberal constitutional society is perfectly captured by Harvard legal philosopher Roberto Unger. The generality and uniformity of law, coupled with the separation of powers of government, "represent the core of the rule of law ideal. Through them, the legal system is supposed to become the balance wheel of social organization." And as Unger adds, historically grounding his critique, the rule of law and its "legal order emerged with modern European liberal society." In contrast to regimes of customary and bureaucratic law, and certainly the law of totalitarian regimes, Unger points out that in "the liberal state, there is a separate body of legal norms, a system of specialized legal institutions, a well-defined tradition of legal doctrine, and a legal profession with its own relatively unique outlook."

Much of popular legal culture, of course, deals with the legal profession itself. In a 1986 American Bar Foundation essay, "Lawyers and Popular Culture," excerpted in Richard Abel's *Lawyers: A Critical Reader*, I provide an overview of how movies have portrayed the profession of law. Much of the remainder of popular legal culture, however, revolves around issues of legal norms, institutions, and doctrine, and how well they work in practice. The notion of the rule of law itself is often at the heart of motion pictures about law and the legal system. A documentary like Errol Morris's *The Thin Blue Line* (1988); a criminal-law film like Joseph Ruben's *True Believer* (1988); a civil-law motion picture like Steven Zaillian's *A Civil Action* (1998); and a film of historical reconstruction, like Yves Simoneau's made-for-television *Nuremberg* (2000)—each has its own rules and conventions to follow, but each at the same time quite transparently deals first and foremost with the overarching question of whether we are to be governed by laws rather than men.

Following Unger, the rule of law is (at least historically) bound up with liberal society and the rise of European liberalism. The latter, in its turn, is inseparable from liberal constitutionalism and those late-

nineteenth century conflicts that marked the age of revolutions—
social and political struggles that gave birth to the original liberal
constitutions themselves. There are differences, of course, between the
American and French revolutions, but for our immediate purpose
what they shared is more important: a bill of rights, a declaration of
the rights of man, a commitment to liberalism and reason, and to the
rule of law as the political backbone of society.

From his vantage point in the twenty-first century, historical sociologist Goran Therborn is able to look back at the eighteenth century
and observe the significance of the American and French revolutions.
The word *revolution* itself could, according to Therborn, "by the
mid-18th century, as in Voltaire, refer to changes in a general sense.
What the term definitely did not denote was a break with a traditional
political system, opening the gate to a novel future." Referring to that
extraordinary political pamphleteer who participated in revolutions
on both sides of the Atlantic, Therborn concludes: "Thomas Paine's
words in early 1791 marked a turning-point: 'It is an age of Revolutions in which everything may be looked for.' "

If republican France declined to institutionalize a cult of national
founding fathers, that was *not* the case with a number of Latin American nations—and, of course, was not the case with the United States.
While celebration of the American Revolution and the Miracle at
Philadelphia loom large in American public education, and characteristic rituals of citizenship such as Independence Day parades and
fireworks mark secular holidays of the first rank, Hollywood has
nevertheless remained curiously aloof from the foundational history
of the country. Contrasting the motion-picture industry's attention to
the Civil War, as well as the first and second world wars, Patrick
McGilligan identifies "only a rare few interpretations of the American
Revolutionary War." He suggests that perhaps the extreme mytholo-
gizing of the revolutionary generation precipitated an absence of quality (fictional) literature surrounding these figures, and that this
absence has likewise discouraged filmmakers from tackling such omi-
nously venerated heroes and events.

Setting to one side the thrilling climax to Alfred Hitchcock's *North
by Northwest* (1959), exactly how would you make a movie about
men like Washington and Jefferson, Mount Rushmore–sized political
figures, national heroes so much larger than life? But consider this

nagging fact: Abraham Lincoln is up there on Mount Rushmore, along with Washington and Jefferson, and neither Lincoln nor the Civil War, as McGilligan points out, have been ignored by filmmakers. The extraordinary and unexpected popularity of Ken Burns's monumental PBS documentary on the Civil War underlines a deep disparity between the kind of treatment movies have provided the "war between the states" and their handling of that earlier historical conflict between American colonists and their British masters.

America's Revolution

One of the few cinematic efforts to depict the Revolution, D. W. Griffith's *America* (1924), was not only dismissed by famed Russian director Sergei Eisenstein, but, more importantly for Griffith and his financial backers, was less than a hit with the American public. One of the challenges confronting filmmakers interested in the American Revolution has been to adequately identify and portray a villain or enemy of the American cause during a period when the United States, certainly in the public mind, generally enjoyed a "special relationship" with Great Britain. Responding to this dilemma, Griffith chose an American turncoat and aspiring dictator, a fictional character like the two sisters in Griffith's film about the French Revolution, *Orphans of the Storm* (1921), to play what McGilligan describes as "the villain of the piece."

Nevertheless, according to the Museum of Modern Art's pioneering film curator, Iris Barry, *America* was still temporarily banned in Britain because of its anti-British sentiment. McGilligan further cites the case of a little-known American film of 1917, *The Spirit of '76*, which was locally censored in the United States and whose director was fined and given a prison sentence because he had shown "British atrocities during the Revolutionary War" at a time when the U.S. relationship with Britain was particularly close. More recently, the mayor of Liverpool, England, purportedly demanded an apology for the portrayal of the city's hero, Lieutenant Colonel Banastre Tarleton, presented as guilty of having committed atrocities against soldiers and civilians in the Mel Gibson vehicle *The Patriot* (2000).

Critics remain divided even today over Griffith's *America*. In his biography of the great silent-film director, Richard Schickel acknowledges that there is "something perfunctory, cramped, and distinctly unfelt about *America*," and, he adds, Griffith's picture "offers nothing in the area of craft and technique that he had not previously surpassed." Garry Wills, however, is somewhat more sympathetic. Allowing for what he characterizes as the film's historical distortions, Wills nevertheless praises carefully crafted scenes of Lexington, the bitter winter at Valley Forge, and the battle at Bunker Hill, the latter based upon John Trumbull's painting. And Wills, like Schickel, heralds the ride of Paul Revere in *America*, even if it manages to reproduce some of Longfellow's original errors.

One final attempt to portray the American Revolution on screen, cited by McGilligan, is the Columbia Pictures musical *1776* (1972) based upon a Broadway show of the same name. The film suffers, in McGilligan's view, because it shies away from the modest political critique implicit in the musical stage version. For example, the show-tune "Cool, Calm, Conservative Men," which presents the architects of the Revolution singing, "We have land / Cash in hand / Self-command / Future planned" is deleted from the film version of *1776*. Careful avoidance of any consideration of the class background of the men who declared the nation's independence necessarily comes at a price. The character of John Adams in *1776* is a composite of the historical John Adams and of his radical cousin Sam Adams.

McGilligan observes that the screenwriters of *1776* employ "actual letters and other historical material in their script in order to lend authenticity to the proceedings," while at the same time they undercut what little real historical content there was to be found in their immediate Broadway source. Similarly, after observing how effectively Ken Burns utilizes "personal memoirs and letters" in his PBS Civil War documentary, Jeanie Attie argues that the film's fixation on one form of realism, quotidian detail and "faded photographs of ordinary men," causes Burns to actually miss the boat with respect to what the Civil War was all about. One consequence of such heavy reliance on letters, diaries, and quotations from archival materials is that viewers are left in the dark as to the larger political and economic context within which the conflict itself unfolded. The "cumulative effect," in Attie's opinion, "is to alleviate the nagging feeling that the Civil War was fought over serious issues."

If the American Revolution was fought over serious issues, they ended up on *1776's* proverbial cutting-room floor. Having reached a deadlock in his effort to formulate a draft of the Declaration of Independence, Thomas Jefferson is visited by his pretty wife, Martha (Blythe Danner), and they spend some private time together. Soon, Jefferson is back at work, writing vigorously, and McGilligan suggests, "we are intended to believe that the Revolution was conceived in Jefferson's bedroom." After being chased about by the flirtatious Franklin and Adams, Martha departs the film, "her dramatic function evidently fulfilled." The transformation of historical events into romantic interludes obviously did not end with D. W. Griffith's conventional reliance upon sentimentality. That American movies have had so little to say of significance, indeed so little to say at all, about the American Revolution remains a mystery.

Produced by Columbia Pictures, Roland Emmerich's *The Patriot* (2000) might have been an exception, but the film is only superficially about the American Revolution. The problem is not that *The Patriot* is formulaic, but, rather, that it represents a formula onto which the images of colonial America have simply been pasted. "American *Braveheart*" is how one critic referred to *The Patriot*, and a typical review points out there are so many similarities between Mel Gibson's *Braveheart* (1995) and *The Patriot* that the latter "feels a bit like a remake set in a different time and country." While critic Roger Ebert enjoyed *The Patriot*, he argues in his *Chicago Sun-Times* review that "there isn't an idea in it that will stand up to thoughtful scrutiny." Ebert is typically blunt: "The British are seen as gentlemanly fops or sadistic monsters, and the Americans come in two categories: brave or braver. Those who have a serious interest in the period will find it a cartoon." We may wish to hold off a little before dismissing out of hand the notion of a cartoon version of the American Revolution. But *The Patriot* contributes little to our understanding of American political and constitutional foundations. Contrary, for example, to Bernard Bailyn's argument in his *Ideological Origins of the American Revolution*, Mel Gibson and his comrades in *The Patriot* are almost uniformly motivated by a desire for revenge against individual British officers, bloodthirsty killers who have murdered loved ones. *The Patriot* could, with a few costume changes, have been a Western, a swashbuckler, or even a gladiator movie.

A British filmmaker, oddly enough, who had earlier directed *Chariots of Fire* (1981), *did* make a film about the American Revolution that deserves our attention—a motion picture sufficiently controversial to compensate for decades of Hollywood silence. Hugh Hudson's *Revolution* (1985), produced by Irwin Winkler and made for Warner Brothers, is not casually titled. Hudson tries to place the American Revolution in the general context of world revolutions and therein lies the source of the film's extraordinary texture and intellectual dimension.

Since it did not bring to fruition any fundamental changes in American social structure—in the distribution of wealth or disparities between rich and poor—historical sociologist Barrington Moore, in his classic *Social Origins of Dictatorship and Democracy*, questioned whether the American Revolution deserved to be designated a "revolution" at all. But director Hugh Hudson's purpose is to show the American Revolution "from the bottom up," and if there are genuinely revolutionary elements present in this particular colonial rebellion against Britain, they receive the lion's share of attention in Hudson's *Revolution*. From the opening sequence, in which American patriots throng the narrow streets of an almost Dickensian urban landscape—carrying aloft the head of King George removed from a toppled public statue—through their revolutionary expropriation, in a pinch, of the boat belonging to illiterate Tom Dobb (Al Pacino), Hudson's American revolution at least *feels* like the French one.

Tom Dobb and his son, historical bystanders and politically indifferent at the beginning, are swept up into the great social events that engulf them. They take on genuinely heroic stature as they rise to the occasion. Apparently identifying more with radical history than with British empire, Hudson presents the British in America as a savage occupation force no less brutal or morally disgusting than the colonial tyrants or rulers in Richard Attenborough's *Gandhi* (1982) and *Cry Freedom* (1987), films about India and South Africa respectively, made just before and after Hudson's *Revolution*. At long last, cinematic decolonization was evidently an idea whose time had come.

The American Revolution provides both a backdrop for and the initiating factor in the rights of passage experienced by Tom Dobb and son as they gradually forget about the trapping business and come to experience the American cause as their own cause, becoming more independent and self-reliant while, at the same time, developing a deep sense of solidarity with all those struggling against the British yoke. "I look around me, Ned," says Tom Dobb, reading the letter he has learned to write to his son by the conclusion of the film, "and I see all kinds of people; men and women, and they got families like mine and we stand together like brothers and sisters." The demeaning depiction of Martha Jefferson in *1776* is replaced here, in *Revolution*, by the strong performance of Nastassja Kinski as Daisy McConnahay, a feminist rebel against the suffocating values of her bourgeois family. Daisy constantly pressures Tom to extend himself, to take risks, and to identify with something larger than himself and his kin—with, for example, the cause of freedom. Her contribution to his education is rewarded with his love. Leader of a group actively supporting the rebels that is assaulted by British troops, Daisy is believed dead during the latter portion of the movie, only to be tracked down by Tom and reunited with him at film's end, in the teeming city of a new nation.

The cool, calm, conservative men excised from history in *1776* are returned to it here; Daisy's own father is a captain of commerce, if not yet industry, who manipulates the wartime market in staples and other supplies for personal profit while feigning support for his daughter and her idealistic endeavors. And it is businessmen and speculators like Mr. McConnahay that the film presents as the principal beneficiaries of the Revolution. Nevertheless, African Americans, Jews, and Indians are all presented as making their contribution to the independence movement, participating in *Revolution* in ways generally ignored by the traditional popular culture of the nation's founding.

Common men and women carry the struggle forward even if they may not have full power to shape its outcome. "We're gonna find us a place," Tom writes a son who has already headed west, "where there ain't no one to bow down to, where there ain't no lord or lady better than you; where you can say what you like and climb as high as you want and there ain't nobody gonna treat no one like a dog in the dirt." It is on this ironic note that Hudson concludes his film, self-consciously refusing to resolve the seeming contradiction between Dobb's optimism and the real world that Hudson suggests is coming, between the democratic nature of the revolutionary process and its undeniably elitist (and constitutionally disenfranchising) outcome, the fact that it ultimately served the interests of the propertied and privileged (and Caucasian) more than anyone else.

The critical reception provided *Revolution* was even less hospitable than that given Griffith's *America* sixty years earlier. Noting the same paucity of films about the American Revolution that struck McGilligan, Leonard Maltin suggested that Hudson's "megabomb" would deter moviemakers from approaching this theme again prior to 2776. Characterizing Pacino's Tom Dobb as much too modern to be compelling, Maltin blames the film's script and acting for its dismal performance at the box office. George M. Fraser argues that *Revolution* "is clear neither in plot nor in photography, and offers little of historical interest." (Fraser's faultfinding with the film's cinematography would at least appear to contrast with Maltin's praise for its production values.)

Baird Searles includes in *Epic*, his coffee-table book on historical films, a full-page photo from *Revolution*: pop singer Annie Lennox as Lady Liberty (listed as "Liberty Woman" in the film's credits), with red-and-white striped sash and flowing red banner. To this illustration, he appends the caption: "Americans look back on their revolution as more dignified than the French, but perhaps the fervor was equally colorful." At least in terms of visual reconstruction, Searles has understood Hudson's attempt to relate the French and American revolutions. In his commentary, he suggests that poor ticket sales may simply suggest that "the moviegoing public did not want the Revolution demythologized," and adds that *Revolution* presented "a colonial America seemingly populated by characters from the 1980s, with Marxist and Freudian overtones."

In spite of what Searles calls "Marxist overtones," Marxist critic Michael Parenti was not convinced of *Revolution's* radical bona fides. Having criticized the film for an inept script purportedly suggesting that colonial resistance arose merely from poor treatment at the hands of "mean-spirited" and "sadistic" British troops, Parenti adds that the film conveys an "oddly counterrevolutionary message." Since soldiers like Tom Dobb are shown being cheated out of their pay by their own officers, the lesson of *Revolution* is that the more things change, the more they stay the same. Corruption always wins out in the end and resistance is just not worth the candle. Thus, for some critics Hudson's film represents a blueprint for revolution, while for others just the opposite.

Patriots

Michael Parenti's critique would have been more on the mark were it directed at *The Patriot*, in which historical context is erased and British violence seems the sole justification offered for revolutionary action. To be sure, it would be a mistake to underestimate the actual impact of at least some British troops stationed in the "New World." The Boston Massacre is just one example where acts by British occupation forces infuriated colonists, were seized upon by the radical popular culture of the period, and used to rally support for revolutionary sentiment. But even the scene in *Revolution* singled out by Parenti, in which Tom Dobb is being cheated, is more complicated than he allows.

Tom is initially interested in redeeming a receipt for his boat, which was commandeered at the beginning of the film. When Tom is inadequately compensated he asks for the rest of his money. "What rest, Mister?" demands the officer. "They've been devalued. That's all those old Continentals is worth now. You take it or leave it." Unwilling to be put off in this way, Tom retorts: "What happened to the 150 acres I was promised?" The officer, with one hand heavily bandaged and a blindfold over one eye, responds, "Listen, you got two arms and two legs and two eyes, haven't you? Now move on, I'm very busy."

But Tom persists and demands to know where he can claim his land. Pounding a cane against the platform on which he stands, the officer yells back: "It was sold by Congress to speculators to pay for the war debt, alright? Now move it!" Tom responds bitterly: "I'm the bloody war debt—we all are bloody war debts." Passing the buck, this frustrated paymaster, himself disabled by war, instructs the ragged veterans before him: "So why don't you go to Congress. . . . Don't tell me. You go to Congress, all of you, and you tell them."

The proof of the pudding is in the eating. The "lesson" or "message" of *Revolution* is, in a sense, whatever film audiences draw from it. Describing, even in full detail, the scene to which Parenti refers cannot, in and of itself, disprove his thesis. But Hudson's treatment of this incident seems to place blame not so much on Tom's officers, even including the one who effectively turns him away but, rather, upon Congress and the speculators, that is, politicians and businessmen. Parenti doesn't mention the film's characterization of Daisy's father or other commercial adventurers who exploit the new nation's turmoil for private ends. Nor, important though it may be, does he mention just what comes next, after Dobb has been told to take his complaints to the new government.

Tom asks where and when he can present his protest and is told that "Congress is coming here, to Philadelphia, they're coming, damn you." "Damn *you*," replies Dobb. "All these men here, we all fought for something and we got it. . . . You take it from us and we're gonna fight again." Is this just complacency, an exchange that teaches struggle is futile? Hudson cannot change the facts or alter the outcome of the revolutionary movement. But he suggests, through Dobb in this sequence, that just as the people got rid of the British, they can also get rid of any new system of exploitation that replaces the regime of colonial administration.

Revolution can easily be interpreted as implying that constitutional democracy or "every generation"—as the labor organizer's ballad goes—"has to win it all again," or fails to do so at its own peril. Recall Jefferson's famous line about the tree of liberty needing to be watered by the blood of patriots every few generations.

It is still fair to question whether Hudson has made Tom Dobb, in Maltin's phrase, too contemporary. In Glenn Silber's exemplary documentary film *The War at Home* (1979), about the anti–Vietnam War movement at the University of Wisconsin, there is a scene where another group of haggard and sometimes wounded veterans stands before a government building and, instead of receiving devalued severance pay, joins in casting their various medals and commendations in the direction of the citadel of power that looms behind them. Their opposition to war is fierce. "We don't want to fight anymore," a soldier tells the crowd of supportive demonstrators congregated around him, "but if we have to fight again," he says, gesturing toward the governmental edifice, "it will be to take these steps."

Woody Guthrie once said that, if called, he would not be afraid to bear arms but that the government might be surprised to find out which way his gun was pointing. Tom Dobb's challenge to his paymaster, and to ruling authority, perhaps anticipates too keenly the alienation and sense of betrayal still to be experienced by future generations who would come to question the veracity of their political leaders. But this is a very different kind of criticism from Parenti's when he asserts that *Revolution* promotes resignation or that it is a "counterrevolutionary" motion picture.

Although Parenti does (briefly) defend a handful of what he labels "independent" films (e.g., *Silkwood*, *Norma Rae*, *The China Syndrome*, *Reds*), his critique of popular culture shares, with Noam Chomsky's analysis of mass media, a tendency to see a range of sources of news, information, and political values as essentially monolithic in their suppression of adversary or dissenting perspectives.

Gareth Jenkins, in a generally laudatory review of Chomsky's book *Deterring Democracy*, questions this particular aspect of Chomsky's theory of social control. Chomsky's Orwellianism, in Jenkins's opinion, overstates the significance of contradictions within the world of ideas and images. For Jenkins, contradictions in social reality, not those from the ideological sphere, place real barriers in the path of ruling power. Of course, juxtaposing ideas and reality in this way will draw a sharp response from some left-wing theorists of the culture industries: political perception can become, or at least help shape, social reality.

While *Revolution*'s Tom Dobb is confronting his military superiors, his son Ned is exploring on his own. He wanders into an assembly hall where another young man is cleaning up after the British have left, trying to get things in order since the Congress will apparently meet in this very room. Describing a mechanical model of the solar system, he instructs Ned: "Mr. Rittenhouse made it. This is the earth and that's the moon." Ned asks how far it is between them and is told: "Two hundred thousand miles."

Viewing the model literally, Ned comments that it "don't seem that far," and his host chuckles. "How do you know for sure?" demands Dobb and the well-dressed young man confidently announces: "I went to Harvard." Manipulating the device, he adds: "See? See how the planets turn? Each makes its own revolution around the sun. See, Mr. Jefferson says that's the idea of America. A revolution. A new turn." This is an instructive scene. Eighteenth-century revolutionaries, sometimes encyclopedia- as well as constitution-writers, were fascinated with applying scientific and mechanical metaphors to the political process. But the astronomical illustration here is apparently lost on Ned, and clearly this key sequence retains an appreciation for class disparity (the rustic Ned, straight off the battlefield, contrasted with the elegant and well-dressed young fellow from Cambridge who tutors him), which structures Hudson's vision of the tension at the heart of the revolutionary enterprise.

In contrast to the class antagonism emphasized in *Revolution*, political theorist Dick Howard describes how a New England merchant elite came together with the common people, the "crowd," in the fight for American independence. While elites experimented with means by which the people could be effectively controlled and the crowd discovered the virtues of flexing its political muscle, a convergence of interests spelled doom for the British system of colonial rule. "Across the thirteen colonies," argues Howard, "a common experience of critical demystification and of political action was leading toward the unity that was the revolution. The Declaration of Independence was nearly anticlimactic from this point of view."

Other commentators focus more, like *Revolution* itself, upon signs of conflict rather than convergence. Colonial historian Alfred Young, for example, talks about the "accommodations" forced upon the merchant elite by "the people out of doors," the crowd which could not necessarily be kept in hand. "The Constitution," he suggests, "was as democratic as it was because of the influence of popular movements that were a presence, even if not present. The losers helped shape the results." Thus in a very practical sense, the Ned and Tom Dobbs of the world and their friends and comrades do shape the results of the revolutionary process; their presence, and the threat they posed to "fight again," compelled Alexander Hamilton and Co. to adopt a far more democratic system of government than they would otherwise have chosen.

Another historian, Linda Kerber, agrees in part with Young and acknowledges that the new Constitution's notion of "the people ranged remarkably lower on the social ladder than any serious republic in living memory had sought to define as active citizens." Nevertheless, the new republic should be evaluated cautiously, in terms of who was *excluded*, as well as in terms of who was included, in the democratic project. "It is the rare Founder," says Kerber, "whether elite or middling, who has left us testimony that he had even the slightest suspicion that black slaves and white women were also part of the civic culture. Indians were explicitly excluded. These were losers who emphatically did not shape results."

Leaving to one side the question of whether (or to what extent) "losers" on the American side had an impact on the outcome of constitutional debates, it is evident that Kerber and Young, like the creators of *Revolution*, feel that the story of the American Revolution cannot honestly be told if women, African Americans, and Native Americans, for example, are systematically excluded from the record and thus denied historical visibility. It remains difficult to understand how a film whose great strength is its unique inclusion of a rainbow coalition of forces that toppled the British can be branded as "counterrevolutionary" or seen as reactionary in design. Hugh Hudson's portrait of "the birth of the nation" could not be more at odds with the vision of D. W. Griffith.

The Disney Version

To the perspectives of Griffith and Hudson, and the makers of *1776* and *The Patriot*, we can add another view of America's constitutional foundations, one aptly described in general terms, by Richard Schickel, as "the Disney version." This angle on the story of American politics might include a coonskin-capped congressman's visit to Washington, D.C., as on the *Davy Crockett* television show or, for that matter, a tourist's visit to Liberty Square at Disney World in south Florida. For our purposes, however, Disney's perspective on the origins of American legal and political order is most dramatically presented in two films from the 1950s, *Ben and Me* (1953) and *Johnny Tremain* (1957).

Published in 1943, Esther Forbes's *Johnny Tremain* won the Newbery Medal for the best children's book of the year; Forbes also won a Pulitzer Prize for *Paul Revere and the World He Lived In*, a biography of one famous rebel who makes an appearance in *Johnny Tremain*. Acknowledging the influence of both Forbes's children's book and the feature film that Disney based upon it in shaping his "early perceptions and understanding of the American Revolution," historian Joshua Brown nevertheless provides a compelling critique of the book's shortcomings. *Johnny Tremain* delivers a "conservative Whig interpretation of the revolutionary cause as amorphous and broad, with rifts and differences based on personality and not conflicting aims rooted in class position and ideology." Perhaps even more crucial, in Brown's view, is what he describes as the "underlying complacence of the book, an upbeat picture of the Revolution that is dismissive of the 'evil' Boston mob and blind to blacks and women, who merely populate the fringes of the plot in benign, but nevertheless racist and sexist, portrayals." In short, Hudson's *Revolution* this book is not.

Another aspect of Forbes's novel not covered by Brown's thumbnail sketch is her emphasis on "patriotic gore," a fascination with violence, pain, and bloodletting that seems to foreshadow *The Patriot*. Early in Forbes's tale, Johnny is working as an apprentice silversmith and, violating a prohibition on Sabbath work, carelessly mishandles molten silver. He severely burns his hand and his fingers are effectively fused, connected by scar tissue. Narratively, *Johnny Tremain* has a kind of Dickensian plot, revolving upon Johnny's secret heritage as a formally unacknowledged member of the aristocratic family headed by Jonathan Lyte. Psychologically, however, the book is about Johnny's desperate feelings of inadequacy owing to his disabled hand and how this injury divides him from experiences apparently critical to his development of self-esteem.

For example, on the eve of the Boston Tea Party, an event central to both novel and Disney film, Johnny is admitted to the inner circle of revolutionary conspirators. Charged with excitement, he debates whether to permit one of the New England radicals, Doctor Warren, to look at his damaged hand. Another leading conspirator who is present in the room, Sam Adams, swears both Johnny and his best friend Rab to secrecy and then asks Rab if he will join in the protest that they are plotting. Johnny, however, standing at Rab's side, is not included in Adams's invitation.

"Was this," Tremain asks himself, "because he thought Johnny too cripple-handed for chopping open sea chests?" Near the end of the book, after Johnny's compatriot Rab has been severely wounded in battle and the boys stoically say goodbye to each other, Rab bleeds to death. At just this point, Johnny finally discovers the courage to allow

Doctor Warren to examine his disabled hand. He knows the necessary surgery will be painful but he is now prepared to suffer what he must like a man. His dying friend had given him a treasured weapon: Johnny's "eye caught on the musket. He took it up, holding it close to the light of the window, fingering and examining it to see those improvements Rab said he had made on it." Only then does Doctor Warren get a good look at Johnny's hand. He warns that he may not be able to restore the hand sufficiently for Tremain to resume his silversmith's craft. "Will it be good enough to hold this gun?" asks Johnny. "I think I can promise you that," replies the doctor and Johnny's decision comes swiftly: "The silver can wait. When can you, Doctor Warren? I've got the courage." The doctor volunteers to go get some men to hold Johnny's arm still while the flesh is cut but the youngster assures the physician there will be no need. He wants his hand fixed immediately so he can put Rab's gun to good use in the American cause. Forbes tells us that Johnny's nostrils tremble, almost as if they could "recapture the gunpowder of yesterday. So fair a day now drawing to its close. Green with spring, dreaming of the future yet wet with blood."

To be sure, even in Hudson's *Revolution*, developing the courage to kill the enemy represents one of the rites of passage into manhood. "Even just wars are horrible and exploitative, *Revolution* argued," according to critic Terry Christensen. And it remains true, in the twenty-first century, that there is no such thing as a "clean war." All wars necessarily involve violence, brutality, and death. Interestingly enough, however, there is an episode near the end of *Revolution* that offers a somewhat different perspective on the psychology of war.

Tom, Ned, and their comrades ambush the British commander, his son, and some other redcoats. The audience has been well prepared for this particularly violent scene and willingly identify with the American guerrillas because of, rather than in spite of, their deadly use of force. Still, Ned Dobb's particular rite of passage into manhood, pictured quite differently here from that of Johnny Tremain in Forbes's novel, is marked by a decision *not* to kill. Clearly given permission by his father to execute the British warlord's son whom Ned has in the sight of his rifle, Ned declines to pull the trigger. This scene is very similar to one in John Sayles's movie *Matewan* (1987), where a young coal miner has a fleeing Pinkerton agent in his rifle sight and, likewise, determines that sparing a life can be more just and honorable than taking one. In Hugh Hudson's revolutionary war, as in John Sayles's class war, there is still some room for humanity, decency, and self-control.

Not surprisingly, much of the "future yet wet with blood" (American involvement in the Vietnam War, for example) is not even dreamt of in the Disney version of *Johnny Tremain*. Nor, needless to say, were the debates that would emerge forty years later over the legal system's handling of high-profile criminal prosecutions and political cases, including the role of defense attorneys representing notoriously unpopular clients. But there was an intriguing if unexpected connection between the two that deserves at least our brief attention.

Recall that, while Johnny is gradually moving closer, on the one hand, to the spirit of revolution and opposition to British tyranny, he is also, on the other hand, trying to establish his legitimate entitlement to full membership among the aristocratic Lytes, one of Boston's most prominent families. Johnny's mother gave him, upon her death, a silver cup bearing the Lyte family crest. The other three members of this unique four-cup set are secure in the Lyte family collection. When Johnny modestly presents his own cup to Jonathan Lyte (Sebastian Cabot), who positively exudes a stuffy British arrogance in sharp contrast to Johnny's healthy and gregarious American egalitarianism, young master Tremain is promptly placed under arrest. The imperious Jonathan Lyte dramatically accuses Johnny of having broken into his home and stolen the silver cup.

Certainly Johnny was invited to the Lyte mansion under false pretenses, thinking he would be welcomed there. More than that, of course, he is being denied recognition of a blood relation, on spurious class grounds, to which the audience is convinced he is entitled. But far worse, for the moment, is the fact that Johnny has been subject to a frame-up and, as a result, is brutally thrown into jail, awaiting trial on a serious burglary charge.

We are shown Johnny lying in a mound of hay, locked behind bars, when several men are admitted to his cell. Johnny immediately recognizes Paul Revere. The famous engraver and soon-to-be Midnight Rider, played by B-Western veteran Walter Sande, ruefully explains to Johnny that "it looks as though Mr. Lyte intends to make an example of you." But Revere tells Johnny not to worry and, gesturing toward another one of Johnny's visitors, explains why: "This is Mr. Josiah Quincy. He's taking your case."

Johnny replies incredulously: "But I can't afford a lawyer, let alone the best one in Boston." Attorney Quincy, played by Whit Bissel—who would soon appear in the political blockbusters *The Manchurian Candidate* (1962) and *Seven Days in May* (1964)—reassures Johnny: "Any innocent man can afford me." Johnny persists, arguing that he is "a nobody," but then is instructed by these radical didacts that we are all nobodies when we stand alone and it is when we stand together, with others, that we realize our true strength. This wholly unsolicited provision of pro-bono legal representation to a youngster with his back against the wall, whom Jonathan Lyte (we discover the following day at trial) wishes *to have hanged*, is a key turning point in the development of Johnny's "revolutionary consciousness," so to speak. "And we happen to believe we must fight together against small tyrannies," Revere concludes the jailhouse sequence, "as well as big ones." And we all know what the "big one" is.

Disney's look back at the colonial criminal-justice system, from the vantage point of 1957, is certainly interesting. Contradictions in the evidence at trial (Johnny had shown his cup to a girlfriend a month *prior* to when Lyte claimed it was stolen) result in his prosecution being dismissed. A judge portrayed as being of no more than average competence and rectitude declines to bow to Lyte's power and prestige. The system works.

Zealous Advocates

Josiah Quincy, an early and bitter critic of slavery, *was* one of Boston's best lawyers; Quincy and John Adams famously defended the British soldiers accused in the Boston Massacre trial. But it is important to record here exactly why they were willing to engage in the representation, not only of such unpopular defendants, but of ones whose politics ran dead against those of Quincy and Adams, true friends of the growing rebellion.

A prosperous Boston merchant, James Forrest, a native of Ireland, came to John Adams saying that Josiah Quincy had agreed to represent the British soldiers if Adams would join the defense. "I had no hesitation," Adams recalled years later, "in answering that Council ought to be the very last thing that an accused Person should want in a free Country. That the Bar ought in my opinion to be independent and impartial at all Times and in every Circumstance." This is a remarkable statement. It suggests that the sense of professional duty lawyers manifest today, certainly in much of the popular presentation of attorneys in fiction and film—and which remains, of course, enormously controversial—was already well developed even *before* the establishment of the United States as a nation. At least *this* aspect of the rule-of-law philosophy and liberal legalism actually preceded the establishment of American constitutional governance.

Josiah Quincy's father wrote him a heartbreaking letter that begs for the son to tell his father it cannot possibly be true: there is no way that young Josiah could have become "an advocate for those criminals" who fired on the patriots that fell in the Boston Massacre. Josiah's response is bracing; he tells his father that his detractors should surely have "spared a little reflection on the nature of an attorney's oath and duty; some trifling scrutiny into the business and discharge of his office" and, specifically, he reminds is father that "these criminals, charged with murder, are *not yet legally proved guilty* and therefore, however criminal, are entitled, by the laws of God and man, to all legal counsel and aid."

The italics are Josiah Quincy's own. One only wonders how many sons and daughters since, newly sworn in as lawyers and having joined the public defender's office or a criminal-defense firm, have not written similar lines to an outraged parent, seeking to have the public faith of a liberal democracy taken to heart in personal as well as professional relations—such unfair criticism from a parent constituting, perhaps, one of Revere's "small tyrannies" that lawyers, in particular, seem fated to endure.

It is essential, then, at least in this instance, to contrast the real Josiah Quincy with the Disney version. Whit Bissel's Quincy tells Johnny Tremain "any innocent man can afford me." But Josiah Quincy instructed his father that all men are presumed innocent. The merchant who asked John Adams to represent the British officer charged with having given the order to fire told Adams, "as God almighty is my Judge, I believe him an innocent man." Adams curtly replied: "That must be ascertained by his Tryal." As far as Adams and

Quincy were concerned, the Johnny Tremains of the world deserved adequate legal representation, not because they could afford it or because they supported the cause of American freedom or even because they were innocent. They deserved representation simply because they had been charged. And that, sadly, is not what Disney's Quincy tells Johnny the burglar in his cell. Why not?

The years immediately preceding the release of Disney's *Johnny Tremain* were marked by the notorious Smith Act trials, contempt citations issued against attorneys for Smith Act defendants, and an anticommunist loyalty oath campaign within the American Bar Association, all of which were a part, according to historian Jerold Auerbach, of a "sustained, invidious, and more successful effort to intimidate lawyers for unpopular defendants and to discipline those whose beliefs or associations were adjudged subversive." What audiences for Disney films needed to see was a Josiah Quincy, not unlike the real one, willing to defend an unpopular client not because he was innocent, however much he might deserve exculpation, but simply because he had been criminally charged by the state. What was important, in the 1950s, was not whether a Smith Act defendant had or had not been a Communist Party member but, rather, that the federal government had charged an American citizen with a serious crime and that the individual thus needed to be represented by an attorney.

"A presumed tradition of professional independence and responsibility," reports Auerbach, "degenerated as the practice of law became 'a hazardous occupation.'" This was the political situation confronting civil-liberties and labor lawyers during the McCarthy period and, as we have seen, the practice of law had earlier become a hazardous occupation for some colonial attorneys like John Adams and Josiah Quincy. Filmmakers could do worse than to honestly portray the dramatic professional lives of early American lawyers with the courage to stand up and put their careers on the line.

Contemporary criminal-defense attorneys, pulling out all the stops, are delighted to muster classical examples like Adams and Quincy, lawyers whose bold statements of the presumption of innocence can be quoted for skeptical reporters on the courthouse steps. But surely men like John Adams and Josiah Quincy, the legal "profiles in courage" to which modern criminal-defense attorneys so confidently allude, would not endorse the tactics now being employed in their name. Insuring that everyone charged with a crime receives adequate legal representation is one thing, but appealing to the politics and prejudices of jurors simply in order to prevail in a particular courtroom battle cannot possibly be what the founders of the bar's historic independence and impartiality had in mind. How could one possibly square such tactics with the legal defense John Adams and Josiah Quincy boldly provided the demonstrators prosecuted for the Boston Massacre?

According to professor L. Kinvin Wroth and Judge Hillar B. Zobel, the editors of John Adams's legal papers, from the moment of the shooting in Boston forward, it appeared that the only way to defend the soldiers responsible would be to show that they had been provoked to use deadly force. "But establishing proof of the danger Preston and his men faced," the editors argue, "meant nothing less than, in effect, prosecuting the entire town of Boston for assault with intent to kill." And John Adams went to considerable lengths to secure precisely the panel of jurors he wanted for the trial of Captain Preston. His efforts did not go unrewarded: the defendant walked. "Characterization of the jury as packed," again, according to the editors of Adams's legal papers, "is not exaggerated."

In his closing argument to the jury in the severed case, where soldiers under Preston's command were charged, Adams embraced a new tactic. One of the victims of the volley of fire that the troops directed at the demonstrators had been an African American, Crispus Attucks. Why not put *him* on trial? The soldiers bravely held their ground crying for the townsmen to stand off. Then, continued Adams to the jury, "to have this reinforcement coming down under the command of a stout Molatto fellow, whose very looks was enough to terrify any person, what had not the soldiers then to fear?" "This," Adams reminded the jury, was "the behavior of *Attucks* to whose mad behavior, in all probability, the dreadful carnage of that night, is chiefly to be ascribed." What a pity that the rabblerouser was among the dead, Adams might have added, as if from the caption to a Daumier cartoon, since it so conveniently insulated him from prosecution! "A *Carr* from *Ireland*, and an *Attucks* from *Framingham*, happening to be here," Adams concluded, "shall sally out upon their thoughtless enterprises, at the head of such a rabble of Negroes, &c.

as they can collect together, and then there are not wanting, persons to ascribe all their doings to the good people of the town."

So much for the heroic victims of Paul Revere's famous engraving—the portrait Adams painted for the Boston jury was one of layabouts and troublemakers, less like patriots and more like Richard Nixon's antiwar bums, deserving what they got. The good soldiers who held their positions as long as they could without firing were ultimately provoked by what Adams called "a rabble of Negroes." Adams's zealous and generally successful representation of his unpopular clients in the Boston Massacre trials did not, of course, prevent him from later becoming president of the United States.

After dumping British tea into Boston's Harbor, Johnny Tremain and Rab, along with their fellow Sons of Liberty, quickly disperse. Critic Leonard Maltin observes that from "an overhead balcony, merchant Jonathan Lyte is aghast, but the British admiral in charge of the harbor comments wryly that 'those Indians seem to prefer principle to profit,' a concept the mercenary Lyte cannot grasp." Then the "patriots march into the middle of town, lighting the liberty tree with their torches." This magical scene is recalled for Walt Disney World visitors by the lanterns hanging from branches of the Liberty Tree in Disney World's Liberty Square.

Although cultural theorist Stephen M. Fjellman fails to remind readers of the relationship between this most memorable scene from *Johnny Tremain* and the Liberty Tree at Disney World, he does record that "forty feet tall and sixty feet wide and weighing over thirty-eight tons, this live oak recalls the original Liberty Tree in Boston under which the self-styled Sons of Liberty gathered in 1765 to protest the Stamp Act." While Leonard Maltin argues that Disney's *Johnny Tremain* "makes real and three-dimensional what most history books put down in flat, hackneyed prose," Disney historian Steven Watts points out that "a political subtext also quickly entered the discussion," adding that contemporary defenders of *Johnny Tremain* characterized the film as a "patriotic celebration of freedom and democracy, one with a direct application to the Cold War struggle."

Fjellman contrasts the Liberty Tree at Disney World with the Swiss Family Treehouse, located in Adventureland. The Liberty Tree is a real tree, Fjellman points out, whereas the Swiss Family Treehouse—based on the tree in another Disney film, *Swiss Family Robinson*

(1960)—is fake, with a prestressed concrete trunk and vinyl leaves. "Disney's relentless presentation of the fake as real," in Fjellman's view, "is often charming." But not always. Fjellman suggests that the "core of Liberty Square celebrates the ascendancy of commerce," and he points to historical omissions in Liberty Square, conceived as a representation of the nation as a whole on the eve of independence, as well as to the stark rewriting of American history in the Hall of Presidents.

The Hall of Presidents is a red brick structure facing the Liberty Tree and Liberty Square Potato Wagon. It houses both a seventy-millimeter movie screen and the famous presidential robots. Fjellman describes the pageant of U.S. history projected on the screen in the Hall of Presidents as "Distory," a sanitized version where there are "no more wars, no flappers, no Depression." The Disney version claims that freedom reigned and individual rights were respected, while ignoring, in Fjellman's view, crucial historical realities: "Indians were being decimated, labor wars were being fought, Woodrow Wilson was throwing leftists out of the country, blacks were being disenfranchised, and women were considered second-class citizens."

Along with providing such inside information as the fact that Liberty Tree Tavern is one of only two restaurants in the entire Magic Kingdom that take reservations, Stephen Birnbaum's travel guide to Walt Disney World also reveals that, unfortunately, the Hall of Presidents "is not one of those laugh-a-minute attractions, like Pirates of the Caribbean or the Country Bear Vacation Hoedown; it's long on patriotism and short on humor." Ironically, this may be one instance where Birnbaum and his team of professional tourists have missed the mark. Historian Michael Wallace, a key onscreen commentator in Ric Burns's remarkable historical documentary *New York* (1999), also visited Disney's Hall of Presidents and reports back that, however unintentionally, this attraction can *always* be counted on for a good laugh.

When the "historical" film described in detail by Fjellman ends, the screen is removed, and suddenly the audience is greeted by a stage filled with realistic American presidential robots. All of the robot presidents actually move and each is introduced by name. Wallace observes that when the "roll call gets to FDR and the more recent presidents, there is a whisper here and there, but when it gets to

Nixon, chortles and guffaws break out." Wallace argues that here the "contrast between the Official History and living memories is too great—Nixon as defender of the Constitution?—and the spell snaps under the strain." When Wallace inquired whether this was perhaps just a bad day for Mr. Nixon, he was told that "no, the crowd always rumbles when RN takes his bow."

It All Started with a Mouse

Along with *Johnny Tremain*, the 1953 cartoon featurette *Ben and Me* represents the major contribution made by Walt Disney during the 1950s to popular conceptions of American legal and political origins. According to film historian Graeme Turner, movie attendance in the United States peaked shortly after the Second World War. By 1953, when *Ben and Me* was released, almost half of American homes surveyed had at least one television set and the motion-picture audience dipped to half of what it had been in 1946. In spite of Disney's near total domination of the animated-film industry in the 1930s (a golden age when, to many, in the view of Ralph Stephenson, the cartoon simply meant Walt Disney's work), Disney Studios emerged from the war with serious financial problems. Leonard Mosley asserts that only "Joseph Rosenberg of the Bank of America had saved them from going out of business." Failing to make money during the war, when so many others in Hollywood had done well, Disney sought out scapegoats. "The bleak situation over money," writes Mosley, "drained him of his dynamic. Misery and worry brought out the worst in him, and he was apt to blame everybody—Jews, blacks, Commies, union workers—for his misfortunes."

Waiting just around the corner, however, were Disneyland and Davy Crockett, theme park promotion, television, and unprecedented merchandizing operations, as well as *Cinderella, Alice in Wonderland, Peter Pan, Lady and the Tramp,* and *Sleeping Beauty.* In his later years, Disney was fond of reminding his fans that it had all started with a mouse—and Mickey, of course, should never be omitted from the Disney success story. "In the seventies," points out Norman Klein, "the permanent rights to Mickey were priced at $750 million, more than the total assets of many of the Fortune 500. One would have to double that figure in the nineties."

The early 1950s, as Bob Thomas suggests, marked the turning point in Disney's fortunes. Disneyland, which even in its earliest planning stages included a True-Life Adventureland featuring a "botanical garden with exotic fish and birds," was inspired in part by Disney's true-life adventure films. Such documentary films had appeared in the early 1950s to be a natural continuation of Disney's wartime informational film production and, significantly, promised to generate much needed revenue during a make-or-break period in the studio's financial history. With *The Living Desert*, their latest true-life adventure almost finished, Walt Disney and his brother Roy had an abortive meeting with Howard Hughes to discuss Disney's acquiring RKO films. "With *The Living Desert* near completion," according to Bob Thomas, "Roy realized that RKO had neither the enthusiasm nor the know-how to sell such an attraction. He established a small sales organization called Buena Vista, after the street where the studio was located." But how was Buena Vista going to sell a seventy-two-minute documentary to motion picture exhibitors? "*The Living Desert*," explains Thomas, "was first booked into the Sutton Theater in New York, along with a cartoon featurette, *Ben and Me*. It was an immediate success, and Buena Vista added more salesmen and released *The Living Desert* in a careful, deliberate way throughout the country. Proportionately, it became the biggest profit-maker in Disney history, earning $4,000,000 after a production cost of $300,000." By this interesting route did prints of *Ben and Me* find their way into projection booths in movie houses across the country.

In 1953, that is. It was the year Notre Dame's Johnny Lattner won the Heisman Trophy, Joseph Stalin died, and a loaf of bread cost six cents. The Korean War ended and Marlon Brando won the Academy Award for *On the Waterfront*. Queen Elizabeth was crowned, *I Love Lucy* was America's favorite television show, and the House Un-American Activities Committee's investigation of Hollywood finally concluded. Simone de Beauvoir's *The Second Sex* had just been published and, the following year, the Dulles brothers' CIA would oust Guatemala's legally elected government. The Vietnamese defeated the French at Dien Bien Phu. Baby Boomers were starting school.

Directed by Ham Luske, who had previously succeeded in "making Snow White move with human grace," *Ben and Me* tells a story about how America got started. Specifically, it reveals how the revolutionary stroke of a pen embodied in the Declaration of Independence was the work, not of Thomas Jefferson (or even his friend, Benjamin Franklin), but of a mouse named Amos. (So, as Walt said, it really did "all start with a mouse"—though not, in this instance, *the* mouse.)

In the bitter winter of 1745, young Amos relates that "these were desperate times" in the Colonies, "jobs were scarce, even for a mouse." As he is almost stepped on and lands unceremoniously in a snowdrift, he adds, "for we were a downtrodden race." The "hard times" social context recalled in Sterling Holloway's wonderful voice-over narration, in the role of Amos, is quickly undercut, in midsentence, by a visual gag. Mice are initially seen as oppressed, metaphorically downtrodden, but as Amos lodges the complaint, it takes on a literal meaning.

The real source of mice politics, however, turns out to be their treatment by cats, or better still, the system of cat-and-mouse social relations. In fact, in a major departure from Robert Lawson's juvenile book of the same name, on which *Ben and Me* is based, the film's writer, Bill Peet, and his assistants in story adaptation (including Winston Hibler, who helped write narration for *The Living Desert*), started "the Disney version," of the American Revolution long before Amos the mouse shows up, cold and starving, on Benjamin Franklin's doorstep.

Disney's *Ben and Me* adds a prologue to Lawson's book, beginning the story of radical social upheaval with Amos's ancestors struggling against an ancien régime in Europe in the sixteenth century: a cat regime, to be specific. In one of the first scenes in the film, purportedly taking place in 1568, Amos's remote ancestor Christopher seeks refuge in the cellar of a London bakery, only to be denied access to a split-open sack of flour by a mean (and hungry-looking) cat. Next comes great-great-great-grandfather Jason, "the first real champion of the rights of mice."

Amos relates that "during the early seventeenth century, the cat population of London had reached alarming proportions and the city was actually threatened by a mouse shortage." At this point, viewers are shown an antiquarian book, opened to the page depicting a cat imprisoned in a large birdcage. Printed beneath this illustration is the inscription: "An ACT demanding that during this present emergency the caging of all CATS be NOW and hereby compulsory under penalty of the STOCKS, MDCXX."

Amos's voice-over narration continues, adding further to the family history, "So in 1620, Jason prepared a petition demanding that all cats be caged. Well, this was ignored." Thus Jason is forced to take his family with him aboard ship to the new world. This sequence is remarkably like that which depicts the founding of New England's colonies in Frank Capra's wartime documentary *War Comes to America*, a contribution to the *Why We Fight* series of propaganda films.

"Jason soon learned," Amos recounts, "that the passengers, men and mice, were all in the same boat. They were all fleeing from the persecution and tyranny of the old country. The name of their good ship was the Mayflower. . . . At last they were free." The screen next is filled with a close-up of one pilgrim's pet kitty who has come along for the cruise. "Meeeooww," purrs the cat, licking his lips menacingly. "Free? Well . . ." adds Amos with obvious chagrin. So mice were still not free, not from the seemingly permanent menace of a familiar feline. The revolutionary rhetoric of solidarity is undercut with the "same boat" figurative/literal doubling joke and then the "free at last" aspiration is diluted with the near scriptural invocation: the [cat] you have with you always.

There is more cat-and-mouse humor to come. A furry Tom awaits in the Philadelphia bakery whose owners have posted a sign, "Apprentice Wanted," one of the "scarce jobs" for which a mouse need not apply, and among Franklin's famous aphorisms Amos locates "a cat in gloves catches no mice," and so forth. But it is already clear how important cat/mice conflicts are by the time Disney's *Ben and Me* picks up with Lawson's story of the charming friendship between Amos and a bumbling Benjamin Franklin.

Later, when there are "rumors of violence" and "loud talk against the stamp taxes and other outrages," torch-wielding demonstrators take to the streets. Caught up in the passion of the moment, Amos (watching events below from high atop a lamppost) slams his fist against the other hand while echoing the slogan, "No taxation without representation!" He immediately loses his balance from the force of the blow and is saved from falling to the ground, head over heels, only because his tail gets caught. There is a call for war and Amos enthusiastically repeats the fist-pounding gesture, only to have his bonny patriot's hat fall down over his eyes. The quotidian nature of a mouse's existence—from almost being stepped on to having a tail to coping endlessly with predatory cats—constantly provides a humorous counterpoint to Amos's cocksure radicalism as well as the serious subject matter implicit in any revolutionary insurgency and its history.

Another alteration of Lawson's book made by Disney's story writers is even more telling. In the *Ben and Me* cartoon history, Amos serves faithfully as Benjamin Franklin's advisor and confidant. He finally gets fed up, however, with Franklin's practical jokes, like employing Amos for a lightning rod—malicious tricks invariably played out at the mouse's expense. Amos moves out of Ben's comfortable residence and returns to the old church vestry, behind the paneling, which provided his family their first home in New England. Eventually, when the crisis between colonies and mother country reaches a boiling point and Franklin is beside himself with uncertainty as to what course the people should take, Ben pleads with Amos to return to his side. Amos consents, but only on condition that Ben promise to sign a "binding contract" guaranteeing that he will treat Amos better than in the past.

The contract is in Lawson, too, in an early chapter titled "The Bargain," but in the book Ben agrees simply to provide Amos's large family (in the church vestry) with cheese, rye bread, and wheat, on a regular basis, and Amos himself with one fur cap, in exchange for Amos's reliable advice and assistance. That's it—the bargain does not reappear in Lawson's account.

But in the film, it comes at the end and plays a much larger role, becoming the "legal document" that alone can restore Amos (with his political savvy) to Franklin's side at a time of great national peril. In exchange for Franklin's binding promise to treat Amos with respect, the mouse will once again render service to Franklin and the Revolution as a one-mouse brain trust. Amos works all night on the contract and delivers it folded to Franklin the next morning, wrapped with the mouse's tail like the ribbon around a barrister's brief.

Before Ben can read it, however, Tom Jefferson shows up, imploring Franklin to help him finish the historic speech over which he has been racking his brain. He's stuck and cannot find the words. At this point Amos insists that Ben read his proposed contract, or else Amos will leave. Franklin raises his magnifying glass to the tiny parchment Amos hands him, and begins reading: "When in the course of human events, it becomes necessary . . ." "Ben!" cries Jefferson, jumping to his feet, as he immediately picks up where Franklin left off, thrusting his outstretched arms to the sky, dramatically reciting those few incandescent words already familiar to every viewer. The image fades from Ben's hearthside and print shop to the echoing chamber of a revolutionary convocation, and then to a heroically posed classical painting of Jefferson and the Signers. The rest, as they say, is history.

The problem is why in heaven's name Amos would begin his bargain with Franklin with language like "When in the course of human events." Franklin is not King George and all Amos really wants is for Ben to stop using him as an experimental subject along the royal road to Edison and the light bulb. Once Jefferson walks in the door, at the moment of rhetorical transposition when Amos's script plays its crucial role, here is Ben's side of the conversation with Tom: "Come in, Red, come in. . . . Of course, Red. . . . But Red, I thought it was finished . . ." In a mere fifteen words of dialogue, Franklin refers to Jefferson three times as "Red." Red Skelton and Red Buttons, maybe. Red Schoendienst and Red Grange, yes. But Red *Jefferson*? Disney Studios thrived on artistic rendering of the familiar, playing out conventions everyone would recognize. But who ever heard of a Red Jefferson? It seems odd that this obscure nickname would suddenly be repeated at this moment for no apparent reason. It's just, well, not Disney.

Reference to Lawson's book not only clears up the mystery but explains what Disney's story writers were up to. In Lawson, "the bargain" between Ben and Amos is not the source for those stirring words that open America's Declaration of Independence. "Red," to be sure, is in Lawson's story but he is not Tom Jefferson. "Red had come up from Virginia," recounts Lawson, "with Mr. Jefferson—in his saddlebag." Red was originally *a mouse*, and a revolutionary mouse at that!

"Scarce had they arrived," says Lawson, "before Red began preaching Revolution to the mice around the Inn stables. He soon had them organized." Red is a revolutionist and political organizer, a "young

firebrand" with "radical tendencies," and although prominent Philadelphia mice are a bit taken aback, even "shocked by the violence of
his theories," they admire his "eloquence and capacity for leadership."
Describing his inspirational polemics delivered to clandestine meetings of radical mouse cadres, Amos relates: "At one of these meetings
Red brought forth for discussion a 'Manifesto,' or list of grievances
which he felt we mice had suffered at the hands of our master, Man.
It began: '*When in the course of human events it becomes necessary for
a mouse to dissolve the bands which have linked him to his master . . .*'
and went on at considerable length."

From Red to Amos to Ben to Tom: this is Lawson's secret history,
a conspiratorial rendition of the founding, a version that ended on the
cutting-room floor at the studio on Buena Vista. Welcome to Bur-
bank.

Power Shift

What happened? Perhaps even the armchair cultural historian needs
but a single clue: Robert Lawson's *Ben and Me* was written and
published in 1939. What took place during the fourteen years separating Lawson's children's book from the Disney version? No one has
put it more clearly and concisely than world-systems theorist Immanuel Wallerstein, who suggests that the conclusion of the Second World
War altered two of the basic premises of the interstate system. First,
the United States emerged as the "uncontested hegemonic power."
Since there were no longer any "significant 'rightist' governments
among the core states," the United States quickly shifted "from being
'left of center' to being the leader of a 'free world' alliance against the
world left, now dubbed 'communist totalitarianism.'"

Second, Wallerstein indicates that 1945 marked the beginning of a
long economic upswing in the capitalist world that dramatically reduced internal social tensions. "The elimination of the need for a
'popular front' alliance internationally," he observes, "ended all need
for it internally in the U.S. Quite the contrary: the period after 1945
was one of sharp suppression of left forces in U.S. society." Thus the
journey from Lawson to Disney, from 1939 to 1953, marked the
transition from "popular front" to McCarthyism, an alarmingly

abrupt transformation of national culture and ideology that goes a long way toward explaining the different versions of *Ben and Me*.

Is it fair to call Lawson's vision of revolution a "popular front" approach? Beyond presenting the Declaration of Independence as a radical manifesto smuggled into the hands of the people at the top by a firebrand mouse named Red, whose violent theories shock even those who would borrow from his revolutionary rhetoric, there's still more. When Red discovers that Franklin and Jefferson have purloined his oratory, he complains about their "theft of his labors," a familiar left-wing charge against the owners of the means of production.

Following his contribution to the American Revolution, Red joins Amos in France for a life-and-death struggle against "the White Mice of Versailles," thereby demonstrating international class solidarity. Rather than cats versus mice, in Lawson it is mice versus mice, the rodents dividing sharply among themselves along class lines. "Patricians!" snorts Red, condemning his new adversaries. "Aristocrats! Oppressors!" A Bolshevik at heart, Lenin of the mousy set, Red declares that the "downtrodden Slum Mice and Sewer Rats of Paris are ripe for Revolution. . . . All they lack is a leader. I will be that leader." Red even recruits Russian mice to join the struggle against reaction but, Lawson records, "Alas for Red's faith in the proletariat! At the first sight of the lavish refreshments spread out in the adjoining rooms his fickle Revolutionists dropped their weapons and rushed for the food."

So Lawson, too, deploys ironic humor to distance himself from left-wing utopianism, demonstrating in the process his own residual cynicism about the staying power of radical political élan and authentic revolutionary commitment. Nevertheless, there is no mistaking the critical distance between Lawson and Disney, between the thirties and the fifties of America's twentieth century. The contradiction is amplified by an additional contrast, that between Northeast and Southwest, between Rust Belt and Sun Belt, or in Carl Oglesby's formulation between "Yankees" and "Cowboys," within recent American political and cultural history.

Popularized in the 1970s by Kirkpatrick Sale in his best-selling book *Power Shift*, this critique of postwar American social and economic transformation is perhaps most fully developed in the singular writing of cultural and political raconteur Mike Davis. Crucially, he describes an "industrial revolution in the old hinterland" as driven by federal taxation policy because "federal fiscal transfers, secured by the historically disproportionate congressional power of the South and West, were the prime movers in the creation of the Sun Belt. Thus in California, Washington, Texas and Florida," Davis concludes, "military spending sponsored the rise of aerospace and electronic industry complexes, while oil depletion allowances and agricultural credits rationalized the regional primary sectors and encouraged downstream diversification in oil technology and agricultural processing/merchandising."

Thus, in Davis's remarkable critique, "immense long-term expenditures on highways, water projects and natural gas pipelines laid the basis for profligate metropolitan development in the desert West." And out of that desert West, after World War II, came not only Disney's *Living Desert* and *Ben and Me*, Disneyland and stationwagon living, but Nixon and Reagan, Watergate and Iran Contra, and the whole new tilt in American political life. Davis convincingly portrays this transformation as anchored in an actual economic reversal; a volte-face in the balance of power that reigned from the Civil War to World War II; a dramatic alteration in "who gets what," inevitably arising from seismic dislocation within the real bases of power.

So it is no accident that since that fateful day in Dallas in November 1963, America has elected three presidents from Texas, two from California, and one each from Georgia and Arkansas: tip of the iceberg of a power shift, indeed. The contrast between Harvard's and JFK's Boston, where Lawson's *Ben and Me* was published by Little, Brown in 1939, and Disney's southern California in the 1950s, base of operations for a genuinely right-wing rising tide, could not be greater.

Rumors about Disney "assisting in setting up the blacklist," according to Norman Klein, "began the saga of anti-Disney lore—about Disney as reactionary—and remains a sore point in animators' biographies and animation histories even today." Eric Smoodin fills in much of the detail to which Klein refers and he concludes that film historians and critics have often pictured Hoover's FBI as antagonistic to liberal or communist writers and filmmakers while "in a sympathetic relationship with such right-wing figures as John Wayne and Walt Disney." Smoodin nevertheless concludes that "the Bureau's information on Disney shows that these relationships were never so simple. . . . He was a chief propagandist but also a producer of potentially subversive movies." The subversive potential in Robert Lawson's *Ben and Me*, at any rate, was considerable and it is precisely his more sympathetic view of revolution—a vision that might have permitted, for example, a very different American reaction to Vietnamese nationalism—that was so carefully extracted from *Ben and Me* in the Disney version. The real evidence of Disney's politics is not in an FBI file but in the images projected by Disney Studios, for better or worse, onto the silver screen.

After citing, as examples of first-rate historical dramatists, Shaw and Schiller, Racine and Corneille, Büchner and Brecht, and then referring to Shakespeare's history plays (admittedly a tough act to follow), historian Michael Kammen observes that it is precisely an appreciation of the "intimate relationship between past and present" that is missing in American historical theater. "By and large," he concludes, "our playwrights have been historically illiterate" and, as a consequence, "they have not served the American Revolution, or their society, well." Beyond the Revolution on stage, Kammen acknowledges without evaluation the Revolution's cinema, including Griffith's *America*, the musical *1776*, and Disney's *Johnny Tremain*. Although he ignores *Ben and Me* and wrote his critique prior to the release of either *Revolution* or *The Patriot*, Kammen would still have to search long and hard to locate within the popular culture of revolution and constitution that facility with historical narrative and modes of historical thought that he feels characterizes the best of continental drama.

That situation may not prevail indefinitely. In a *Newsweek* cover story titled "Founders Chic," RFK biographer Evan Thomas says that, like the generation of Americans that came of age during World War II, the revolutionary generation is "hot." We now have "a new appreciation for the courage and the vision of the Founders" and, in Thomas's view, rightly so. Citing the popular success of David McCullough's biography *John Adams*, Thomas argues that "Americans are nostalgic for an earlier era of genuine statesmen" and indicates that by "humanizing the Founders, McCullough and others have rescued them from the sterility of schoolbooks and, vividly and often movingly, showed them overcoming their fears and flaws." Motion pictures, even more than popular biography, are adept at such portrayal.

Any effort to map the constitutional foundation of American law and politics on film, however, must begin with what we have now: an odd assortment of cinematic projections of liberal revolution, radical means calculated to secure moderate ends, rebellion on behalf of the rule of law. Constitution making itself, in such sharp contrast to its treatment within American historical and legal scholarship, has seemed an almost taboo subject for the makers of theatrical motion pictures.

Beyond the whirlwind of revolution and the Miracle at Philadelphia, how else might we define a constitutional cinema, the genre of rights and fundamental law? If broadly conceived, the category might include pictures that focus on constitutional liberties (Robert Collins's *Gideon's Trumpet*, made for television and based upon the book by Anthony Lewis, as well as Alan Parker's *Come See the Paradise*) or the civil rights movement (Alan Parker's *Mississippi Burning* and Mykola Kuilish's *The Road to Brown*). Since the Constitution provides citizens with a blueprint for the structure of American government, as well as a Bill of Rights, movies which deal with the separation of powers in action—films about the relationship between American courts, legislatures, and the executive branch—could also be counted.

To be sure, unlike the work of trial courts, that of *appellate* courts (very briefly, for example, in Steven Soderbergh's *Traffic* and Barbet Schroeder's *Reversal of Fortune*) and the U.S. Supreme Court (again, briefly, in George Stevens's *Talk of the Town* or, more substantially, in Ronald Neame's *First Monday in October* and Alan Pakula's *Pelican Brief*) has hardly preoccupied filmmakers. And Jennifer Selway tartly observes that *First Monday in October* (1981) is a motion picture in which "the rule is disproved that any film starring Walter Matthau can't be all bad."

Across the continent from California's movie capital, in Washington, the actual U.S. Supreme Court stubbornly remains immune to live television and radio coverage. But again, perhaps not indefinitely. Without apparent damage to the rule of law, considerable national attention was devoted to the rapid audiotape release of oral argument before the Supreme Court in the bitter, postelection, Bush/Gore legal confrontation. And the trail for such audiotape release was blazed almost a decade earlier by Peter Irons and Stephanie Guitton in *May It Please the Court: 23 Live Recordings of Landmark Cases as Argued*

Before the Supreme Court. A Supreme Court cinema, reflecting the drama of high-court politics, like live coverage of the Court itself, is long overdue. The legislative branch of the federal government (Frank Capra's *Mr. Smith Goes to Washington*, Otto Preminger's *Advise and Consent*) and Congressional investigating committees (Peter Yates's *The House on Carroll Street* and Irwin Winkler's *Guilty by Suspicion*) are a very different story. Films that focus on or at least include serious treatment of the House and Senate have certainly established an important niche within the history of Hollywood film. Politicians and the executive branch on film (Orson Welles's *Citizen Kane*, Robert Rossen's *All the King's Men*, Franklin J. Schaffner's *The Best Man*, with a screenplay by Gore Vidal) and movies that focus on the president of the United States (John Frankenheimer's *Seven Days in May*, Oliver Stone's *Nixon*, Barry Levinson's *Wag the Dog*, Mike Nichols's *Primary Colors*, Rod Lurie's *The Contender*) probably now deserve a book of their own.

Nevertheless, the greatest visibility in cinema of the legal process itself is still to be found in films dealing with crime, criminals, and criminal trials and it is to that motion-picture genre which we turn in the next chapter.

Chapter 3

Criminal-Law Films:
Crime-Control Versus
Due-Process Cinema

IF HEGEL WAS right, an appreciation for dialectical oppositions can greatly enhance one's insight into the nature of existence, including the experience of historical development and change. Harvard law professor Duncan Kennedy, present at the creation of the critical legal studies movement, wrote a famous law-review article identifying a tension he saw running like a red thread through the history of American law: that between individualism and altruism. Historian Arthur M. Schlesinger, Jr., has described American history as a whole in terms of the "cycles of American politics," an oscillation in governmental commitment to public purpose as against private interest. In *Law and History*, I point to the complex Hegelian architectonic of American legal development, akin to Schumpeter's dialectic of "creative destruction."

Core genres within the culture of American legal cinema can similarly be portrayed in terms of a central and animating contradiction or dialectic specific to each. The rule of law itself can be seen in terms of a contradiction between adherence to the principle of a government of laws and not of men, on the one hand, and the obvious fact, on the other, that even in liberal legal systems, as Franz Neumann conceded, it is men and women who rule. Whether we call this irony or contradiction, it provides the dramatic conflict, the antagonistic foundation, on which much popular legal narrative and film has been constructed.

Crime Control

The cinema of crime and criminal law, a vast and important genre of legal motion pictures, can readily be approached in terms of its central contradiction, which not surprisingly simply mirrors the central conflict structuring the Anglo-American criminal process: the dichotomy between crime control and due-process values within an adversary system of criminal justice.

It was the due process / individual rights orientation of lawyers like Josiah Quincy and John Adams (when they accepted British soldiers as clients) that so irritated radical defenders of "the people out of doors" in Boston. And it was the crime control / social order propensity of John Adams and the Federalists, once in power, which was behind the Adams administration's attempt to enforce the Sedition Act of 1798. Even if the alien and sedition acts merely reflected, as legal historian Stephen Presser contends, "fear that the sort of instability of life and liberty that prevailed in revolutionary France might be brought to the shores of America," the crime-control impulse reflected, even then, a desire to at least temporarily subordinate the rights of individuals to the presumed larger social stake in law and order, on which individual liberties themselves ultimately depend.

Two centuries later, during the 1960s, while Students for a Democratic Society were drafting, in Port Huron, Michigan, a statement of political faith that emphasized "the absence of individual freedom in modern American life," Richard Nixon, Spiro Agnew, George Wallace, and a phalanx of angry politicians were running for office on a "law and order" platform, promising to get tough on crime. "Nixon and the Republicans," according to historians George Brown Tindall and David E. Shi, "offered a vision of stability and order that a majority of Americans—soon to be called 'the silent majority'—wanted desperately." At just this time, as the country was rocked by violent demonstrations and a "police riot" at the 1968 Democratic National Convention in Chicago, Stanford Law School dean Herbert Packer published his book *The Limits of the Criminal Sanction,* in which he outlined in the clearest possible terms the essential character of the conflict in values structuring the American criminal justice system.

Packer described what he called a "crime-control model," which was committed to keeping crime under tight control to insure public order, arrayed against a "due-process model," devoted to the primacy of individual liberty and concomitant limitations imposed upon official power. Advocates of the crime-control model sought to repress crime almost no matter the cost in terms of personal freedom. Their opponents, at the other end of the criminal procedure spectrum, were predictably fond of a familiar homily: it is better to let ten guilty men go free than to convict a single individual who is innocent.

The Boston Massacre took place in 1770. Exactly two hundred years after redcoats opened fire on either patriots or a "motley rabble of saucy boys," depending on your point of view, Ohio National Guardsmen shot and killed four students during an antiwar demonstration on the Kent State University campus. Crime-control advocates defended the use of force to secure public order both in 1770 (the British colonial regime) and in 1970 (the governor of Ohio). Due-process proponents were outraged. In filmmaker Sidney Lumet's original series *100 Centre Street* (2001), the central dramatic conflict reproduces precisely Herbert Packer's crime-control / due-process dichotomy, embodied in the sharply juxtaposed perspectives on life and law held by two criminal court judges, Joe Rifkind (Alan Arkin), Jewish and liberal, and Attallah Sims (LaTanya Richardson), African American and conservative.

Judge Rifkind, exercising routine bureaucratic discretion, releases on his own recognizance a juvenile offender charged with subway turnstile jumping. A packer at Macy's, defendant William Floyd cannot pay a $250 fine and, in the alternative, has served two days of a possible three-day sentence when Rifkind says "we're not going to wreck his life over 240.20," and releases Floyd on the basis of time served. Rifkind then meets Judge Sims for dinner at a fancy Italian restaurant. After telling the judge that she never met a sentence she didn't like, Rifkind asks her, "Attallah, has there ever been a case where you were moved by the circumstances surrounding the criminal?" She replies she has not, and when Rifkind asks, "Not once?" she shakes her head. "OK," Rifkind begins hypothetically, "how about this, a black man . . ." But she immediately cuts him off, interjecting: "Oh come on now Joe, don't start with that crap. . . . Listen, if I can make it anyone can; straighten up and fly right like the old song says." Rifkind laughs and says, "You're a tough broad, Attallah, but that's why I love you," and the sincerity of his affection, despite their different judicial philosophies, is evident. "Your bleeding Jewish heart is going to drop you in it one of these days. And I love you, too." The soup arrives.

Judge Sims's words prove prophetic. After scenes in which the recently reprieved William Floyd brutally beats the owner of a Chinese takeout over $4.75 worth of greasy eggrolls and, in court, Judge Sims seems especially harsh toward an HIV-positive teenage prostitute strung out on drugs, Floyd, on a roll, shoots and kills a twenty-two-year-old female cop on her first patrol, while holding up a downtown delicatessen. Whatever the apparently bottomless depths into which Judge Rifkind is then dropped, all of New York City is judging him.

If the key issues, seen through the optic of the crime-control / due-process antinomy, remain central concerns of popular legal culture today, it was in the 1960s, perhaps, that this particular battle was most fiercely waged, both in the movies and in the streets, and it was from within the maelstrom of the first Nixon administration that the quintessential crime-control motion picture, Don Siegel's *Dirty Harry* (1971), emerged.

Far more in the style of a war film than a crime film, *Dirty Harry* opens with a close-up of a stone wall, on which are inscribed these words: "A tribute to the Police Officers of San Francisco who gave their lives in the line of duty." The camera then pans down through a long list of names and the years of death, even without any of the film's credits being superimposed over this somber introductory series of shots. Siegel then immediately cuts to the film's action.

Deploying a classic mask shot, in which a portion of the screen area is darkened, Siegel trains the audience's line of sight through the scope of a rifle. A maniac sniper shoots and kills a young lady taking a dip in the brilliantly blue water of her penthouse pool, high above the streets of San Francisco, and threatens further mayhem if the city does not immediately fork over $100,000. Enter police officer Harry Callahan (Clint Eastwood), his own wife mysteriously dead, quietly resolved to put the killer out of action in his own way, even though the liberal mayor (John Vernon) wants to play ball with the nut. Callahan takes time out from eating a hot dog to shoot a few urban gangsters holding up a downtown bank in broad daylight and, in the process, introduces into American cinema the famous line "Do I feel lucky? . . . Well, do you punk?" Meanwhile, the sniper (calling himself Scorpio in the scribbled notes he leaves at crime sites), true to his word, shoots a randomly selected African American boy in the street and narrowly misses killing a priest.

Harry Callahan and his new partner, Chico Gonzalez (Reni Santoni), a graduate in sociology from San Jose State, obviously need to get down to a little serious police work. Scorpio has kidnapped a fourteen-year-old girl, Ann Mary Deacon, and buried her somewhere beneath San Francisco with only a few hours of available oxygen supply. Good old Harry, always stuck with the dirty assignments, gets to make the connection and, ransom in hand, manages to get set up and beat up, puts a knife in the killer's leg, and is finally saved from execution only by the gunplay of his sidekick Chico, while sweet Ann Mary Deacon, the audience worries, breathes none too easily. Though wounded, the police officers' prey has escaped again.

With Chico himself fallen in battle and hospitalized, like Callahan's previous partner, Harry is now on his own. Still, he catches up with the long-haired predator in an abandoned Keezar Stadium, bloodies his leg a little with one carefully placed shot from his patented .44 magnum handgun, and then steps on the wounded limb. After crying out, "I want a lawyer" and "I have a right to a lawyer," Scorpio can no longer stand the pain Harry is inflicting and divulges an underground burial location where Miss Deacon, once she is dug up, is very pale and very dead.

But at least Harry got even, right? Wrong. Apparently the district attorney and the brass upstairs do not take kidnapping and murder seriously, because—one, two, three—Scorpio is free. Because Harry got the truth out of his prisoner by slightly illicit means (torture), the solid case evaporates. And guess who is out on the streets again? Nothing if not persistent, Scorpio soon kidnaps a bus full of schoolchildren and wants the city of San Francisco to pick up the cost of an airline ticket (with some serious spending money thrown in) to some-where—maybe Morocco, where drugs are supposed to be cheap—but definitely out of Callahan country.

Once again invited by city hall to play the uncaged killer's game, this time Harry refuses and instead goes after a little sweet, potentially suicidal, revenge. Jumping onto the hijacked vehicle from a highway overpass and forcing the bus to crash, Callahan finally corners his prey outside an isolated quarry and mine shaft. Callahan gets the drop on him and then repeats, for emphasis, the crowd-pleasing line, asking whether this particular punk feels lucky. Apparently without first checking with his broker, this punk *does* feel lucky and stupidly goes for his gun. Harry blows the little rat's guts into the river. Probably out of a job for his unorthodox police work (and who wants to fight a losing battle against crooks coddled by the courts anyway?), dirty Harry Callahan quietly takes his badge from his wallet and skips it across the surface of his last target's watery grave.

Dirty Harry is a product of a chaotic, even hysterical, moment in American social history, and perhaps only Sam Peckinpah's *Straw Dogs* (1971) and Arthur Penn's *Little Big Man* (1970) compete with *Dirty Harry* in terms of their ability to draw the audience into an unambiguous identification with extremely brutal and violent con-duct. It is hard not to experience the conclusion of the Penn film, for example, as a delirious celebration (for better or worse) of the Custer massacre. In all three films, a visceral and larger-than-life moving image of righteous killing is substituted for classical tragedy as the means by which an audience becomes emotionally cleansed, if that is an adequate characterization of the kind of cathartic release this sort of cinema delivers.

Paul Taylor, writing in the 2001 edition of Britain's wonderfully hard-edged collection of film "blurbs"—the *TimeOut Film Guide*—says that *Dirty Harry*'s critics "were immediately thinking of effects ('Every frame votes Nixon')," but adds that in his view "Siegel's am-biguity wins out." And Geoff Andrew, in the same film guide, asserts that in *Little Big Man* "[a]mbiguity, both toward fact and character, is the keynote." Most remarkable of all is Chris Petit's claim, again in *TimeOut*, that in Peckinpah's *Straw Dogs* "'[c]ivilized' man's con-frontation with irrational violence is handled with impeccable logic."

Indeed, "looking back," Petit concludes, "it's hard to see what the charges of gratuitous violence were all about."

Did they show the same prints of these films in Britain as in the United States? Or is this another case of "you had to be there"? In retrospect, what seems most striking about these films is the way in which they *unambiguously* revealed some of the legal, historical, and sexual fault lines along which the political landscape shook during the 1960s. Paul Taylor's throwaway line about *Dirty Harry*, "[s]eminal law and order cinema," gets right to the heart, not only of how *Dirty Harry* was received at the time it was made, but of what it represents structurally and generically: the right-wing pole or extreme of the criminal-law film's dialectic.

In *Dirty Harry*'s defense, Taylor says it is "more than a little embarrassing when critics trust audiences less than filmmakers do." Embarrassing to whom? One need only try to imagine the same kind of comment being made about "the critics" failing to trust the essential intelligence and better instincts of audiences for Leni Riefenstahl's *Triumph of the Will* (1935) or Veit Harlan's *Jud Suss* (1940). Fortunately, Chris Petit, who liked *Straw Dogs*, nevertheless regards *Triumph of the Will* as "still one of the most disturbing pieces of propaganda around."

A routinely insightful, remarkably reliable, and progressive film writer, Patrick McGilligan points out in his 1999 biography of Clint Eastwood that even Eastwood acknowledged "he had realized right from the onset of the project that *Dirty Harry* contradicted the 1966 *Miranda vs. Arizona* decision of the U.S. Supreme Court, which protected criminal suspects by assuring them they would receive a 'Miranda warning' of their constitutional rights before any interrogation by police." And at the critical point in the film, where Ann Mary Deacon is found dead but at least Scorpio is finally in custody, Callahan is shocked to learn that Scorpio must be released. After Harry graciously acknowledges he had some luck cracking the case, the rug is pulled out from under him and he is told in no uncertain terms by District Attorney William T. Rothko that he's lucky he is not being indicted on a charge of assault with intent to commit murder.

"Where the hell does it say you've got a right to kick down doors, torture suspects, deny medical attention and legal counsel?" Rothko demands to know. "Where," he continues, his tone becoming nastier, "have you been? Does Escobedo ring a bell, Miranda? I mean you must have heard of the Fourth Amendment?" he asks derisively. "What I am saying," Rothko bluntly adds, "is that man had rights." Behind his desk—tan suit, button-down shirt, regimental tie, black horn-rim glasses—he is all lawyer, all rules. Everything Harry hates, even about his side of the legal fence.

The *Miranda* ruling, adds McGilligan, "was generally regarded as a victory for liberals." In fact, liberal Supreme Court justice Abe Fortas had stated in defense of the *Miranda* decision, "we deal not with the criminal against society, but the state and the individual." Not exactly the way Harry Callahan would have put it. "Dirty Harry was a character who gladly bent the *Miranda* rules," concludes McGilligan, "and Clint's dialogue excoriated mushy academics, stupid prosecutors and judges, inept government officials."

In the summer of 2000, the United States Supreme Court decided a case, by a margin of seven votes to two, that reaffirmed their 1966 *Miranda* decision. "The big surprise" in the case, according to a *Nation* magazine editorial, "was [Justice William] Rehnquist himself, whose vote with the majority left dissenting Justices Antonin Scalia and Clarence Thomas to flail on the conservative margin." If one of the most right-wing Supreme Court justices since the Second World War could convince himself that *Miranda* warnings are truly mandated by the Constitution's Bill of Rights, then maybe it really is time for Harry Callahan to discard the badge. More importantly for our purposes, however, this may be a sign that the world movies reflect has been transformed to a point where crime-control cinema must now reinvent itself.

To be sure, police vigilantism, like that of Harry Callahan (or by Harry Callahan's police department *adversaries* in director Ted Post's counterpoint, *Magnum Force*), has occasionally been replaced by citizen vigilantism, both on film (e.g., Charles Bronson in Michael Winner's three *Death Wish* pictures) and in life (e.g., Bernhard Goetz on New York's subway trains). Law professor Susan Estrich, in her book *Getting Away with Murder*, ranks vigilantism as one of the nation's "top ten sympathy defenses" and provides a long list of cases in which individuals acting alone or as part of a mob effectively utilized the defense to escape punishment for homicide. Citizen vigilantism rep-

resents the sinister underside to movements for "popular justice"—
grassroots alternatives to legal formalism whose reflection in film is
surveyed in my contribution to a group of essays collected under the
title *Legal Reelism*.

In the movies, even judges (Michael Douglas in Peter Hyams's *The
Star Chamber*) and criminal-defense attorneys (Glenn Close in Richard Marquand's *Jagged Edge* and Gary Oldman in Martin Campbell's
Criminal Law) have been pressed to take law into their own hands.
But didn't Atticus Finch, too, bend the rules in the end when his
children were endangered, in Robert Mulligan's screen adaptation of
Harper Lee's *To Kill a Mockingbird* (1962)? Perhaps this stalwart
cinematic entry in the "rule of law" pantheon deserves just the kind of
subtle critical reconsideration at which the British *TimeOut* critics
appear to excel.

Due Process

If *Dirty Harry*, more than any other film, seems to distill key elements
of crime-control cinema, what are the crucial characteristics of due-
process films within the criminal-law genre? Two crime films, taken
together, are illustrative in this regard: a contemporary equivalent of
the Hollywood "B movie," *Shakedown* (1988), and a major star vehicle, *True Believer* (1988). These two films, made in the same year,
evidence a stage of evolution, a turning point, in the developing due-
process film formula.

Admittedly, James Glickenhaus's *Shakedown* is hardly an original
or pathbreaking film. "No celluloid cliché," says James Christopher,
"that could possibly fit into *Escape from New York* or *Dirty Harry* is
left unstitched" in *Shakedown*. But its very conventionality, each
stitched cliché, can help draw together important elements of the
due-process film's fabric. *Shakedown* includes a strong woman character in the role of an assistant district attorney. The inclusion of
women attorneys, in fact, represents a significant trend in criminal-law
films over the last twenty years (e.g., *Jagged Edge, Suspect, The Accused, Physical Evidence, The Client, Guilty as Sin*).

Susan Cantrell (Patricia Charbonneau) performs a function in
Shakedown similar to that of Debra Winger's character, Laura Kelly,

in Ivan Reitman's *Legal Eagles* (1986), or even that of Mrs. Christine Manson, wife of Dr. Andrew Manson, in King Vidor's 1938 film version of A. J. Cronin's novel *The Citadel*. She is keeper of the conscience and moral lightning rod for a professional husband/boyfriend torn by the conflict between public obligations and private desires.

Tempted to abandon a criminal client he believes is innocent, and ready to move into corporate legal practice via a well-chosen marriage to the daughter of the corporate firm's name partner, Roland Dalton (Peter Weller) briefly revives a former liaison with Cantrell.

Having breakfast on a porch overlooking Manhattan's Central Park, Cantrell challenges her old flame: "So you're going to take fourteen years of legal aid work and chuck it out the window?" Dalton is irritated. "You don't get it, do you?" he replies. "I mean you got me as some kind of retrograde Clarence Darrow or something. . . . You keep thinking I'm leaving legal aid because I want to be something else. I'm outta here, babe, because it's kicking the life out of me." He gives up trying to sound high-minded. "So what if I want things, Susan. People want shit, you know? I want things!"

Although, as it turns out, Susan Cantrell helps movitave Dalton's renewed commitment to fighting the good fight, she is not at the dramatic center of the film. What *Shakedown* has in common with *True Believer* is its focus on the importance of a zealous criminal defense, regardless of the odds, and its disdain for the precise, calculated, almost impersonal logic of official coercion, including criminal conspiracies perpetrated by police and prosecutors. Traditional due-process films like John Ford's *Young Mr. Lincoln*, discussed earlier, Henry Hathaway's *Call Northside 777* (1947), or Alfred Hitchcock's *The Wrong Man* (1956), dealt with efforts to vindicate the innocent. But later due-process films go further and brand government officials as frame-up artists. In this respect, *Shakedown* and *True Believer* mark a turning point.

In *Shakedown*, the finale is virtually a kind of auto smash-up cartoon, a "heady mix of sleaze and comic book heroes" that causes *TimeOut's* James Christopher to predict for the film "a long life on the video shelf." Having stuck with his client after all, and having nearly been executed by rogue cops as a reward, Dalton crashes a taxicab into an official police cordon blocking his entry to the criminal-courts building where, exculpating evidence in hand, he plans to save his client from conviction. Officers attempt to arrest him on the spot (and no doubt have a jailhouse accident planned for him) as the cover-up continues.

But Judge Maynard (Augusta Dabney) marches into position between Dalton and the secretly drug-dealing cops, telling the police in no uncertain terms: "On the streets you are the law but on the steps of this courthouse, I am the law. If this police officer does not lower his gun," the robed judge now instructs her bailiff, "arrest him for obstructing justice." Admittedly, "Mr. Big," the conventional hoodlum who wears fancy clothes and rules from on high over a criminal empire where cops are mere errand boys, is not brought down to earth or to justice without the standard pyrotechnics. Nor is he subjected to the rule of law without some extralegal crime fighting by a lawyer / unorthodox cop duo, a buddy team that turns up in modified form in films as different from each other as Brian DePalma's *The Untouchables* (1987), Alan Parker's *Mississippi Burning* (1988), and Alan Pakula's *Presumed Innocent* (1990).

Joseph Ruben's *True Believer* revolves around an intense characterization by James Woods of politically hip criminal-defense attorney Eddie Dodd. The element of altruism or conscience helping to regulate decision making in *Shakedown*, injected by Susan Cantrell, or by Laura Kelly in *Legal Eagles*, becomes a kind of moral Marshall Plan in *True Believer*. The film includes an idealistic young lawyer fresh off the staff of the University of Michigan Law Review (Robert Downey, Jr.), a private investigator who still clings to her faith in Dodd, as well as the immigrant mother of a purportedly unjustly convicted, Korean-American gang member, all of whom totally commit themselves to waking up Eddie from his marijuana-induced indifference. They want desperately to remind him that the words of the U.S. Constitution actually mean something—or, at least, *should.*

True Believer, according to *New Yorker* film critic Pauline Kael, "can be said to be about Dodd's finding his lost ideals, but it's basically about pace and drive. The director doesn't use the movie to congratulate himself on sharing Eddie's ideals; he uses it to make us share the excitement of Eddie's recovering those ideals." Of course, it can be argued that director Joseph Ruben's emphasis upon the medium rather than the message makes the message about keeping in touch with the progressive, if idealistic, values of youth more self-effacing and thus provisionally attractive than would be the case were the message broadcast over a loudspeaker. This may be Ruben's way of responding to the old Hollywood adage "If you have a message, send it by Western Union."

But there is another way to look at *True Believer*, beyond noting Eddie Dodd's revitalized radicalism or the "marriage of purpose and adrenaline" that keeps the film hurtling forward to its conclusion, the release of falsely convicted Shu Kai Kim from Sing Sing. Consider actor Kurtwood Smith's performance in the role of district attorney. Eddie Dodd first begins to wonder if Shu Kai Kim just might be innocent when the DA, out of the blue, offers to let the Korean convict out of jail in only a few years if Dodd refrains from his effort to reopen the case. This deal or bargain represents a proffered exchange. It is designed by the DA to keep under wraps the *real* trade-off, the original Machiavellian justification for the state's decision to frame Shu Kai Kim for a murder actually committed by a valued police informant. The notion that "the end justifies the means," a classic prescription for authoritarian tyranny, may constitute the real target of *True Believer*.

At a certain point, the transformation of the due-process genre of criminal-law film into a kind of jurisprudential critique of the entire political system necessitates a generic category of its own. We will explore that possibility shortly, under the heading "Underground Film." But first it is worthwhile to consider ways in which the crime film, narrowly conceived, might still reinvent itself.

Breaking Out of the Double Bind

The crime-control/due-process tension remains so sufficiently sharp and ideologically contemporary that entire television series can and will be spun from this central conflict, rotating the moral and dramatic tensions again and again around the same dynamic confrontation. And crime films with contemporary urban settings, "the naked city" or "asphalt jungle" of modern society (e.g., *City Hall*), historical settings (*L.A. Confidential*), organized-crime milieu (*Goodfellas*), police misconduct (*Training Day*), or that focus on especially disturbing forms of criminal behavior (*Silence of the Lambs*), will continue to draw enthusiastic audiences.

But in his updated conclusion to Carlos Clarens's classic *Crime Movies* (1997), Foster Hirsch describes what he believes to be a certain exhaustion in the crime genre. In the case of Quentin Tarantino's *Pulp Fiction* (1994), for example, which is "[c]oated with references to other movies and pop-culture artifacts," and which Hirsch calls "terminally hip postmodern collage," he worries that criminal law and procedure, "the criminal way of life" itself, has become "removed altogether from any ethnic or sociological reality and suspended in a world that could exist only in the movies or, as the title informs us, in the pages of a pulpy paperback."

Taylor Hackford's *The Devil's Advocate* (1997), a film in which John Grisham appears to meet Anne Rice, may be another example of what Foster Hirsch is getting at. *Chicago Sun-Times* critic Roger Ebert says that the movie "is neither fish nor fowl: It is not a serious film about its subject, nor is it quite a dark comedy, despite some of [Al] Pacino's good lines." Sam Mendes's *American Beauty* (1999) seemed to suffer from the same defect: it was too broadly drawn to be serious but neither sufficiently subversive nor sharp enough for black comedy. Nevertheless, *Devil's Advocate*, by literally identifying legal practice with satanism and thus pandering to anti-lawyer sentiment to an unprecedented degree, may have achieved greater popularity with movie audiences and been given more credence by some critics than Ebert allows.

Beyond the gothic horror of *Devil's Advocate*, where might the criminal-law film be headed—gaining its second wind and exploring new territory beyond the now familiar crime-control/due-process impasse? In 1970, Yale law professor John Griffiths published a law-review article in which he proposed a "third model" of the criminal process. Specifically referring to Herbert Packer's crime-control and due-process models as, in reality, just one model, a "battle model!" with two contradictory poles, Griffiths complained that "Packer consistently portrays the criminal process as a struggle between two contending forces whose interests are implacably hostile: the Individual (particularly, the *accused* individual) and the State." Griffiths characterized this dichotomy as essentially a double-bind situation. No one in their right mind would willingly sacrifice either of the central interests (ordered liberty or individual rights) ideologically portrayed as necessarily contradictory in Packer's opposition.

But Griffiths sought a way out of this conflict by proposing an alternative family model of criminal process—a model that started by abandoning the notion of absolute irreconcilability between the individual and society, between personal liberty and state power. Based on an idealized version of family solidarity rather than a psychodynamic portrait of the way many nuclear families actually work, Griffiths's family model looked a lot like the informal, nonadversarial, communitarian approach to criminal justice that anthropologists had frequently identified among Native American tribes and other traditional cultures. Without further exploring Griffiths's approach to criminal procedure but still following his cue, we might look for an alternative criminal-justice cinema, a new synthesis or attitude, structuring a different way of making films about crime and criminal law.

That might be what director Robert Altman is looking for in *The Gingerbread Man* (1998); the family-model option proposed by Griffiths stands in the background of Altman's latest entry within the crime movie / film noir category. Based on a story by John Grisham, *The Gingerbread Man*, according to *Memphis Flyer* critic Hadley Hury, writing from deep inside Grisham country, is "a dark jewel of a film in which the use of noir elements is not the usual matter of a few stylistic" flourishes but provides instead a "window on a seductive, unsettling, psychological state—the classic noir state of the center not holding." The center that does not hold in *The Gingerbread Man* is, as Hury argues, a psychological center, but it is also, metaphorically speaking, a legal center. A reliable and predictable opposition of criminal-justice forces delicately balanced between crime-control and due-process commitments gets knocked out of alignment, just as "weakness, corruption, and the mess they make of things" throws the lives of the film's characters into absolute chaos and confusion.

Rick Magruder (Kenneth Branagh), a brilliant southern criminal-defense attorney, has just won a big trial in Jacksonville, Florida, and is driving back up to his home in Savannah, Georgia. An overhead tracking shot follows Magruder in his red Mercedes sports car as he explains over a cell phone why he does not mind having destroyed a police officer's career on cross-examination: "He blew procedure, lied on the stand, suppressed evidence—come on Terry, I'm a big supporter of cops but there is only one set of rules whether you read them or not." Terry, evidently a reporter, asks Magruder about the morality of his trial strategy. "Morality in law?" laughs Magruder. "Who told you that, the great lawyer fairy? I've got to protect my client." The due-process slant on criminal law (including its presumed indifference to crime control and social order) from Herbert Packer's "battle model" has been firmly established as Magruder's worldview a couple of minutes into the film, before Branagh's face has been shown on camera and while the opening credits are still running. This kind of swift generic shorthand is only made possible by a deep and pervasive, if unconscious, familiarity with both legal and cinematic conventions, shared by audience and filmmaker alike.

Magruder then calls home and the baby-sitter answers, telling Magruder she is watching him on television at that very moment, being interviewed on Court TV. He wants of course to talk to his kids, and his daughter immediately says, "One of the guys on TV said you are a snake oil salesman and I told Jeff you couldn't be because you're still a lawyer, right?" She scolds her little brother, Jeff, saying she *was* right; Dad tells the kids not to fight and that he is on his way home; and that's the central dynamic of the film: will Rick's legal commitment to due process / client loyalty interfere with his personal commitment to being a good father and caring for his children? In short, the "battle model" versus the "family model."

Later, when Magruder's girlfriend (Embeth Davidtz) has her car firebombed and he goes to the police for help, he gets the cold shoulder. "This place is full of guys," a police-detective acquaintance (not a friend) tells the angry lawyer, "who are fed up with bustin' their chops bringing in scumbags, particularly ones that shoot at the cops, so that you can waltz in as some champion of civil rights and get 'em off." The detective tells Magruder that if he has a complaint to make, he can file it at the front desk, and on his way out the door a receptionist suggests, tongue in cheek, "You got a car fire, maybe you ought to call the fire department."

While Magruder has become quickly (and recklessly) obsessed with his new girlfriend, it is his children who remain the most important thing in his life. When the kids become the target of a creepy kidnapping threat, he understandably panics and starts loading a revolver from his desk drawer to go after the culprit he thinks is responsible. Magruder's law partner is alarmed and asks him what he is doing. "These are my kids, Lois." But she still hesitates: "Maybe he's just trying to scare you." Acknowledging his vulnerability, Magruder responds as he races out the door, "Yeah, well, he's doing a pretty good job."

There is a remarkably similar scene to this one in Orson Welles's *Touch of Evil* (1958), a film with its own version of the crime-control/due-process tension within the battle model of criminal procedure. Charlton Heston plays a rather lawyer-like, cabinet-level, three-piece-suit, Mexican, drug-enforcement official named Vargas; Welles himself plays Hank Quinlan, a corrupt local cop on the Mexican-American border (the film was actually shot, mostly at night, in Venice, California). Quinlan has been fabricating evidence, putting people behind bars, and developing a tough reputation for years—until Vargas shows up. In a run-down apartment building on an oppressively hot summer afternoon, Vargas lectures the arrogant Quinlan on the principle of legality, the values structuring a due-process orientation toward criminal justice administration: "A policeman's job is only easy in a police state."

Welles as director subjects Vargas, however, to a severe test, forcing the liberal police official to make a choice—and in the process Vargas discovers an unexpected limitation upon his own commitment to the due-process model. His pretty American wife (Janet Leigh) is kidnapped by motorcycle gang members, headed by that appropriate queen black widow, Mercedes McCambridge (fresh from starring in Nicholas Ray's fabled Western *Johnny Guitar*). In the end, the elite drug-enforcement administrator (Heston/Vargas) manages to trap the hapless, overweight ("It's either the candy or the hooch") Welles/Quinlan, a symbolic figure for the perverse intercourse of law with pure political expediency who is also, practically and cinematically speaking, human slime floating like an oil slick beneath an abandoned concrete bridge in the film's concluding sequence.

But Vargas has to transgress a few rules himself to catch the crooked cop. The scene where Vargas busts up the smoke-filled, punk mariachi bar, with the warning, "I'm not a cop now, I'm a husband!" is one of the most visually riveting examples of black-and-white film-noir cinema one can imagine. Welles, like Altman later in *The Gingerbread Man*, seems to be taking aim at the durability of due-process, rule-of-law values when subject to the pressure cooker of extreme psychological stress. Both directors tend to leave viewers' solid convictions on such matters in a shambles, along some dark little alleyway, as night falls on a windswept Venice or rain-drenched Savannah.

Cultural historian Michael Denning regards the antifascist popular art of Orson Welles as the crowning achievement of that 1930s "popular front" art which managed to survive postwar reaction and McCarthyism. Denning tries to extract Welles's politics from the critique of (and fascination with) power evident in so many of his films. John Berry, on the other hand, an assistant to Welles in the Mercury Theater, interviewed by Pat McGilligan and Paul Buhle in their book *Tender Comrades*, describes Welles's politics as no more complex than "a wonderful, warm, human conception of what life should be." Admittedly, Denning says that "Welles's ambitions, accomplishments, and failures remain the most fitting emblem of the *unfinished* labors" of the popular front's cultural cadre. He also argues, however, that *Touch of Evil*, which Welles himself described as an attack on the abuse of police power, is an antifascist, pro-due-process film.

Denning describes the "framing of young Manolo Sanchez by the corrupt policeman Quinlan" in *Touch of Evil* as the "metamorphosis" of a California criminal case, tried in 1942–43, which had drawn Welles's attention. In "the Sleepy Lagoon case," Chicano teenagers landed murder convictions that Welles and other liberals regarded not as an example of blind justice but, rather, an expression of the "Nazi logic" of the Los Angeles police department. And Welles was on to something: the Sleepy Lagoon murder convictions were reversed on appeal. Manolo Sanchez in *Touch of Evil*, however, was *guilty*—he actually committed the murder Quinlan tries to pin on him through outrageously illegal means. In a sense, Welles's corrupt cop has more in common with dirty Harry Callahan (Clint Eastwood), who, as we have seen, utililizes unconstitutional methods in his effort to enforce a rough justice. *Touch of Evil*, like *The Gingerbread Man*, allows plenty of room for interpretation.

In the latter picture, Robert Altman's Rick Magruder ends up killing the wrong guy and having to face the consequences. He begs the Savannah police to try to understand that he was only protecting his family and himself under the circumstances as he understood them to be. But the chief of police questioning Magruder responds: "You all never gave that same courtesy to Officer Watson down in Jacksonville, did you? You put that guy up on the stand. . . . He was just trying to protect himself. You punched holes the size of cow chips in a twenty-year career."

To the battle model of criminal procedure John Griffiths juxtaposed a family model—one where human or personal values would predominate, rather than the formal rules and official roles conventionally assigned within the administration of criminal justice in an adversary process. *Touch of Evil* and *The Gingerbread Man* suggest that when those same values, love and concern for family members, are interjected into the drama of criminal-law films, they can radically upset our normal or routine response to the battle model of criminal justice, and can throw into disarray the standard rules of a cinematic genre. Neither cops (contrast *Dirty Harry*) nor defense lawyers (contrast *True Believer*) emerge unscathed from *The Gingerbread Man*.

From this angle, we can appreciate the way in which a film like Steven Soderbergh's *Traffic* (2000) can also be seen as a movie that breaks the mold of conventional, crime-control/due-process cinema. Griffiths wants his readers to see the crime-control and due-process models of criminal procedure as opposites and yet, at the same time, as two sides of the same coin. A similar perspective is reflected in the original, six-hour British *Masterpiece Theatre* production of Alastair Reid's *Traffik* (1989), which deals with the international structure of the heroin business. And the same point of view governs *Traffik*'s feature-length, American, theatrical-release version, starring Michael Douglas and Benecio Del Toro, which substitutes cocaine for heroin and the US/Mexico center/periphery relation for that of Britain/Pakistan.

This approach to the international marketing of heroin or cocaine, conceived as a business enterprise with both legal and illegal components, represents an ideal way of portraying the presumed antinomies of criminal justice as part of a single unified and coherent process. Packer's crime-control and due-process models, on this view, really *are* two sides of the same coin. Oversimplifying only slightly, drug kingpins, located at the production end, and their conservative political opponents, at the consumption end, complement each other and constitute one gigantic commercial transaction—cops and crooks need each other.

"What we wanted to do," observed *Traffik*'s British producer, Brian Eastman, "is to treat the drug business like the car business; not show it in the usual black-and-white morality, but put in perspective of how the world drug trade looks, and force people to think a little more closely about it as a world industry." And it is just this element of *Traffik* that drew American interest a decade later. "Laura Bickford, one of the producers for *Traffic*," points out *filmcritic.com* writer Max Messier, "was attracted to the original miniseries because of the interesting stories, the social commentary on drug usage, and the implication of The System itself being the major perpetrator of drug addiction."

Traffic was a huge critical success in the United States, and Soderbergh won the Academy Award for best director. While there was some criticism of *Traffic* from the left for occasional racial stereotyping, and *Salon*'s Charles Taylor was disappointed by the film because of its seeming willingness to take the government's war on drugs seriously, critics were otherwise nearly unanimous in describing Soderbergh's "dope opera" as, in the words of film writer J. Hoberman, "exemplary Hollywood social realism." In the December 27, 2000, *Village Voice*, Hoberman specifically contrasted *Traffic* with the previous year's best-picture Oscar winner, arguing that a "terse domestic squabble" between harried, upper-middle-class parents, played by Michael Douglas and Amy Irving, had a "bitterness far beyond the smarmy histrionics in *American Beauty*."

Roger Ebert initially found *Traffic* fascinating, "simply because it shows how things work—how the drugs are marketed, how the laws are sidestepped. The problem is like a punching bag. You can hammer it all day and still it hangs there, impassive, unchanged." Every part of the system is carefully coordinated to fit with every other part, a continuum within which crime control and due process are rendered perilously abstract reflections of outmoded legal ideologies. Only gradually did a right-wing backlash develop against *Traffic*, for purportedly declaring the drug war a failure at the very moment law-and-order advocates were arguing that America, with tougher criminal penalties and mandatory sentencing, had finally begun to win the war on drugs. Conservative Republican senator Orrin Hatch may privately have regretted his decision to make a cameo appearance in Soderbergh's film. But it was at least as easy to argue that *Traffic* simply paralleled the statements President George W. Bush made in Mexico, characterizing illegal drug traffic as essentially a "demand side" problem, than that the film advocated surrender to the forces promoting legalization of cocaine use.

Perhaps the real predecessor for *Traffik/Traffic* was William Friedkin's *To Live and Die in L.A.* (1985). Admittedly, this visually stunning crime film—including one of Friedkin's finest automobile-chase sequences—does not have the social-realist ambition of the subsequent British and American "dope operas." But it does betray a similar fascination with technical detail (the business of counterfeiting instead of drug dealing) and, more importantly, Friedkin and writer Gerald Petievich introduce an uncharacteristic ambivalence, even a disinterest, into the kind of moral discourse that normally wraps itself like an electrified fence around crime-control and due-process narratives. "Hero and villain merge," suggests *film.com* reviewer John Hartl, in a picture where there is "little difference between the cold-as-ice criminals and their pursuers, who frequently endanger the lives of innocent citizens." Popular-culture critic John Cawelti identifies a similar "generic transformation" going on even earlier, in Roman Polanski's *Chinatown* (1974). After describing the traditional myth or formula structuring the American hard-boiled detective narrative, Cawelti argues that *Chinatown* deviates from the formula to the point that, by the end of the film, the myth is turned upside down. "Instead of bringing justice to a corrupt society," says Cawelti, "the detective's actions leave the basic source of corruption untouched."

Beyond family and social-systems theory "third models" of the criminal-justice system—and cinema—there is another alternative conception that constitutes a significant development of the crime and criminal-law motion-picture genre. There is no clear line separating this alternative cinema from the due-process dialectic and its evolution inside the crime-movie tradition, but at a certain point, the transition from defense attorneys heroically providing the wrongly accused with zealous advocacy to lawyers and their allies taking on the entire political system requires a separate category of its own—or at least separate treatment within the context of criminal-law films.

This cinematic confrontation with ruling power represents a popular-culture equivalent of the radical arts project to which avant-garde artist Hans Haacke once referred as "framing and being framed." Painters frame pictures of political and corporate corruption; filmmakers working in the crime genre frame images of criminal defendants, themselves framed by the very forces of law and order. Once defense attorneys are portrayed, not just as representing clients or unraveling a case, but as following deceptively innocuous leads back to an original and all-encompassing source of criminality, a central historical conspiracy, then the due-process narrative has been effectively reconstructed.

Underground Film

As suggested in the previous discussion of *True Believer*, the due-process genre, pushed far enough, threatens to become a jurisprudential critique of the entire political system. Kurtwood Smith's bone-chilling defense of his conduct, at the climax of *True Believer* (where a young gang member's liberty is casually subordinated to reasons of state), is reminiscent of another speech Smith made while playing a CIA-linked undercover operative in William Tannen's *Flashpoint* (1984).

Masquerading as DEA Agent Carson, Smith asks Southwest border-patrol guard Bobby Logan (Kris Kristofferson) why a rising star like Bobby had apparently exiled himself to the desert. When Logan replies, with disgust, that the reason is "politics," Agent Carson explodes: "This whole fucking nation is politics. . . . You work for the same law that pays all our salaries: the law of supply and demand. Think about it, whiz kid. That's the American way, pal. Supply and demand. And when the supply is lacking, you create it." Whether it is fear of drug-related street crime, illegal immigration, or left-wing subversion, Carson contends, the government creates such anxiety— *must* create it—since one of the functions of the state is to engineer social consensus and insulate power from criticism, hopefully even from visibility.

"Who are you?" asks Bobby Logan in *Flashpoint*, as it gradually dawns on him that, in speaking with Carson, he is not talking to your basic, dollar-a-dozen DEA agent. "I'm a fixer," says Smith, smiling obliquely, "I fix things." In *True Believer*, what is being fixed is the mess made by cops managing, rather than combating, the cocaine economy. The only eyewitness in *True Believer* who claims that Shu Kai Kim is innocent is an odd fellow confined to a mental institution, who also thinks that John F. Kennedy was assassinated on orders from the telephone company. By the end of *True Believer*, everybody in the film is wondering what the phone company had against Kennedy!

And that is exactly what Agent Carson has to fix in *Flashpoint*: an unraveling cover story about who was responsible for events in Dallas in November 1963. Some viewers or critics may regard not just assassination-conspiracy movies but also films about the criminal-justice system, in which police and prosecutors emerge as a deceitful and potentially draconian force (*The Formula*, *The Border*, *The Star Chamber*, *Suspect*, *Lone Star*), as further regrettable evidence of what Richard Hofstadter famously called "the paranoid style of American politics."

Clandestinism, responds Carl Oglesby in his book *The Yankee and Cowboy War*, is not the figment of paranoid imagination, exploited by Hollywood like any other popular fad or frenzy, but is, rather, a "disease of republican twilight. Its coming bespeaks the degeneration of the constitutional republic into the military empire." Surely military empire could not dominate American political life without men in uniform being permitted to hold positions of substantial responsibility for the making of foreign or domestic policy. Yet was that not the case during the notorious Iran-Contra Affair? Were not key aspects of American foreign policy turned over to current or former military officers, operating on the periphery of existing institutions like the National Security Council and the Central Intelligence Agency?

Challenged by counsel for the congressional committee investigating Iran-Contra, Lieutenant Colonel Oliver North responded that he did not see how he could have acted other than in strict secrecy without the Russians finding out what the United States was doing in the Middle East or Central America. Confronted with the fact that, according to the CIA, the Russians were well aware of what the U.S. was doing, North was forced to acknowledge that this was true. Was it not, counsel asked, the American people who were supposed to be kept in the dark?

In a sharp attack upon the jury that found O. J. Simpson not guilty, former L.A. prosecutor Vincent Bugliosi said that for jurors to have returned the verdict they did, they must have been willing to believe that the whole L.A. police department and forensics unit had conspired to frame Simpson. This, Bugliosi claimed in his book *Outrage*, was equivalent to taking seriously films like Oliver Stone's *JFK*. But a lot of people *did* take *JFK* seriously and, as surely even Bugliosi is aware, a majority of Americans still do not believe the Warren Commission's lone-gunman theory as an explanation for the Kennedy assassination. So many popular television series (e.g., *The X-Files*) and motion pictures have been made to whet the conspiratorial appetite that this particular narrative disposition now deserves a category all its own.

Even prominent philosopher and literary observer Richard Rorty feels compelled to point out that a brilliant book like "*Snow Crash* capitalizes on the widespread belief that giant corporations, and a shadowy behind-the-scenes government acting as an agent for corporations, now make all the important decisions. This belief," Rorty continues, casting his net over a wider range of novels, "finds expression in popular thrillers like Richard Condon's *Manchurian Candidate* and *Winter Kills*, as well as in more ambitious works like Thomas Pynchon's *Vineland* and Norman Mailer's *Harlot's Ghost*." Is American fiction and film doing the nation a disservice by picturing the legal system or, for that matter, American government itself as "just a false front," as Rorty put it?

Before we look more closely at the nature of conspiracy films themselves, it is worthwhile acknowledging the importance of secrecy as well as briefly charting its real-world political history. Secrecy, under certain circumstances, can become a threat to democracy, the rule of liberal legalism or the rule of law, as we have described it. The three essential elements of the democratic state are popular sovereignty (and an inevitably hard-won *universal* suffrage), civil rights and liberties, and public government. The historic struggle to establish the power of parliaments and legislatures against kings and dictators and to secure such basic liberties against state power as the right to speak or organize trade unions has proved essential to the construction of modern democracy.

But the guarantee of *public*, rather than *secret*, government remains on a par with the first two components of a free society and may indeed have become the most precarious of the three pillars supporting constitutional rule in the United States. Classic authoritarian techniques of rule—attacking civil liberties or assaulting parliamentary opponents (even abolition of the legislative body itself)—have proved tempting, yet often elusive, to contemporary political leaders uncomfortable with democratic institutions.

Of course the desire to provide some sort of legal justification, however strained, for official conduct remains. After the Bay of Pigs fiasco, according to historian and biographer Richard Reeves, President John F. Kennedy turned to Richard Nixon, a bitter adversary, for advice as to what course of action to follow next. "I would find a proper legal cover and I would go in," Nixon recommended. "There are several justifications that could be used," he continued, "like protecting American citizens living in Cuba and defending our base at Guantanamo. The most important thing at this point is that we do whatever is necessary to get Castro and Communism out." Thus a perceived need to provide some semblance of "legal cover" for governmental action (however illegal the action may be) remained strong, as did willingness to employ the standard, all-purpose justification of anticommunism, at least until recently, when Western rulers were denied that excuse by an internal collapse of the Stalinist system. President Ronald Reagan and his secret government used their commitment to saving Nicaragua from communism and their support for the William Casey–manufactured Contra army (which Reagan dubbed the moral equivalent of our Founding Fathers) as justification for trading American arms for hostages held by Iran (contrary to stated U.S. policy) and for bankrolling and equipping Contra "freedom fighters" (contrary to U.S. law). The deployment of retroactive as well as "mental" presidential findings during Iran-Contra (ultimately no more credible than outright, illegal destruction of documents, which also occurred) carried the effort to fabricate legal cover stories to a pathetic, perhaps tragicomic extreme.

But to whatever lengths contemporary politicians seem willing to go in an effort to evade democratic accountability, abolition of the legislature itself (at least in the United States) appears beyond their grasp. Admittedly, Truman and Eisenhower transformed the national-security bureaucracy into a new and competing branch of government. After John F. Kennedy was removed from power, Lyndon Johnson created his own Gulf of Tonkin incident and prosecuted a savage and unpopular "police action" in Vietnam without a congressional declaration of war. Richard Nixon had his enemies list and bugging devices, and successfully conspired to run against the opposition candidate of his choice. Reagan's "can do" National Security Council staffer Oliver North bragged of his willingness to lie to Congress if he felt the end justified the means.

But to actually dissolve the legislature seems a political gambit about which American authoritarians can only fantasize. In Gregory LaCava's film *Gabriel over the White House* (1933), the president "suspends" a deadlocked U.S. Congress for the duration of the Great Depression. And not long thereafter, with respect to the judiciary, President Franklin Roosevelt *really did* at least try to pack the U.S. Supreme Court. But by the end of the twentieth century, if not by the 1930s themselves, deployment within domestic politics of such extraordinary measures as outright redesign or elimination of a branch of government had apparently been declared off limits by the ground rules of the liberal capitalist state.

For this very reason, an historical shift in "the rules of the game," the third component of constitutional democracy has become absolutely crucial to the maintenance of a free society: *public government* is critical if secrecy is to be prevented from providing the cloak behind which those who seek democracy's subversion can achieve their main aims *without* actually having to risk construction of a police state or straightforward abolition of the legislature. Richard Nixon may have engineered the "Saturday night massacre"; George Bush may have secured the presidency in 1988 through "flagrant misrepresentations" of his part in Iran-Contra; but Nixon could not abolish the courts and Bush could not avoid an eventual confrontation with the record (and the electorate) in 1992, unless he chose (like Lyndon Johnson) not to run again. Where contemporary authoritarians have done their greatest damage to the democratic state is in secret, not in public where they realize they could actually lose. Not without reason did legislators once again, in the wake of the Clinton presidency, debate whether legal limitations might still be placed upon the constitutional authority of the executive branch to grant pardons to individuals not yet prosecuted—pardons essentially insulating them from potential criminal liability and, at the same time, a president departing office from political accountability.

What brought down Nixon's regime was the bungled burglary of the Watergate complex. What Reagan and his co-conspirators did not count on was Nicaragua shooting down the Hasenfus plane. Even Rodney King's assailants ended up being convicted of felonies for one reason: someone had a video camera, ready and able to make public the secret brutality of the Los Angeles Police Department. Without the videotape, the beating would have been hard to prove. Secrecy is a final refuge for the totalitarian impulse within modern constitutional democracy.

Under the rubrics of *sottogoverno*, or subterranean government, and "cryptogovernment," Italian law professor Norberto Bobbio organized the critique of an entire spectrum of totalitarian political techniques. They range from influence by hidden centers of financial leverage and management of that part of the economy that "belongs to the sphere of invisible power, beyond the compass . . . of democratic and jurisdictional control," to "actions carried out by paramilitary political forces which operate behind the scenes in collaboration with the secret services." In spite of thousands of pages of law reviews and legal textbooks devoted to American constitutional law and its practice, as well as tens of thousands of law-school classroom hours devoted to separation-of-powers analysis and the endless parsing of Supreme Court cases, only during the last several decades has this public/secret dichotomy, what Bobbio describes in a European context as the new "opaqueness of power," been thrust onto the stage of national politics in such a way as to virtually compel its introduction within the canons of political theory. Thus only now can we acknowledge the systematic study of *subterranean government* as one of the most interesting developments in the history of jurisprudence in our time.

During the avant-garde sixties, "underground film" meant movies unlikely to be shown in regular theaters, even at midnight on a Friday or Saturday. "Underground" thus meant unorthodox, lacking commercial appeal, somehow on the periphery. Luis Buñuel's *Un Chien andalou* (1929) fit the bill, but so did Tod Browning's *Freaks* (1932) (banned for thirty years outside the United States, according to David Quinlan), as well as the daringly formalist cinema of artists like Andy Warhol. In 1969, Parker Tyler published his manifesto, *Underground Film: A Critical History*, in which underground film refers to experimental and avant-garde filmmaking arising from the same "steady pressure against the world of existing plastic forms," which had generated action painting and pop art, minimal art and color-field painting. "Underground filmmakers had always operated on the fringes of the American culture," reports motion-picture historian Douglas Gomery, "but in the 1950s and 1960s they worked with more intensity than ever before."

Lines separating underground from experimental or independent filmmaking have not always been clearly drawn. "Independence" may refer to a relation between financial backers of an individual film and the Hollywood studio system (or, today, the corporate giants that absorbed the major studios); or, for that matter, between a filmmaker and those same investors. It can imply a degree of autonomy in a film's distribution and exhibition or the distance between a film's content (or even form) and the reigning conventions of a particular film culture. "The independent producer of an iconoclastic film," argues Michael Parenti, "who might not be able to get studio financing, has to rely on personal funds and sympathetic individual investors. Sufficient backing may take years to procure, as was the case with John Sayles's *Matewan*, the story of class warfare in the West Virginia coal mines."

In fact *Matewan* (1987), as well as Martin Ritt's *The Molly Maguires* (1969)—which was made for Paramount, then a Gulf and Western corporation—represent literally *underground* film: moving pictures actually photographed beneath the earth's surface, employing a narrative derived from and designed to comment upon the social relations of the mineral-extraction industry and its history within the labor movement. This particular sort of underground film appears in many different national film traditions and reveals the extent to which film artists across cultures have found mining an inherently dramatic social context within which to situate stories about moral and political issues. From John Ford's *How Green Was My Valley* (1941) and Carol

Reed's *The Stars Look Down* (1939), to Adolfo Aristarain's *Time for Revenge* (1981), films organized around the mine itself and the lives of those who toil underground, and which focus on the conflicts generated by this often dangerous category of employment, have left their mark on film history.

The master discourse in this particular area of cultural expression, however, almost certainly was inscribed more than a century ago by the French novelist Emile Zola, in his famous *Germinal* (1885). Zola's avant-garde naturalism, a "stylistic exaltation of the material universe," in Sandy Petrey's phrase, proved an incomparable means of conveying the actual experience of being inside a mine. The opening pages of *Germinal*, where Zola initially situates his reader within the alternative universe of "Le Voreux," the world of the mine, of its workers and owners, of the system of industrial capitalism itself, are unforgettable. "While Etienne lingered by the fire warming his poor raw hands," writes Zola, "Le Voreux began to emerge as from a dream."

It is this dream, with all of its strangeness and violence and mystery, that French film director Claude Berri manages to capture from the very first frames of his own motion-picture adaptation, *Germinal* (1993). Reviewing Berri's film, Jill Forbes suggests that for "late-twentieth-century audiences, the mining environment of 'Germinal'—like the lost countryside of the Pagnol films—is highly exotic. It is not just that the pits have closed (earlier in France than in Britain), but the culture of solidarity they generated has all but disappeared too." Zola acknowledged that the central drama of *Germinal* was the struggle between capital and labor, and F. W. J. Hemmings, like Forbes in her observation on the contemporary fate of proletarian solidarity, remarks in his introduction to the Everyman Library edition of Zola's most famous work that the "struggle between capital and labour has lost its priority over the years, to be replaced by others more urgent."

We might paraphrase Forbes and Hemmings by suggesting that the character of social conflict within a world organized along capitalist lines has indeed been transformed during the past century, and that the very nature of societies governed by capital, especially in terms of new networks of flexible accumulation, has been reconstituted almost from the ground up. Certainly, during the period when Zola wrote, it was still possible to construct convincing archetypal representations—

images of the "capitalist system"—which were instantly recognizable and carried with them a profound capacity to express the essence of the social regime for which they provided a basic metaphor. The mines and furnaces, pits and smoking chimneys of capitalist industry provided, perhaps, an illustration without parallel. But the task of coherently representing the modern world-system of control in literature and film has been rendered infinitely more complex, precisely as a result of the social restructuring alluded to above.

Immanuel Wallerstein even suggests that "urbanization of the world and the increase in both education and communications" have made it much more difficult for ideology and security managers, the politicians and public-relations people employed by any society, to come up with new justifications for persistent and dramatic disparities in wealth and power. The old apologies, a century after they were initially skewered by novelists like Balzac, Hugo, and Zola, seem to work no more. "Such political awareness," concludes Wallerstein, "is reinforced by the delegitimization of any irrational sources of authority." Though this may be a somewhat optimistic view of "political awareness," the fact remains that the modern state has been compelled to resort more and more to secrecy, to the deployment of invisible power, in order to preserve its paramount position.

Advances in popular sovereignty, political suffrage, and legislative representativeness, accompanied by a deepening of demands for human rights and civil liberty, have all put considerable pressure on the state to accomplish traditional managerial (and repressive) tasks under infinitely more democratic and thus constraining conditions. The now commonplace globalization of poverty and violence, by themselves, would cause Zola's Etienne Lantier to find the "social problem" unrecognizable today. Thus the current predicament of the progressive writer or filmmaker: how to render the unrecognizable visible, to capture an image of a system whose control tower seems to be located nowhere, to render in fiction or film a system almost without transparent reference points, frequently organized out of the way, from below, by an invisible state.

A link was forged between the world of Zola and our own, between the capitalism of late-nineteenth-century France and that which emerged victorious by the end of the twentieth century, in a lecture delivered by University of Wisconsin social historian Harvey Goldberg at the time of the Watergate crisis. Discussing Zola's famous involvement in efforts to uncover the truth in the notorious Dreyfus Affair, Goldberg observes that "the Dreyfus Affair is a kind of trial run for Watergate, a kind of trial run for those 15 or 20 years of CIA covert operations, a trial run if you please for a whole schema of political assassination of foreign revolutionaries or uncomfortable political leaders at home." Then, with characteristic melodramatic flair, Goldberg drives home the political conclusion: "The point is that with the Dreyfus Affair you are into a very continuous exercise in *raison d'état*, in public lying, into what we now call cover-up. You are into a kind of conspiracy to protect the establishment from too much open and critical thinking, from too much public discussion, from too much intervention by the popular classes into the political process."

All the techniques of the clandestine state, the technology of state secrecy whose historical outline was sketched in the earlier political analysis grounding our critique of cinema, the foundation for an inquiry into the form and content of the underground film—all of that Goldberg sees as already implicit in the tentative machinations employed by the French government in its effort to disguise the savage injustice perpetrated by its conviction and imprisonment on Devil's Island of the army officer Alfred Dreyfus. But how can contemporary motion-picture directors find just the right image, a calculated visual means of conveying the experience of conspiracy and cover-up, designed to reveal the technical apparatus of government secrecy on which authoritarian rulers have come to depend? What would an underground film tracking the emerging system of subterranean government actually look like?

What we are seeking here, in short, is the cinematic expression of what Fredric Jameson calls "totality as conspiracy," in his book *Geopolitical Aesthetic: Cinema and Space in the World System.* "Archetypal journeys back beyond the surface appearance of things," suggests Jameson, "are also here dimly reawakened, from antiquity and Dante all the way to Goffman's storefront/backroom" and even to Marx's request that we follow the captains of industry "into the hidden abode of production, on whose threshold there hangs the notice 'No admittance except on business.' "

Jameson proposes the thriller genre as the perfect medium to perform tasks assigned to a contemporary version of underground film, arguing that the "promise of a deeper inside view is the hermeneutic content of the conspiracy thriller in general," and in fact nominates Sydney Pollack's *Three Days of the Condor* (1975) as a prime candidate. The "representational confirmation" in *Condor*, asserts Jameson, "that telephone cables and lines and their interchanges follow us everywhere, doubling the streets and buildings of the visible social world with a secondary secret *underground* world, is a vivid, if paranoid, cognitive map." As we shall see, it is the *legal* "conspiracy thriller" that delivers one of the most compelling versions (and visions) of contemporary underground cinema.

Sydney Pollack directed the first Grisham film, *The Firm* (1993); the second, released later the same year, was made by Alan Pakula. The book Pakula brought to the screen was virtually written for him to direct: *The Pelican Brief*. Even a cursory review of Pakula's "conspiracy trilogy" (*The Parallax View, All the President's Men, The Pelican Brief*) will demonstrate why a focus upon the spatial or architectural properties of his movies may qualify Alan Pakula as the contemporary underground filmmaker par excellence.

The Parallax View (1974)—at least until appearance of Oliver Stone's controversial *JFK*—has been generally regarded as the most interesting of the Kennedy-assassination-inspired films. Warren Beatty plays the role of Joe Frady, a newspaper reporter who reluctantly comes to believe in the existence of a professional organization of assassins called the Parallax Corporation. This company is available to handle the kind of assignments that the modern corporate state occasionally requires and yet cannot publicly employ legitimate governmental entities to handle. The investigative journalist manages to infiltrate the organization in search of his headline, but realizes too late that he is in over his head and, in the end, is made a "patsy" for the film's violent conclusion.

Formally, Pakula utilizes a "multiplicity of landscapes," following in the footsteps of Hitchcock's *Saboteur* (1942) and *North By Northwest* (1959), in order to geographically situate the conspiracy thriller within the quotidian discourse of the travel brochure and, in Jameson's apt phrase, "the meanings of the space of daily life as such." Other formal devices, however, cause Michael Ryan and Douglas Kellner to fault *Parallax* as political cinema: "The members of the corporation are depicted as faceless businessmen, the dark lighting and extreme long shots of the concluding tribunal scene make the commission of inquiry into impersonal functionaries of corporate society. . . . [A]rchitectural space and scene construction operate to make Frady seem overwhelmed."

That, one could rather easily reply, is the whole idea. Surely, between the Rolling Stones' "Shout it out, who killed the Kennedys . . . well, after all, it was you and me," and *JFK*'s rather concrete evocation of identifiable suspects, there is plenty of room for a film like Pakula's, which asserts, however abstractly and metaphorically, that it is the system itself that constitutes (and thus alone can accurately represent) *the system*, with conspiracy seen (or, where successful from the system's point of view, the Parallax view, *not* seen) as the totalizing moment of contemporary history.

Jameson describes *All the President's Men* (1976), which we have already discussed in the context of realism and film, as "that muted new version of *The Parallax View* which is Pakula's Watergate film." The formal bridge between the two films is an architectural one: the "wings and causeways of the sports arena in which the second senator has just been shot," and from whose inadequately lit, concrete and steel suspended ramps Joe Frady emerges, only to be himself eliminated, open directly into the "cavernous parking garages" where Bob Woodward (Robert Redford) will surreptitiously meet an invaluable (still unnamed) source from deep inside the Nixon-Haldeman conspiracy. Like Jameson in his identification of a "light-dark axis" around which *All the President's Men* is organized, Ryan and Kellner observe a symbolic opposition between the film's shadowy underground parking garage and the fluorescent lighting of the *Washington Post* newsroom.

One of the most satisfying moments in Pakula's Watergate film, in the view of Jameson, occurs just after Bob Woodward meets with his underground (and unidentified) source for one of the last times. "Woodward breathlessly turns to confront his pursuers," says Jameson, "only to find the lights of the empty streets of a sleeping Washington staring him in the face." Whether or not one prefers, like Jameson, to describe this climax in terms of the "empty Mallarmean category of an encounter with the absolute Other," it effectively consummates the film's formal project of locating purely cinematic means for portraying the invisibility of government by conspiracy—what

Norberto Bobbio, as we have seen, described as the opaqueness of power. We may also utilize this scene as a bridge into our final architectural site, so to speak, the visual structure around which *The Pelican Brief* (1993), the final panel of Pakula's conspiracy triptych, is built.

Woodward's source, the character played so sardonically by Hal Holbrook, has just finished running through a list of a dozen crimes committed by the Republicans trying to get Richard Nixon reelected, when Woodward, momentarily stunned, asks, "Do the FBI and Justice know this?" Pakula cuts from a close-up of Redford to one of Holbrook, smoking a cigarette, and before the source can answer Woodward's question, as if on cue, there is suddenly the sound of a car nearby with the ignition switch turning, roar of the engine, then tires squealing as the car bursts into gear and out of the underground parking facility at high speed. There follows a shot of Redford's head spinning to see what's happening, then a shot of Holbrook, then of the car itself, back to Redford, and finally a terrific, almost abstract-art shot of a bare concrete wall and single light fixture (cf., Mondrian and Rothko): Holbrook has disappeared. The sequence Jameson describes, out on the wet streets after Woodward laboriously climbs to the main level, follows this scene immediately but does not come close either in terms of sheer terror or ultimate meaning. Back in the garage, the underground itself, is where it is at.

Besides turning it into a film, the single most important contribution Pakula made to Grisham's novel *The Pelican Brief* was the addition of a harrowing sequence, near the end, in the bank's parking garage. Reporter Gray Grantham and law-student extraordinaire Darby Shaw are nearly victims of a deadly car bomb only moments after heroically tracking down and getting their hands on precisely the political dynamite they were after. Fortunately Darby picks up the cue, either from earlier in this film, when her constitutional-law professor was murdered, or from the previous Pakula film about Watergate, which dealt in a sense with the same conspiracy. It's what turned Woodward's head, too: the sound of a car key in the ignition. The vicious dog in *Pelican*, barking at such an inopportune moment for the bad guys, is just extra, perhaps the evil twin of the president's own dog: biting the hand that feeds you. Woodward said, after all, that he too was a Republican.

"The existence of this lower level," says Rosalind Williams in her cross-disciplinary *Notes on the Underground*, "is revealed gradually, through mysterious occurrences and accidents." Williams's remarkable book assays the literary and political force field wherein secrecy and the underground, conspiracy and the topography of power, intersect. From Zola's *Germinal* and the mines and furnaces of industrial capitalism's nineteenth-century landscape, through the surreal modern concrete and glass cityscape of John Boorman's *Point Blank* (1967) or Errol Morris's *The Thin Blue Line* (1988) and the sinister parking structures of John Frankenheimer's *Seven Days in May* (1964) or Alan Pakula's "conspiracy trilogy," the architectural rendering of political space has remained a crucial focus of social critique in the arts. One need only recall the "mysterious occurrences and accidents," the gradual process by which young physician Hugh Grant in Michael Apted's *Extreme Measures* (1996), is drawn from his promising medical practice into the lower depths, through which flow "dark conspiratorial waters," as *TimeOut's* Trevor Johnston says, in "parts of the city he didn't even know existed." From Edgar Allan Poe and H. G. Wells through Pakula and Apted, the subversive attraction of the underground metaphor has been hard to resist.

In perhaps the most exhaustive treatment of the subject imaginable, *Conspiracy Theories: Secrecy and Power in American Culture*, Mark Fenster acknowledges that "[t]here *are* elements of secret treachery in the contemporary political and economic order." But in his chapter dealing specifically with conspiracy theory *as narrative*, "*JFK*, *The X-Files*, and Beyond," Fenster compellingly identifies fundamental contradictions within conspiracy theory as a narrative form. "Conspiracy theory represents the desire for," says Fenster, "and the possibility of, a knowable political order; yet, in its disturbing revelations and uncertain resolution it also implicitly recognizes the difficulty of achieving transparent, equitable power relations in a capitalist democracy." In other words, conspiracy theory as narrative or cinematic genre tends to tie itself in knots. "Despite its professed intentions of uncovering the plot," concludes Fenster, "the classical conspiracy narrative is inherently ambivalent about uncovering 'the truth' of power and the possibilities of a different future." Would not any conceivable political resolution simply set the stage for another round of crime and cover-up?

Actual Innocence

Motion-picture audiences themselves may already have begun to resist an increasingly predictable conspiracy narrative. The basic pattern has now been repeated in fiction, film, television, video games, and almost every form of popular entertainment. Within just a year of his comments on *Extreme Measures*, Trevor Johnston could describe Richard Donner's appropriately named *Conspiracy Theory* (1999)—in spite of having Julia Roberts and Mel Gibson in the cast—as plagued by "increasingly desperate chases" designed simply to mask a "lack of confidence in a narrative with too few suspects and the same old CIA bad guys behind it."

So the crime-film and criminal-law genres may, once again, be compelled to revise themselves and reorganize the structural elements of the crime narrative sufficiently to pour some new wine into old wineskins. If systems theory (crime as an autonomous and self-contained business operation) and underground conspiracy (crime as contemporary political metaphor) have, to a point, provided useful patterns for a third model of criminal-justice film—beyond crime-control and due-process cinema—perhaps other alternatives are already visible on the horizon.

The classic due-process movie, narrating a gripping story of how an innocent defendant is narrowly saved from prison or the gallows by a gritty reporter or gutsy lawyer, represents a cinematic vehicle badly in need of having its battery recharged. "Of the traditional crime genre films," Nicole Rafter points out in *Shots in the Mirror: Crime Films and Society*, "courtroom dramas have the dimmest prospect for revival." They have, in her view, devolved "into witless reliance on depleted traditions, so much so that even the advent of women lawyers has been unable to resuscitate them." What, if anything, could? They just might get a much needed shot in the arm from new perceptions of social reality. Rafter does acknowledge, in her insightful study, that "new social issues" will always constitute an important source of material for the revival of crime films and, however ironic it may seem, it is no longer possible to ignore "actual innocence" as a new social issue in American life.

We may all have become accustomed to the kind of argument advanced for years by Alan Dershowitz—that most criminal defendants are guilty and that defending the guilty is not a less important job than defending the innocent, it is just harder. But something new has indeed been discovered under the sun of criminal justice: innocent people get convicted in American courts every day. The unbelievable has become scientifically irrefutable, as Barry Scheck, Peter Neufeld, and Jim Dwyer make transparent in their best-selling exposé, *Actual Innocence*. What made all the difference, as documented in A&E's *The Hunt: DNA* (2001), is the dramatic reduction in the cost of state-of-the-art DNA technology and its increasingly routine use both at trial and as a device for checking results previously obtained under conventional procedures within the criminal-justice system.

The DNA revolution in criminal-justice technology is not, of course, the only possible "new social issue" which could both recast and reinvigorate the crime film genre. Jim Dwyer, co-author of *Actual Innocence*, co-wrote another book, in 1994, that, at least in retrospect, points toward a different way in which social reality has helped criminal-justice cinema achieve a new lease on life. That book, *Two Seconds Under the World: Terror Comes to America*, dealt with the first World Trade Center bombing; and the culmination of the events which it describes, on September 11, 2001, has not only paved the way for a generic reconstitution of criminal-law films but, in fact, a need to review the existing subgenre of motion pictures about terrorism.

Watching Edward Zwick's *The Siege* (1998), for example, after witnessing what initially appeared to be a Roger Corman or Tim Burton–style science fiction movie with airliners crashing into the World Trade Center, provides an eerie experience indeed. Visual truth can clearly be stranger than matinee-movie fiction. "Which poses the larger threat to democratic institutions," asked Richard Schickel, in his 1998 *Time* review of *The Siege*, "terrorism or the hysterical response to it?" In *The Siege*, wrote *USA Today* critic Mike Clark, "[h]ate crimes go up, retail sales go down, [and] Wall Street closes" after terrorists "kill and maim scores of Manhattan society's finest." Audiences that craved motion-picture realism and believable action, and rewarded them at the box office, had not necessarily wished to have their future foretold on film, to see the silver screen turned into a crystal ball.

"Crime movies of the early twenty-first century," predicted Nicole Rafter, will "fill our mental reservoirs with a vast supply of imagery for thinking about crime, criminals, and the role of criminal justice institutions in society." Her prediction is already coming true, underscoring once again the significance of popular culture as a record of our time.

Chapter 4

Civil-Law Films:
The Cinema of Tort Liability

GANGSTER-FILM THEORIST Jack Shadoian begins his critique of American crime movies by asking himself what is accomplished within the gangster genre that cannot be achieved just as effectively within other cinematic genres. That is an excellent way to begin thinking about all kinds of genres, including the legal/lawyer one. What is it that is really specific to this genre and does not exist in the same form outside? The overlap between the legal genre and a host of others (gangster, prison, melodrama, Western, science fiction, *social*-science fiction, slapstick comedy, and so forth) immediately complicates the question in interesting ways.

Considering the public's addiction to the facts of crime, it is hardly surprising that the legal-trial genre is dominated by the high drama of criminal trials. It would, however, be erroneous to think that criminal trials exhaust the canon of courtroom confrontation in fiction and film. There is still the civil side. There are, for example, a civil-law cinema of psychiatry in court and separate categories for contract and property law on film. Indeed, a small group of surprisingly complex movies, rich in legal ideas and references (*The Addams Family, Beetlejuice, The 'burbs, Batman Returns, MouseHunt,* and *Nothing but Trouble*), constitutes the vital core of property-law cinema. While there are, in addition, films touching upon such civil-law issues as libel and slander, divorce, child custody, denaturalization, and no doubt others, in this chapter we will focus on movies dealing with torts, what lawyers succinctly refer to as noncriminal wrongs.

The Master Discourse

Criminal-law films, as we have seen, can readily be divided into two dominant forms: crime-control and due-process cinema. The dominant form or "master discourse" of tort cinema, however, was established in four films made between 1982 and 1997: *The Verdict, Class Action, Philadelphia,* and *The Rainmaker.* It is important to note the similarity between these four films, which taken together can be seen as expressing a single story or narrative, in spite of the fact that each film is directed by an individual stylist or auteur: respectively, Sidney Lumet, Michael Apted, Jonathan Demme, and Francis Ford Coppola. The force of generic conventions was sufficient to effectively restrain the otherwise strong personalities and cinematic idiosyncrasies of these four directors, while working within the master discourse.

In *The Verdict* (1982), Paul Newman plays Frank Galvin, a down-on-his-luck, alcoholic negligence lawyer who almost forgets to show up for the case of a lifetime. Oddly, this cornerstone of tort cinema is most usually debated by lawyers and law professors as a film about ethics and professional discipline, rather than for the legal context of the film itself, its substantive law focus. Of course, *The Verdict* is about good and bad lawyering. Of course, the film's audiences were at least as interested in whether Galvin would rally in time to save the day as they were in whether he had an obligation under the ABA code of professional responsibility to notify his clients, for example, of a settlement offer. But the film is also, crucially in my view, about medical malpractice, one of the most important areas within the entire field of American tort law.

Galvin represents the family of a plaintiff who has suffered irreversible brain damage as a result of the way anaesthesia was administered during a routine medical procedure. In the movie's decisive scene, Galvin examines a nurse on the witness stand who effectively implicates the defendant physician in a plot to alter documents in order to hide his own responsibility for causing grievous harm. Galvin's closing argument to the jury—"Act as if you believe and faith will be given to you"—provides a remarkable restatement of Dean Prosser's general theory of torts: the courts are there to do justice, but we have to believe in the system itself before we will take the risks, and go to the trouble, to make use of those courts.

Now there is, on the one hand, a certain similarity between *The Verdict's* story line and that of some criminal-trial films. Take, for example, *True Believer*, discussed in the previous chapter as a classic due-process/criminal-law film. Again, James Woods plays Eddie Dodd, a down-and-out, formerly brilliant, now pot-smoking defense attorney basically available to any drug dealer who will take him on as counsel and can pay the fee in cash. Just as Frank Galvin gets that unique, dreamed-of, potentially redemptive case, so does Eddie Dodd. For each lawyer, the big case moves gradually from the periphery of consciousness to the very center of their being. It becomes an obsession. Winning is not just winning any longer. Justice in a particular case, economic survival, professional prestige, personal salvation, and the credibility of the legal system itself—all hinge on their heroic struggle to see that the rule of law prevails.

Prevails over what? In *True Believer*, it will be recalled, it is the cops and the district attorney who set up Dodd's innocent client to take the fall for something he did not do. The target of Galvin's advocacy in *The Verdict*, however, is quite different: physicians and the hospital where they practice medicine and the high-powered malpractice defense firm that represents them at trial.

Again, the stories themselves are structurally similar. Art critic Lawrence Alloway, in a very interesting essay on violent American movies written to accompany a film series shown at the Museum of Modern Art in New York, points out that motion pictures "are dominated by conventions and can be grouped in cycles. . . . In movies the actors are as stereotyped as, say, the young hero or the old warrior types in Renaissance portraiture." So the cross-generic (criminal-law film / tort-law film) superimposition of Eddie Dodd onto the silhouette of Frank Galvin should come as no surprise.

And we can even apply Alloway's offhand illustration to the particular iconography of tort cinema. Just as we find "the young hero" in *The Rainmaker's* Rudy Baylor, we can also see "the old (or aging) warrior" in *The Verdict's* Frank Galvin. "Situations," Alloway further argues, "are as recurrent in movies as the set themes of speeches in Seneca's plays, such as the 'simple life' speech, the 'haunted grove' speech, and the 'king must be obeyed' speech, to quote E. F. Watling."

A highly significant example of the sorts of recurrent situations identified by Alloway, but within the genre of tort films, is what might be described as the "how I almost didn't get the client" scene. In *The Rainmaker* (1997), Rudy Baylor (Matt Damon) has to get past rusty gates and barking guard dogs to get the signatures of an exhausted mother and a war-injured veteran, who is "not right in the head," on a contingent fee agreement so that he can represent their son who is dying of bone cancer. Bleeding from the nose onto crucial documents, the son heroically signs his own name to the contract.

In *Philadelphia* (1993), a homophobic attorney, played by Denzel Washington, actually rejects his first opportunity to represent HIV-positive fellow lawyer Andrew Beckett (Tom Hanks), who has been fired from his prestigious law-firm position for alleged incompetence, right after being promoted within the firm. Crusading plaintiffs'-rights attorney Jedediah Tucker (Gene Hackman), in *Class Action* (1990), stands in line to get his client, whom he reels in by telling him that "these bastards think they can do anything they want [but] they don't always get away with it. . . . Once in a while people like us, this law firm, we stop them. This is going to be one of those times."

In *The Verdict*, Frank Galvin tapes a note to his office door and goes to a bar to drink scotch and play pinball while his clients cool their heels in the hallway of a dingy office building where Galvin stores his metal filing cabinets but is generally too hungover to practice law—he has had four cases in court in the last three years. Again, *True Believer* is cut from the same cloth. Eddie Dodd is almost too stoned to answer the door to his office (he now also lives in the back room) when an elderly Korean woman, mother of the falsely imprisoned Shu Kai Kim, comes to beg for Eddie's help. And just as Frank Galvin has a colleague and friend (Hank Warden) sober him up just in time and guide him along the way, Eddie Dodd has an idealistic young assistant who points Eddie in the right direction.

Who "They" Are (villains)

But what is crucially *different* about the tort-film genre, or subgenre, as I suggested above, is the target: "who *they* are," as a grizzled Edmond O'Brien put it in Sam Peckinpah's *The Wild Bunch*—who it is viewers can look forward to seeing impaled in the last act. Like every criminal-law teacher, I spent years telling first-year students that the reason the plaintiff in criminal-law cases is always the government is that these are public, not private, actions. And movies, in their way, reflect the same reality: the villain in tort cinema is private, not public, power.

So private parties, yes, but why villains? It makes perfect sense to ask why the master discourse of tort cinema, engraved frame by frame on public consciousness by *The Verdict*, *Class Action*, *Philadelphia*, and *The Rainmaker*, should have developed the way it did, *when* it did. We are now, and have been at least since Reagan's election in 1980, in a period of development in the history of American tort law and litigation that seems, on balance, to have drawn the line on liberal state capitalist transformation of tort liability. This conservative backlash is often peddled under the heading "tort reform." We might reasonably anticipate a tort cinema during this period that would mirror the current "structure of feeling" (as Raymond Williams would have put it)—the value system, in short, of a vigorous, antilawyer, antiliability, corporate rollback of progressive tort law and practice. But that is not what we have been getting from Hollywood torts. How come? Maybe the persistence of state capitalist tort values in the present period (see, for example, antitobacco and antifirearms litigation) is pushing proplaintiff moving pictures to the fore. Maybe Hollywood is still run by communists (that, for the record, is a joke). Perhaps the movies enjoy something more than merely "relative autonomy" from the social and economic infrastructure. But I can think of another explanation which seems to me better than these.

The targets on which these four films train their sights are, respectively, negligent physicians and the medical-malpractice defense bar, the automobile industry, employers who discriminate against minorities and the disabled in their hiring practices, and the insurance industry. In other words, crooked corporate America. Perhaps the sharpest expression of this sort of targeting is provided in a movie which, if not a tort film per se, at least features Ed Norton as a kind of "tort character." It is actually difficult to classify David Fincher's *Fight Club* (1999). Richard Schickel at least tries to locate the film, suggesting that it works "*American Beauty*–Susan Faludi territory, that illiberal, impious, inarticulate fringe that threatens the smug American center with an anger that cannot explain itself."

Schickel's description seems to fit perfectly another Norton film, Tony Kaye's *American History X* (1999), made the same year as *Fight Club*. It also fits rather well a football-hooliganism film, Alan Clarke's *The Firm* (1988). Clarke's brutal British essay on soccer violence, starring Gary Oldman as Bex Bissek, is actually something of a blueprint for *Fight Club* since the English "firms" of the title are fighting clubs that challenge competing crews of football supporters to a game of up-the-ante, at least until Bex goes too far and gets himself killed. What makes *American History X* and *The Firm* quite superior pictures is not so much their surface realism as their social acuity—they are utterly convincing. It is hard to imagine their main characters surviving in their respective social milieus *without* the occasional bit of physical nastiness. Not so *Fight Club*'s angry young men, who may well be professionals and businessmen by day but hardly seem persuasive as urban anarchists by night—the two just don't mix.

Ed Norton's disgust with his job in *Fight Club*, more like that of Russell Crowe's character in Michael Mann's *The Insider* (1999), is, however, absolutely convincing. Norton explains his work to a woman who happens to be sitting next to him on an airplane, while the audience is treated to a series of shots of a grotesquely burnt-out automobile chassis: "I was a recall coordinator. My job was to apply the formula. A new car built by my company leaves somewhere traveling at sixty miles per hour. The rear differential locks up. The car crashes and burns with everyone trapped inside.

"Now," continues Norton methodically, "should we initiate a recall? Take the number of vehicles in the field a, multiply it by the probable rate of failure b, then multiply the result by the average out-of-court settlement c. A times b times c equals x. If x is less than the cost of a recall, we don't do one." The friendly woman sitting next to Norton, carefully eating her airline dinner with measured strokes of knife and fork, stops cold. She is appalled.

"Every time the plane banked too sharply on takeoff or landing,"

Norton recalls in voice-over, "I prayed for a crash or a midair collision . . . anything. Life insurance paid off triple if you died on a business trip." Just as Norton's job description is punctuated by images of other recall coordinators climbing around a charred and twisted vehicle making jokes about how the people inside died, his prayer for an air disaster is immediately illustrated by the hallucinatory depiction of an inflight air catastrophe, followed by a nightmarish disintegration of the plane fuselage. Looks like no survivors. That is basically Norton's view of modern living in a business society: "On a long enough time-line, the survival rate for everyone drops to zero." A human life, at least in the view of the corporate number crunchers, has little or no value.

Or so it would seem, as the history of the manufacture and marketing of tobacco products in America unfolds. No film has targeted the tobacco companies more effectively than Mann's *The Insider*. Powered by strong performances from Al Pacino and Russell Crowe and backed by an exquisite musical score, *The Insider* is Michael Mann's best film. But moral corruption in the tobacco (and television) industries is exposed by First Amendment–driven electronic-media reporters, not by tort-law-driven plaintiffs' attorneys. The only thing that might qualify *The Insider* as a tort film would be the desperate effort by disingenuous lawyers from "CBS corporate" to deploy tort doctrine (an exaggerated fear of "tortious interference" suits brought against the network by big tobacco) to kill an explosive news story. *The Insider* belongs primarily to the "journalist as hero" genre of motion pictures (*Call Northside 777, Z, All the President's Men, Defence of the Realm*).

Courageous criminal lawyer Eddie Dodd's world can easily be turned on its head, and both the police and district attorneys, *True Believer's* nemeses, can be made into heroes with a snap of the fingers (television series like *Law and Order* do so every night of the week). But Frank Galvin's or Rudy Baylor's world? The system that employs someone like Ed Norton in *Fight Club* to do what he does? Corporations like big tobacco switching places with the victims of medical malpractice or insurance fraud or abandoned product recalls, with a snap of the fingers? Now, there is a challenge.

A steep challenge, to be sure, though not (depending on your view of business ethics) because corporations are inherently bad. Rather, in terms of popular American storytelling, there do not seem to be readily available narrative structures within which corporations can be portrayed as champions. In *Marxism and Form*, Fredric Jameson describes how the European novel had to go through a period analogous to what Marx described in economics as the stage of capital accumulation—only in the case of fiction, it is the stage of primitive accumulation of narratable forms. Corporate America in the movies seems to me a tad short on narratable hero figures and formations. From Robert Wise's *Executive Suite* in the 1950s through Oliver Stone's *Wall Street* in the 1980s, business has tended to look less like a public profession than it has a highly specialized branch of organized crime.

Let us assume, for a moment, that this is actually the main stumbling block. "As persons appropriate from the common repertoire of legal schemas and resources," say legal sociologists Patricia Ewick and Susan Silbey, "they are constrained by what is available, by legality as it has been previously enacted by others." And just so with motion-picture producers, story consultants, screenwriters, and directors making films about torts. Lots of models of lonely, struggling lawyers who ultimately prevail on behalf of the little guy, but precious few scenarios in the script file which you would headline "Corporation Makes Good." The corporate entity, according to lawyer and popular raconteur Gerry Spence, "has been created to perform but one function: to seek profit. In the fulfillment of that objective, it is as mindless as any machine and as soulless as any cement mixer."

So what's a corporation to do? It's difficult to imagine how the kind of thirty-second public-relations promotion corporations put on television could be turned into a feature-length film. Several pages into *Fortune* magazine's 1999 "Fortune 500" issue, Hoechst AG of Frankfurt, Germany, has a two-page spread whose theme is spelled out boldly: "Imagine, lovesickness being the only thing that can cause a heartache." The picture and print add up to the notion that Hoechst chemical company is putting its heart into putting an end to heart and circulatory diseases. Better, obviously, than bravely committing your company to employment of slave laborers in Nazi Germany, a crime for which Hoechst, as part of the I. G. Farben chemical combine, was convicted at Nuremberg.

Could Hoechst's glossy-business-magazine-advertising approach somehow imply a story line, the model for a narrative structure that could be incorporated into some new tort-film discourse? Or, failing that, could the tort film be given new life from a generic transplant? In Henry Hathaway's *Call Northside 777*, crusading big-city reporter P. J. McNeal (Jimmy Stewart) clears the name of Frank Wiecek (Richard Conte), an innocent man wrongly convicted of killing a cop. Just as defense attorney Eddie Dodd clears his client's name and springs him from prison, and journalist McNeal accomplishes the same trick in the Hathaway picture, could the movies find a way to do the same thing for business? Could a motion picture manage to tell the story of a victimized corporation, wrongly accused of negligence in the popular press and in civil court, only to be exonerated by a no-nonsense jury in the film's upbeat ending?

"It is fashionable at the moment," writes Andrew Solomon in his brilliantly crafted study of depression, *The Noonday Demon*, "to excoriate the pharmaceutical industry as one that takes advantage of the sick." Solomon observes to the contrary that in his experience "people in the industry are both capitalists and idealists—people keen on profit but also optimistic that their work may benefit the world, that they may enable important discoveries that will put specific illnesses into obsolescence." Given the feverish efforts of antipsychiatry activists to enlist prominent tort lawyers in their struggle to make drug companies legally liable for treatment-coincident suicides (depressed psychiatric patients who kill themselves or others while on medication even though they do so simply because they are depressed), then it seems clear that raw material for the "corporation makes good" scenario is certainly out there, just waiting to be discovered by ambitious motion-picture-studio story departments, like the one portrayed in Robert Altman's *The Player* (1992).

In contrast to what he characterizes as a populist civil-trial narrative, law and politics professor Jeffrey Abramson describes a "Hamiltonian narrative" that tells "a mirror-image story, about victimized corporations and fraudulent plaintiffs served by the big industry of trial lawyers." The only film Abramson identifies as telling the Hamiltonian story, however, is Atom Egoyan's *The Sweet Hereafter* (1997), based upon Russell Banks's novel, a movie about a small town victimized by tragedy, and perhaps law, but without a victimized corporation at the center. Review after review of the film describes how the emotionally devastated residents of a community in British Columbia are preyed upon by ambitious plaintiff's attorney Mitchell Stevens (Ian Holm). Legal sociologist Austin Sarat says that *The Sweet Hereafter* shows how civil litigation can be "as dangerous to the social health of a community, as to the psychic health of persons in mourning." But the relationship between tort law and corporate conduct is really not at issue.

In *Time*, Richard Schickel says the ambulance-chasing behavior of Egoyan's tort lawyer, Stevens, cannot be explained by greed; Roger Ebert in the *Chicago Sun-Times* goes so far as to argue that *The Sweet Hereafter* "is not about lawyers or the law, not about small town insularity, not about revenge." What *is* the film about? Certainly, *The Sweet Hereafter* deserves to be described as a powerful statement about the terrible inadequacy of various legal yardsticks for measuring liability and compensating loss. The complexity of human tragedy and loss sometimes cannot be comprehended by law or any other social system. However this idiosyncratic film is ultimately interpreted, it should not be seen as a harassed corporate culture's response to Abramson's populist, antibusiness, civil-trial narrative.

But if not *The Sweet Hereafter*, what about Stephen Zaillian's *A Civil Action* (1998)? Could a reclusive and rather unsympathetic old-line Boston law-firm attorney rise to the occasion and clear the name of a victimized corporation, a company falsely accused of, say, poisoning the drinking water of a whole Massachusetts community?

Civil-Action Cinema

That is at least one way of looking at *A Civil Action*, which deals with a court case arising from leukemia deaths attributed to chemical pollutants contaminating the water supply of Woburn, Massachusetts. The attorney for Beatrice Foods, Jerome Facher, played by Academy Award–nominated Robert Duvall, does get his corporate employers off the hook. And Jan Schlichtmann, played with remarkable conviction by John Travolta, does have some of the negative personal characteristics of Walter Matthau's plaintiff's attorney, William Gingrich, in Billy Wilder's *The Fortune Cookie* (1966). Many fans of Jonathan Harr's detailed legal account, on which *A Civil Action* is based, did not find the film nearly tough enough on the judge, the corporations, or Schlichtmann's opposing counsel. So one might regard the movie as an important new departure in tort cinema.

But one of the two corporations featured in the film, W. R. Grace and Co., did not see it that way. On the contrary, they even set up a web page on the internet to get the truth out, suggesting that Jonathan Harr's book and the subsequent film effectively falsify by what they leave out. Interviewed at Grace's headquarters in Boca Raton, Florida, by a *Miami Herald* business reporter, a Grace spokesperson expressed disappointment that the producers of *A Civil Action* failed to provide W. R. Grace with any opportunity whatever to help tell the story of the Woburn tragedy.

The rather deferential *Herald* reporter did not ask, for example, whether Grace felt that Steven Spielberg should have granted the German government or, for that matter, a representative group of Nazi war criminals an opportunity to edit the *Schindler's List* shooting script prior to production. But Grace's protests were themselves sufficient to make the point. *A Civil Action* picks on the same culprit as other mainstream tort films: corporate America. Thus, *A Civil Action* follows the same pattern or genre code established in *The Verdict, Class Action, Philadelphia,* and *The Rainmaker*—and not just with respect to the crucial issue of villains and heroes either. The film also includes its own remarkable version of the mandatory "how I almost didn't get the client" scene, where Jan Schlichtmann actually has to park his Porsche by a highway bridge and climb down onto the muddy shoals of a polluted stream, in his expensive leather dress shoes, to see for himself just what has been done to the unsuspecting residents of Woburn by Beatrice and W. R. Grace.

There is one big difference between *A Civil Action* and the other tort films I have discussed here. To be sure, the dragon who must be slain by the lawyer/knight errant is, in all five films, as I have said, a private power broker or megathug. But in *A Civil Action*, unlike in the other films, the bad guys win. As soon as I read that Harr's book was being made into a movie, I was both intrigued and perplexed by the enterprise. How could the end of *A Civil Action* be accommodated to the "is the jury limited in its damage award to the amount the plaintiff is seeking?" scene which, more or less, provides a stunning, and deeply satisfying, climax to the master-discourse films? Conversely, if the facts were made to fit the fiction—cf., John Ford's *The Man Who*

Shot Liberty Valance (1962): "When the legend becomes fact, print the legend"—would the filmmakers actually show Beatrice and Grace *losing*, perhaps even being forced to apologize onscreen to the Woburn parents who lost their children, something that has not happened to this day? "Because movies generally contain conflict, climax, and closure," argues attorney Tonja Haddad, commenting on legal films where attorneys cut corners in order to win, "and audiences prefer to see the 'good guys' prevail, the lawyers in these movies, despite their unethical behavior, are the heroes who allow justice to triumph."

Contrary to convention, as I see it, the people who made a movie out of Jonathan Harr's *A Civil Action* decided to take their chances and let the chips fall where they may. The chemical polluters basically get off scot-free in *A Civil Action*; and it is the admirable (and I think quite heroic) but nevertheless defeated—nearly destroyed in fact— Jan Schlichtmann who ends up holding the bag. When he turns down what he regards as a pathetic settlement offer from Jerome Facher, Schlichtmann explains that a settlement would not be right, would not be fair to the children who died. Facher brutally responds that it stopped being about them the moment the first pleadings were filed. In the final scene, where Schlichtmann is shown as a petitioner in bankruptcy court, the presiding judge asks him what he has to show for all his years of high-flying trial lawyering, where are the objects by which people in our kind of society measure their personal worth? Clearly, these are critical scenes.

Although it is not what Facher meant, in one profoundly important respect the case *did* stop being primarily about the children as soon as lawyers got involved. Once the case was absorbed by the American legal process, it was less about children, facts, personal responsibility, or justice than it was about money. And corporations have more money than everyone else. They can pay their attorneys more and last longer and generally win, certainly when they are dragged into court, kicking and screaming, by the powerless.

John F. Kennedy was fond of quoting Harry Truman's remark that ten million Americans can afford to send lobbyists to Washington to look after their interests; everybody else has to depend on the president of the United States. If most Americans have to depend on tort law to enforce their interests against the structure of corporate power, they haven't got a chance. That, I think, is the meaning of *A Civil Action*, and it is not something that can readily be fit into the reigning tort-film paradigm—elaborated in *The Verdict*, *Class Action*, *Philadelphia*, and *The Rainmaker*. So, in this sense, *A Civil Action* does indeed cause a new wrinkle in the otherwise smooth fabric of the tort-film genre. In this case, a nonfiction source helped replenish, indeed change the stock, piling up in the great storehouse of (tort cinema's) narratable forms. That is exactly how all literary and cinematic genres change over time, reflecting new, and sometimes bitter, realities.

Precedents

At the same time, however, *A Civil Action* is not itself without cinematic forerunners. Both with respect to its "true life" source and, significantly, its bleak conclusion, *A Civil Action* closely tracks Mike Nichols's *Silkwood* (1983). Both films have the guts to "name names" (Beatrice/Grace in *A Civil Action* and Kerr-McGee in *Silkwood*), and while one would not normally think of the Nichols picture as a "tort film," since it lacks lawyers and trials, it targets nuclear power in the same way that each of the tort films I have discussed arraigns a particular company or industry.

The climax of *Silkwood* comes when Karen Silkwood (Meryl Streep), attempting to deliver key documents about Kerr-McGee's doctoring of atomic fuel rods to a waiting *New York Times* reporter, is apparently run off the road in her Honda and killed. "Amazing Grace" floods the soundtrack as Nichols reveals this appalling conclusion to the Karen Silkwood story. Although Karen herself, through her decision to join the union and her commitment to stopping Kerr-McGee in its tracks may, in a sense, have "been lost, but then found," the documents she was carrying that night have *never* been found. In 1979, a federal court required Kerr-McGee to pay the Silkwood estate 10.5 million dollars in damages as a consequence of the corporation's negligent treatment of Silkwood on the job.

Between Silkwood's death in 1974 and the release of Nichols's film about her battle for plant safety in 1983, another film was made about the nuclear-power industry, and this one too seemed based, in part, on

Silkwood's experience. In James Bridges's *The China Syndrome*, released in 1979, virtually simultaneously with the Three Mile Island near meltdown, a television station employee is shown driving at high speed to get photographs documenting plant-construction fraud to a public regulatory hearing on nuclear-power plants. He too is run off the road and killed and, in this "fiction film," even less ambiguity marks who is responsible for the deadly vehicular ambush.

Some critics might tend to regard *Silkwood* and *China Syndrome* as poor examples of precursors for *A Civil Action*, since they are less "tort films" than "conspiracy films." Catching some of the same flak directed toward Oliver Stone's *JFK*, the two nuclear-power films may be written off as further examples of what we have already characterized, following Hofstadter, as "the paranoid style of American politics."

It is important to recall, however, a simple fact familiar to any lawyer: the essence of conspiracy is not secrecy—let alone paranoia—but, rather, *agreement*. In other words, what makes a conspiracy charge so appealing to prosecutors is that it can be made out simply by providing sufficient evidence that two or more individuals have entered into an agreement to commit a crime. The defendants do not have to actually commit the crime itself—the agreement is the conduct part of the crime of conspiracy.

What *The China Syndrome*, *Silkwood*, and *A Civil Action* have in common is just this sense of agreement, the notion that the people who run the television stations, the courts, the regulatory agencies, and industries that are hazardous to our health have basically entered into an agreement to make sure that nothing is allowed to threaten the bottom line: profits. Law is routinely outmatched when confronted with this agreement, this horizontal plane of combined social action, also known as "social class."

Remake

Nothing underscores the originality of *A Civil Action* more dramatically than the fact that the film was remade, but with a different ending, within about fourteen months. Of course Steven Soderbergh's *Erin Brockovich* (2000), like *A Civil Action*, is based on actual events whose outcome determined the film's conclusion. But lots of movies are based on "actual events"; there is always a question of which stories get chosen to be made into motion pictures. The story of Erin Brockovich's war against California's Pacific Gas and Electric Co. had to be told, not simply because of its inherent interest, but also because it could provide the basis, in a way, for a "cinematic antidote" to *A Civil Action*. It is otherwise hard to believe that the first two American dramatic films about legal cases arising from corporate water pollution would be made back to back, about a year apart. *Erin Brockovich* could do what *A Civil Action* could not: provide its audience with a Hollywood ending. Both films name (corporate) names, both have the "lawyer meets with disgruntled clients en masse" scene, and both even include an "expensive shoes" scene (John Travolta ruins his trying to get down to the Woburn river; Julia Roberts does not like the ones worn by the smug, upscale woman litigator, who Roberts feels wants to "steal" her case).

But while *Erin Brockovich*, for which Julia Roberts won the best-actress Oscar, fits reasonably comfortably (Brockovich is a paralegal rather than attorney) within the master discourse of tort cinema, *A Civil Action*, as we have argued, does not. Jeffrey Abramson acknowledges that Jonathan Harr's *A Civil Action*, and by implication the film based on Harr's book, "is a story without a happy populist ending." In spite of the extreme similarity between *Erin Brockovich* and *A Civil Action*, their different endings imply radically different conceptions not only of the tort process, but of the nature of American justice.

The real remake of *A Civil Action*, even though it is a television documentary rather than a fiction film, is *Trade Secrets: A Moyers Report* (2001), one of the most powerful indictments imaginable, not only of chemical companies and their indifference to the harm they cause, but also of the failure of liberal democracy to protect its citizens from predatory capital. And that is the point: *Trade Secrets* is a documentary. Or better, since the documentary form by itself does not guarantee accuracy, *Trade Secrets* is a documentary film that pulls no punches. So just as in *A Civil Action*, *Trade Secret*'s chemical companies get away with it.

Describing the process by which Karl Marx became a Marxist, Ernest Mandel records that while still a young man, as soon as Marx "tackled a current political problem—namely, the new law on the theft of wood—he came up against the problem of social classes. The state, which ought to embody the 'general interest,' seemed to be acting merely on behalf of private property, and, in order to do this, was violating not only the logic of law but even some obvious principles of humanity."

When a serious journalist or filmmaker tackles a current tort problem, like that of the Woburn catastrophe, he or she comes up against the problem of social classes. The Massachusetts court, which should have embodied the general interest of the commonwealth, violated not only the logic of law but even some painfully evident principles of humanity in effectively insulating chemical companies from any real responsibility for the harm they caused. In *A Civil Action*, Jan Schlichtmann is compelled to relearn the same early lesson taught to Marx by the new law on the theft of wood. It seems to be a lesson that we are unable, or perhaps unwilling, to learn once and for all. In *A Civil Action*, Jan Schlichtmann takes to heart Frank Galvin's advice, "Act as if you believe . . ." and as a consequence, his life virtually disintegrates. By contrast, the master discourse represents (in dialectical tension) both a fantasy about the tort system and the dream of a better world.

Chapter 5

International-Law Films:
Sovereignty, Idealism, Consensus

LIKE THE DOMESTIC law of tort liability, international law and legal institutions represent a juridical field of practice that has developed its own popular culture, however obscure, and the nature of whose representation on film has yet to be theorized. This chapter provides an initial foray into that unexplored cinematic terrain: international law on film. After a brief look at one existing approach to international relations on film, I will organize my critique around three major categories of international legal culture and ideology: sovereignty, idealism, and consensus.

International Relations

The study of international law in the United States is generally though not exclusively confined to law schools. The ancillary disciplines of diplomatic history and international relations ("IR" in popular academic shorthand)—located outside legal education but still generally within universities, schools of foreign service, or military academies—are not without a first effort to chart their popular culture: Robert W.

Gregg's *International Relations on Film*. Although international law and international relations are not the same thing, a book on IR cinema is not a bad place to begin the project of formulating some general ideas about how international law is portrayed in the movies. Professor Gregg, an IR teacher, approaches films about international relations much as a classroom instructor would, utilizing motion pictures as a tool for study, an alternative source of information about a specific subject.

Gregg initiates a discussion of how films that touch upon IR issues can tell us something that the traditional textbooks and professors' lectures cannot—or at least have not. As with some other initial efforts to outline the structure of a cinematic genre, what Gregg leaves in and what he leaves out—how he divides up the material of IR study and the categories into which he fits separate groups of motion pictures—constitute the most interesting aspect of his work. The dilemmas of sovereignty, nationalism and its discontents, civil strife and intervention, espionage and subversion, decision making and crisis management, the tragedy of war, economic interdependence and development—all receive attention as subdivisions within the genre of IR cinema. In each of these categories, Gregg has identified films that virtually anyone familiar with IR would include, as well as a few that might not immediately come to mind but still, on reflection, clearly belong. At times, he reaches to include films whose relation to IR appears remote.

It is easy in retrospect to fault Gregg for failing to devote a chapter to terrorism and international relations on film. But there certainly are a number of films worth considering, including Carol Reed's *Odd Man Out* (1947), Otto Preminger's *Exodus* (1960), Gillo Pontecorvo's *The Battle of Algiers* (1965), John Frankenhiemer's *Black Sunday* (1977) and *Year of the Gun* (1991), and Mimi Leder's *The Peacemaker* (1997), in addition to *The Siege*, discussed earlier in the context of criminal-law cinema's response to new social issues.

In a discussion of the emergence and significance of the sovereign state, Gregg's inclusion of a film like Fred Zinnemann's *A Man for All Seasons* (1966) seems inescapable. Henry Cornelius's *Passport to Pimlico* (1949), a postwar British comedy, initially appears a rather odd choice, but Gregg's analysis of the film suggests a perfect fit within the sovereignty subgenre. "A London neighborhood," Gregg observes, "opts to declare its independence from the crown following the discovery in a local bomb crater of an old and forgotten treaty that proves it really is a part of the medieval kingdom of Burgundy." Complications that ensue—illustrating the burdens, as well as benefits, of sovereignty (especially economic ones)—soon cause Pimlican nationals to wonder if political and territorial independence is all that it's cracked up to be.

Gregg is right to point out that William Friedkin's *The French Connection* (1971) alerted audiences to international aspects of the heroin trade. But in spite of its surface realism (even documentary touches), *The French Connection* remains a classic crime film with an especially original chase scene. Since the movie's perspective is basically that of New York narcotics cop Jimmy "Popeye" Doyle (Gene Hackman)—a street-level view of drug dealing—*The French Connection* lacks the sophistication of either *Masterpiece Theatre's Traffik*, or the American version, *Traffic*, made a decade later and discussed earlier in this book within the context of criminal-law cinema. "Viewers are familiar with countless dramas about drugs," observes Terrence O'Flaherty, "told from the sordid standpoint of addicts or the hazardous viewpoint of the police [but] *Traffik* takes a different look at heroin—as a well-organized, high-profit business." Thus a different kind of film from either *The French Connection* on the one hand or Ted Demme's *Blow* (2001) on the other, *Traffik* includes an interesting subplot involving the relationship between treaty negotiation, political corruption, and media manipulation in both Britain and Pakistan. Both versions of the film do a better job of analyzing the international character of illegal drug transactions than crime films like *The French Connection*.

Gregg's book was published prior to the release of Roger Donaldson's *Thirteen Days* (2000) so, in his discussion of international decision making and crisis management, he relies instead upon films like Stanley Kubrick's masterpiece *Dr. Strangelove* (1963). Jim Goddard's *Reilly: The Ace of Spies* (1983), Gregg argues, provided viewers insight into the way "policymakers may ignore danger signals because they are inconsistent with their mental image of another country." In this instance, intelligence officer Sydney Reilly (Sam Neill) warns political leaders in both Britain and Russia of the impending Japanese invasion of Manchuria, to no avail, thus illustrating "Jervis's dictum that decision makers see what they expect to see."

Gregg's chapter on espionage and subversion is one of his best. In a field where it would be easy to go wrong, he manages not only to identify crucial films (e.g., *Across the Pacific, The Spy Who Came in from the Cold, The Ipcress File, Russia House*) but also Sam Fuller's *Pickup on South Street* (1953) and Sydney Pollack's *Three Days of the Condor* (1975), movies which certainly figure as revealing signs of the times (*Pickup* is right-wing, *Condor* left-wing) but might have been missed by less cinematically savvy writers attempting to identify benchmark IR films. Gregg's highlighting of *Foreign Correspondent* compensates, to a degree, for his omission of other Hitchcock espionage classics (e.g., *The Thirty-Nine Steps, Saboteur, North by Northwest, Topaz,* and *Torn Curtain*).

Law as Ethics

The one chapter of *International Relations on Film* that deals directly with questions of law and legal culture is titled "Ethics and International Law." The way that Gregg identifies international law with a system of ethics or morality is a tip-off to his skeptical—and typically IR—orientation toward how international law works. After describing the legal role performed by government in domestic political systems, Gregg asserts that "[i]nternationally, there is no such government, much less one possessing a preponderance of force and enjoying a monopoly of the legitimate use of force." Thus, in the absence of police, courts, compelled legal compliance, and so forth, international society is as formally anarchic, on this view, as would be domestic society in the absence of such institutionalized legal structures and processes.

One wonders how Gregg reconciles this view of international law with contemporary political history. As Rick Atkinson describes in *Crusade,* his book on the Gulf War, the force authorized by the United Nations for the purpose of evicting Iraq's military from Kuwait was not only effective but, in fact, overwhelming. Similarly, NATO's use of force in the Balkans in 1999 not only secured an end to ethnic cleansing perpetrated by the Serbian regime in Kosovo but set the stage for war-crimes trials, following principles laid down at Nuremberg at the end of the Second World War. Against the odds, former Yugoslav president Slobodan Milosevic is taken into custody and brought within the jurisdiction of international legality. Reflecting on these same developments, law professor David Westbrook concludes that "[i]nternational law is now, if as yet only intermittently, enforceable, and the hoary criticism of international law, that it is not law because it has no enforcement mechanism, has been answered on its own terms."

International law today can be defended as a system of genuinely legal as well as moral rules and values. Thus the portion of Gregg's analysis that deals with movies touching upon international moral debates (e.g., was the United States justified in its use of atomic weapons against Japan?) remains interesting without really getting into the subject of international law. His discussion of human rights, however, places him firmly on international legal terrain. And here, as in so much of his book, his choice of films (*The Wannsee Conference*, *Judgment at Nuremberg*, *The Killing Fields*, *The Year of Living Dangerously*, *The Official Story*, *Beyond Rangoon*) provides at least the architecture for sustained analysis of the really crucial issues.

Sovereignty

Gregg utilizes *A Man for All Seasons* to highlight the emergence of the sovereign state as the dominant political institution in the world system—and not without reason. In *A Man for All Seasons*, as Gregg points out, "the conflict is between [Henry VIII of England] and his lord chancellor, Thomas More, who refuses to swear an oath accepting the king as supreme head of the church of England." To be sure, Zinnemann's film, reflecting the particular concerns of Robert Bolt's fluently written play, presents the essential drama as one of conscience versus convenience, legal principle versus political pressure.

In reality, however, the historical issue involved in More's resistance to royal authority was whether a universal institution, the Church, would continue to hold sway over local political rulers. "With the emergence of the state system," observe Anthony Clark Arend and Robert J. Beck, "there also developed a new theoretical doctrine to explain the status of the state—the doctrine of sovereignty." And as Arend and Beck explain, the doctrine of sovereignty became the ordering principle of a new state system that necessarily superseded the authority of universal doctrines and institutions. Individual states (and their rulers) became the final arbiter of their own conduct and no "pope or emperor had temporal control over them."

Thus Thomas More fought his battle against the state on the wrong side of history, as it were, and fell victim to the emerging authority of secular rulers like Henry VIII. "In 1648," conclude Arend and Beck, "the doctrine of sovereignty achieved 'codification' with the adoption of the Peace of Westphalia, which brought an end to the devastating Thirty Years War." One of the principles of the Peace of Westphalia was an agreement that there would be no interference with the right of sovereign leaders to determine what religion would prevail in their national territory. Here was a principle that Thomas More's supranational allegiance to the Church could not survive.

The decline of theocratic universalism generated ideological as well as political transformation. Crucial to the new ideology that accompanied the rise of the sovereign state, according to legal philosopher Roberto Unger, "is the notion that social relations are and ought to be an object of human will. Such a conception contrasts with the earlier and more universal idea of society as the expression of an order that men do not and ought not control." Thus the historical development of sovereignty, and the social consciousness which it reflects, eventually leads to the decline of monarchy and its ideology—the divine right of kings—as well as the eclipse of theocratic universalism. This aspect of state sovereignty and its politics is alluded to in the first sequence of Roberto Rossellini's *The Rise to Power of Louis XIV* (1966).

The films opens, as Peter Brunette explains, "with a static, painterly long shot of peasants at a dock across the river from a castle." This scene serves "as a kind of earthy counter to everything that follows," as the peasants speak "disparagingly of the English king who has just been beheaded, and briefly complain about the prerogatives of wealth and authority." We will return to Rossellini's cinema of historical reconstruction in our concluding chapter, but the point here (illustrated by both *A Man for All Seasons* and *The Rise to Power of Louis XIV*) is that by the end of the seventeenth century, sovereignty and the paramount legal status of separate nation-states had eclipsed the theocratic worldview and the social universe to which it had lent an aura of legitimacy.

International law, a system of legal rules that transcends and binds individual states, is a modern form of universalism and consequently has had to fight an uphill battle against the dominant world system of sovereign states. It has been the tenacious survival of the doctrine of sovereignty and its accompanying list of rights exclusive to states that has prejudiced many against the idea of international law *as law*. Despite remarkable and unanticipated changes in the world since the fall of communism, many contemporary political observers (following the traditional view of "positivists" in legal scholarship and "realists" in diplomatic history and IR) still cling, like Robert Gregg, to a generally skeptical view of international law.

Could Gregg have found support for his doubts about international law within popular culture itself? In Bryan Singer's *X-Men* (2000)—a film that loyally transfers to the screen some of the most cherished of all Marvel comic-book characters—the United Nations is a target of Magneto's Brotherhood of Mutants. It is hard to say whether the inadequacy of the UN and its puny officials in coping with X-Men high jinks reflects a popular perception of the UN as a "paper tiger" or, instead, mirrors the formulaic ineptitude routinely assigned to merely human governments and armies within the conventional rules of science-fiction cinema. The U.S. President and Congress, after all, fared little better in Tim Burton's *Mars Attacks!* (1996). At least one UN official, however, in "Patient X"—broadcast on network television during *The X-Files* 1997-98 season—brandished an actual booklet copy of the UN Charter. Confronting an armed band of soldiers on a desolate frontier, assistant to the UN's special representative to the secretary general, Marita Covarrubis (Laurie Holden), is at least able to accurately cite chapter and verse from the charter. Not that it has any effect on her unruly opponents, who seem to share the realist and IR skepticism toward international law.

In the absence of an international government above the level of states, supported by effective institutions able to secure enforcement of that superior will, international law can be seen as little more than a rationalization for the political balance of power structuring international society at a given moment in history. If not in the United

Nations (or the North Atlantic Treaty Organization), where can international law be founded other than in the customary practice of states themselves, in their voluntary self-subordination to shared principles of law? And if their obedience is merely voluntary, what does it have to do with law? The "conception of legal obligation as growing out of customary practice," concede international law professors Henry Steiner, Detlev Vagts, and Harold Hongju Koh, "is of course antagonistic to the assertion that only those commands issuing from the state that are backed by threats of force merit characterization as law."

Idealism

At the end of the nineteenth century, it was apparent to all that the sovereignty of the state was unimpeded by notions of international law, and war itself was regarded as the "litigation of nations." In international law, "aggression" was not even defined, let alone effectively prohibited. A couple of decades later, the catastrophic human consequences of the First World War served as a wake-up call, not just for politicians and diplomats, but for whole populations as well. The mass public in industrialized societies had come face to face with the horrors modern warfare could inflict—upon both soldiers and civilians. However idealistic it may have seemed in the wake of world war, imposing real limitations on the destructive power of militarism and armed conflict had to be placed on the legal and political agenda if civilization was to survive.

Contemporary motion pictures, to be sure, like Jean-Jacques Annaud's *Enemy at the Gates* (2001) are unprecedented in their capacity to visually capture the nearly unimaginable horror of combat—the way war feels to those doing the fighting. Yet few films better illustrate either the reaction against militarization inspired by world war or the theme of idealism pervading international law and diplomacy than Henry King's Hollywood biopic *Wilson*. Made in 1944 by Twentieth Century–Fox, "*Wilson* was not so much about the man," argues Terry Christensen in *Reel Politics*, "as about the peace treaty ending World War I and the need for international cooperation, 'the dream of a world united against the dreadful waste of war.' [Producer Darryl]

Zanuck's epic argued that the League of Nations and collective security might have prevented World War II."

While the notion that war is an inescapable if regrettable feature of social life was regarded by some as sober realism, idealists countered that, far from being part of human nature, armed conflict could be banished, and that institutions like the League of Nations, if adequately supported, held out the possibility of outlawing war. President Wilson's personal battle for ratification of the League of Nations treaty by the U.S. Congress failed, and the story of his heroic crusade admittedly did not have a happy ending. But *Wilson*, released in theaters across the country near the end of the Second World War, "implied that America had to make that happy ending through the United Nations or face the consequences." Wilson's lonely advocacy of the League of Nations, the ambitious plans of the founders and supporters of the United Nations, pacifism and antinuclear movements, resistance to positivist skepticism waged by proponents of international law and diplomacy—all of these forces illustrate an idealist side to the unfolding dialectic of international political history.

Neither the League of Nations nor any other regime of international legality, however, could possibly succeed until after a genuine resolution of the key modern historical conflict: the struggle between liberal and authoritarian capitalism. Only the kind of global social and economic reordering that came at the end of World War II could provide a foundation for the institutionalization of international legal principles. And even that institutional initiative, symbolized by the United Nations, would be relatively powerless in the face of a new bipolarity in world affairs: the Cold War. Only after the fall of communism and the deadlock in the UN Security Council was finally broken could the UN become a dominant world political force.

The most extreme forms of skepticism toward international law are now on the defensive. Even rational skepticism can become a self-fulfilling prophecy. And Henry Kissinger's Machiavellian "end justifies the means" philosophy of world power has proved to have costs of its own. "This realpolitik," observes Alan Furst's protagonist in the novel *Dark Star*, "was very alchemical stuff. It started with politicians and their intellectuals, all this doing what had to be done, but it had a tendency to migrate." If the law of nations is no pipe dream, international law's effectiveness at any given point in history nevertheless hinges on an economic, military, and political context within which the possibility of real change, as well as its limits, are negotiated. The end of the Cold War, regardless of whether it constitutes Francis Fukuyama's widely discussed "end of history," represents a watershed in the historical development of international law.

The globalization of capitalist social relations and the corporate form of economic organization have clear implications for the relative independence and authority of the sovereign state on the world scene. The once unparalleled authority of sovereign states is increasingly undermined by world trade and business entities and by the multinational firm itself. So resolution, between 1940 and 1990, of the conflict between liberal and authoritarian capitalism and, then, between capitalism and communism, makes possible a new consensus about political values and interests on which a credible regime of international law can finally be constructed.

Consensus

To *A Man for All Seasons* and *The Rise to Power of Louis XIV* (sovereignty) and *Wilson* (idealism), we may now add another key motion picture to our preliminary sketch of international law's popular culture: David O. Russell's Gulf War film, *Three Kings* (1999). And to sovereignty and idealism, we can add a third theme in this developing cultural and legal critique: consensus. Whether or not one agrees that President George Bush's war to eject Iraq's military from Kuwait represented the first battle on behalf of a "new world order," it was certainly the product of a remarkable political consensus, one which found Americans and Russians voting together in the UN Security Council in a way they had not done before.

It will be recalled that when the UN Security Council authorized the use of force in Korea in 1950, the representative of the Soviet Union was boycotting the Council and was not present to veto the proposed UN or, more accurately, U.S. use of force in Korea. But the Russian, albeit no longer Soviet, representative was indeed present, and voting with the United States, on the day in 1990 when the Security Council authorized the use of force in the Gulf for the purpose of restoring Kuwait's territorial independence.

Another name for that independence, to be sure, is national sovereignty, and the Gulf War could still be seen as a war fought on behalf of the legal rights of the sovereign state. But the supremacy of the nation-state, as the final arbiter of international legality, is certainly placed in question when the UN Security Council displays the kind of consensus it did in the Gulf War—a consensus sufficient to provide legal authorization, under the UN charter, for a use of force designed to secure restoration of peace and security in the Middle East.

There is another way in which the Gulf War can be seen as a war designed to shore up an old, rather than new, world order. In a critical sequence in *Three Kings*, an American soldier who has been captured by the Iraqis is being brutally interrogated. An Iraqi captain, who claims his son was killed during the U.S. bombing of Baghdad and that he was, himself, trained in torture techniques by the Americans during Iraq's war with Iran, demands to have the American explain to him why the United States is making war in the desert. The American replies that he is fighting because Iraq invaded Kuwait and "that is wrong." The Iraqi scoffs and tries to force the American to taste the real reason for the war by pouring oil down his throat.

Describing this same scene, *Village Voice* critic J. Hoberman argues that, unlike much contemporary American cinema, *Three Kings* refuses simply to "consign the Arab foe to absolute cultural Otherness. Russell not only visualizes bombed Iraqi children but even has the guts to point out that, having tilted toward Iraq during its war with Iran, the U.S. helped to train Saddam's killers—even if he does put the thesis that Desert Storm was fought for Kuwaiti oil in the mouth of the scariest of the movie's 'wog' villains." If we are convinced by this "war for oil" argument, regardless of who is making it, then the Gulf War must be seen as little more than old-fashioned imperialist or "gunboat" diplomacy masquerading as UN peacekeeping or peace restoration.

Three Kings, rather evenhandedly, includes this thesis without subscribing to it. The film's action does not begin until *after* the Gulf War has ended, when its protagonists launch a freelance mission of their own to convert to their possession some of the gold bullion that they believe the Iraqis have stolen from Kuwait. But *Three Kings* remains, in essence, a war film. What kind of war film? "Our heroes," suggests *Salon* contributing writer Andrew O'Hehir, "have stumbled into the middle of a civil war, in which the Republican Guard is systematically wiping out anti-Saddam insurgents, who are under the painfully false impression that the Americans will support their rebellion. [But once] [George Clooney's] Archie [Gates] sees a village woman shot dead in front of him, we know what's coming."

If we emphasize the crazy but charming gallantry of Archie Gates, then *Three Kings* looks like more of the same, rather than something original and important. "Sure," says Massachusetts Institute of Technology film critic Michael Frakes, "*Three Kings* is the first film to address certain issues about the Gulf War and it does a good job of presenting them, but it has a very traditional plot structure."

Perhaps. But the *Voice*'s Hoberman is clearly onto something when he argues that *Three Kings* "at least deserves credit for rethinking the combat-movie genre in the weird we-are-the-world terms that Desert Storm established." What exactly might that mean? The Gulf War was fought to reinforce the international legal principle of sovereign equality of states: no nation has a right to annex another nation. Thus most Arab countries supported the UN action in the Gulf. *Three Kings* begins as the Gulf War ends. It is about another war, a *civil* war in O'Hehir's reference, between Iraq's Republican Guard, on the one hand, and national and ethnic minorities resisting Saddam Hussein's regime, on the other. When push comes to shove, the American commandos are not so much soldiers of fortune (though they would like to be) as they are existential volunteers for the party of humanity, willing in a pinch to deploy not just violence but their considerable strategic intelligence on behalf of human rights.

To put it bluntly, *Three Kings* reflects a Gulf War seen, in hindsight, through the optic of NATO's bombing of Yugoslavia in 1999. The Clinton administration's effort to stop the violence and ethnic cleansing in Yugoslavia took place, of course, before the release of *Three Kings*, and it is not being suggested that events in the Balkans actually contributed to the *making* of the film. But the timing of the movie's release necessarily made the crisis in Yugoslavia a factor in the way that audiences looked at *Three Kings* and therefore, in a sense, what they understood the film to mean.

As well it should have. The Vietnamese revolution may have threatened, or at least was perceived by the United States as a threat to, Western economic and military hegemony. The Gulf War, at least in the view of Iraq's soldiers in *Three Kings*, was a war for oil, another conflict in the checkered history of international petroleum politics. But it is harder to sustain this critique in the case of NATO's action in Yugoslavia. If the United States acted to protect Albanian Kosovars from the Serbian regime in Belgrade for the humanitarian reasons that political leaders like Bill Clinton, Tony Blair, and Václev Havel stated, then *Three Kings* can be seen as a film that helps to define and interpret the transition in American foreign affairs from the end of Cold War bipolarity to a new era of international consensus on human rights.

As smart and fresh as *Three Kings* still looks today, we already need another avante-garde war film to update the status of that human rights consensus. Where do human rights stand now, in a world suddenly torn in two either by a clash of civilizations or its simulacrum—a world engulfed by terror and counter-terror yet one in which soldiers (and states) must still face the sort of questions that are confronted by *Three Kings'* ragtag band of would-be-royalty? Is their decision to take their chances with the anti-Saddam rebels less believable than Humphrey Bogart's throwing in his lot with anti-Nazi-resistance forces in Michael Curtiz's *Casablanca*? It is no small virtue that motion pictures invite us to think about ourselves and our history in this way.

Chapter 6

Films of Comparative Law
and Politics: Germany

JOHN HENRY WIGMORE, the most important figure in the history of American evidence law, graduated from Harvard Law School only a few years ahead of Henry Stimson, in 1887. While Stimson went immediately into corporate-law-firm practice, working for Sherman Evarts at 52 Wall Street, Wigmore went instead to teach law at Keio University in Tokyo during the early years of the Meiji constitution. Stimson, a Republican, would become secretary of war in the Roosevelt administration during the Second World War; Wigmore established a framework for the rules of evidence that came to govern the practice of litigation in the United States. But it was Wigmore's initial "career move" after law school that represented a harbinger of things to come.

Between the wars, Wigmore produced an impressive and highly unusual three-volume work titled _Panorama of the World's Legal Systems._ He found the subject of comparative law to be of incandescent interest, almost electrically charged. And the time was right: within recent years, he observed, "the realms of archaeology, epigraphy, papyrology, philology, 'et id omne genus', have vastly enlarged; so that today there remain virtually no civilizations unrevealed in available materials for study." Wigmore was convinced that until the student of law understood a legal system different from his or her own, the student's own national legal tradition could not be seen objectively, in its true light. The study of comparative law, in Wigmore's view, provided real perspective on the nature of one's native legal rules and institutions—a legal culture already so familiar that it probably had come to be regarded as natural, inevitable, the only way that things could possibly be done in a rational world. Just as Bertolt Brecht employed distancing effects in order to "estrange" theatergoers from their all too familiar world, Wigmore sought to utilize comparative law and legal knowledge of other societies in order to permit the law student, lawyer, and educated reader to see law as contingent, something that could be altered and improved.

For that very reason, as well as to put the development of tort law in historical perspective, my earlier book *Law and History* includes a detailed comparison of the development of tort law in Germany and the United States in the nineteenth century. And, in the same vein, it is possible to compare the tort- and property-law films or criminal-law-and-procedure movies of different countries with a similar end in view. A number of American law professors now teach seminars on trial practice and comparative law that feature a sampling of films from different national cinemas, movies that capture the essence of the trial process in different cultures and societies.

Firmly committed to this comparative principle, most of this chapter is devoted to a jurisprudence, so to speak, of German film, with special reference to films directed by Werner Herzog and Rainer Werner Fassbinder. Why Germany? If Wigmore was right, any country will do—so long as it is not one's own—for the purpose of rendering national legal and political traditions somewhat strange. But Germany is particularly helpful in placing the American legal system in sharp relief because its national legal culture has provided such a strong challenge to that of liberal legalism and the rule of law.

The triumph of liberal legalism in parts of Europe and North America, in the eighteenth and nineteenth centuries, represented something novel in political history. In his book on the French Revolution, *The New Regime*, Columbia University historian Isser Woloch writes that the "law quickly became the Revolution's transcendent deity." Like Woloch, historian R. R. Palmer characterizes the democratic revolutions of the eighteenth century as liberal and legalistic. They were revolutions fought, however paradoxically, in order to establish the rule of law.

Eventually, in the third and fourth decades of the twentieth century, liberal constitutional systems (in a popular front with the left worldwide) would constitute a backbone of resistance to the seemingly unstoppable march of fascism and authoritarianism. At the end of the eighteenth century, however, when liberal constitutionalism first came to power, the complex structure of authoritarian capitalist society remained nascent in Europe's countryside and on islands washed by the cold Pacific in northeast Asia.

In the previous chapter, on the cinema of international law, we described how a film sequence shot by Roberto Rossellini captured the essence of state sovereignty. Here, in our introduction to the cinema of comparative law and politics, we look more closely at Rossellini's effort to portray the rise of the modern state in France, and at his interpretation of the Italian state that emerged from the defeat of fascism at the end of the Second World War.

It is useful to preface discussion of Germany's legal and political development with reference to French and Italian history. Wigmore provided a panorama, as he put it, of the *world*'s legal systems. Identifying crucial moments in the political history of three European countries, and their reflection in film, is at least a step in the direction of a more comprehensive comparative cinematic jurisprudence. One could, for example, compare the treatment of terrorism in German, French, and Italian films; the treatment of government taxation policy in the motion pictures of Japan, China, and India; or the treatment of banditry in the films of Spain, Mexico, and the United States. Perhaps, eventually, one could explore different views of a single legal theme or issue as it cuts across a wide range of individual national cinemas. Wigmore's three-volume *Panorama*, first published at the end of the silent film era (still in print today and readily available in used bookstores), could itself be employed as a starting point for what might be titled "A Cinerama of the World's Legal Systems."

Finally, a portion of this chapter is devoted to the debate over realism in legal cinema. Perhaps the most common standard of value employed in the critique of movies about law is a form of realist inquiry: Is that what the law actually says? Could that happen in a real courtroom? The question of realism, in fact, turns out to be more complicated than it first appears. Our evaluation of Rossellini's *historical* realism here introduces the subject of realism to which we return, in a more narrowly legal context, in the final chapter. The primary focus of this chapter, however, remains a cinematic critique of the nature and practice of German authoritarianism.

Historical Reconstruction: France and Italy

Roberto Rossellini's motion picture *The Rise to Power of Louis XIV* (1966) tells not merely the story of a monarch's determined embrace of the political power within his reach but also, as Peter Brunette points out in his exemplary treatment of Rossellini's film career, "the first signs of the formation of the modern state and the rise of the bourgeoisie." At first, it may seem odd that the rise to power of the bourgeoisie should be reflected in this story of Louis's clever manipulation of court politics to his own ends. When Cardinal Mazarin dies, Louis selects Colbert as his chief minister, takes control of the governing council (banishing his mother from power), and, after defeating the opposition to his authority represented by Fouquet's intrigues, imposes Colbert's plan for trade and industry upon the nation. "Although Louis XIV and Colbert were utterly dissimilar," in the words of Philippe Erlanger, the French historian from whose biography of Louis XIV Rossellini's film is essentially drawn, "their cooperation was necessary for the achievement of a grand design, and they valued one another at their true worth."

If the revolutionary transformation of French society, a project that would transcend even the Sun King's "grand design," later required the violent removal of a king, royal policy under Louis XIV had already begun to reveal a shift toward the merchant class. "In France and England," according to social historian George Rude, "the merchant class was more developed than anywhere outside Holland. . . . In France, Louis XIV's wars had created a fertile breeding-ground for contractors, bankers and financiers." The death of Mazarin, followed by Colbert's appointment, sets the tone for Rossellini's cinematic treatment of this historical transformation.

The deliberate way that Colbert systematically outlines for the king his ambitious program of political and economic reform, and what Jose-Luis Guarner calls "that flat tone of everyday conversations between ordinary men" that marks Colbert's delivery, underscore Rossellini's down-to-earth method of recounting historical events. "As a counter-weight to aristocracy," says Rude, referring to the real Colbert in a way which would apply as well to Rossellini's Colbert, "it had been the royal policy to draw into the service of the state the sons of men enriched by trade and finance (Colbert is an obvious example), so much so that Saint-Simon, an aristocrat, contemptuously dismissed the period as *'un règne de ville bourgeoisie.'* "

Rossellini's *Rise to Power of Louis XIV* deserves our attention as one of the most prominent historical reconstructions ever to achieve such a high degree of analytical rigor. The entire film, Brunette observes, is based upon only about ten pages of Erlanger's biography. Screenwriter Jean Guault's dialogue for the first portion of the film, however, comes from the pages of Louis de Rouvroy Saint-Simon, Mme. de Sévigné, and especially Voltaire. The movie is able to focus upon the minutiae of daily life while communicating, at the same time, the importance of grand political developments signified by seemingly trivial details. By deemphasizing conventional "character psychology," concludes Brunette, Rossellini "opens up a wider space for the representation of 'history' itself."

Auden said that history is the secular conscience of the West; Orwell argued that those who control our understanding of the past control the future. History is controversial and represents politically contested terrain. It comes as no surprise that claims to historical accuracy made on behalf of movies generally, or specific films, can generate heated disagreement. Condemnation of Oliver Stone as historian provides a familiar example. Similarly, one of the finest American historians, Eric Foner, responded to Steven Spielberg's critically acclaimed *Amistad* (1997) by writing an op-ed piece in the *New York Times* discouraging secondary-school teachers from recommending the picture to their students. *Amistad* "is by no means a work of history," asserted Foner, "and it is certainly not appropriate for use in the classroom." Foner suggested teachers direct their students instead "to the local library, where they will find several shelves of books on slavery and slave resistance." So much for historical films.

By contrast, John Womack, Jr., author of the definitive *Zapata and the Mexican Revolution*, finds Elia Kazan's biopic *Viva Zapata!* (1952) to be historically accurate. Despite inevitable distortions that result from condensing the Mexican Revolution into a taut narrative, Kazan's film, according to Womack, "quickly and vividly develops a portrayal of Zapata, the villagers, and the nature of their relations and movement that I find still subtle, powerful, and true." Was Kazan (or *Zapata*'s screenwriter, John Steinbeck) a better historian than Steven Spielberg? Do Eric Foner and John Womack look at historical films the same way? And what would they think of Rossellini's historical cinema?

Given the overlap between movies of historical reconstruction and documentary film, it is not surprising that Rossellini makes an appearance in Erik Barnouw's history of nonfiction film. Interestingly enough, however, it is not Rossellini's later, historical pictures that are mentioned by Barnouw, but rather his early, neorealist cinema. For example, Barnouw characterizes Rossellini's *Rome, Open City* (1945) as poetic documentary or "documentary-like fiction." However "documentary-like" they may be regarded today, Rossellini's neorealist films remained fiction films, and it was just such films that he decided to stop making at a key point in his career. As Rossellini told an interviewer in 1972, he "abandoned commercial, traditional cinema in the late '50s," and with his embrace of the historical-reconstruction film, beginning with *The Iron Age* (1964), was rejuvenated as a filmmaker. Rossellini had found, as Peter Brunette says, "the perfect medium—the didactic, essayist film made for television."

His five-hour-long *Iron Age* was followed by *The Rise to Power of Louis XIV* and *Man's Struggle for Survival* (1967–69), which was more than twice as long as *Iron Age*. *Socrates* (1970), *The Age of the Medici* (1972), and five other monumental histories would appear prior to Rossellini's death in 1977. Two other films Rossellini made during this period are worth noting. In September of 1973, RAI-TV in Italy broadcast Rossellini's *Force and Reason*, an interview Rossellini had filmed with Chile's president, Salvatore Allende, in 1971. *Force and Reason* was shown immediately after the world was shocked to learn that Allende had been assassinated in the right-wing military coup that overthrew Chile's democratically elected government. A second film, *Italy: Year One* (1974), shown in the United States at the Los Angeles Film Exposition shortly after its Italian release, is a historical film that can still be distinguished from Rossellini's other work of historical reconstruction in that it is about relatively *current* history: the decade of political crisis in Italy between 1944 and 1954.

Separating the two main chapters of the Italian director's life in motion pictures, Tag Gallagher suggests that during the later phase, Rossellini's "historical neorealism attempts to analyze progress, to reveal its successes and foibles," whereas the earlier "neorealism attempted to draw a portrait of a relatively static situation." While spectacle was uncharacteristic of Rossellini throughout his film career, he was especially hostile to it in his cinema of historical reconstruction. "Sensationalism," he said, "is the first lie. You can't arrive at the truth through lies. I think we must evolve to a new kind of spectacularity, and what greater spectacle is there than knowledge?" Rossellini's amusing twist on the meaning of spectacle clearly sets him apart from the practitioners of epic cinema.

Gallagher argues that Rossellini's essay films, his historical neorealism, should be seen as a "critique of spectacle." Gallagher concedes that Rossellini's historical cinema, including *Louis XIV*, "has its moments of pageantry as pageantial as that of Hollywood, and it has its melodrama too," but he nevertheless contends that Rossellini's cinematic theorems and his historical vision remained intact; the essayist had not lost his way or surrendered to the spectacle under his examination.

At times, Rossellini appeared to believe that he had effectively transcended the distinction between art and life—that he was actually filming history as it is, rather than merely representing or reconstructing it. "An historical event," he stated in 1974, "is an historical event. It has the same value as a tree or a butterfly or a mushroom. I don't choose the tree. I must get the tree which is there. . . . I refuse to accomplish my creative act." Tag Gallagher appears to agree, suggesting that Rossellini's "camera, one might say, becomes the eye of history." On the other hand, Gallagher qualifies this seeming embrace of Rossellini's claim to provide an essentially unmediated representation of history, observing that the director's films "are less interested in doing deep justice to a given historical era than in putting forth a prescriptive reading of historical progress."

It was description, however, not prescription, that Rossellini boldly stated his films accomplished. Brunette is more skeptical of Rossellini's "firm, and apparently untroubled, view that pure information, pure knowledge, can be conveyed neutrally." But as far as Rossellini was concerned, his cinema of historical reconstruction had succeeded in virtually eliminating the distance separating image and referent: images (at least *his* images) are signs for very little other than the "naked purity" of historical fact itself. Rossellini's film theory oddly seems to combine the claims to neutrality of blindfolded justice with the visual acuity of an unblindfolded Justitia with 20/20 vision!

Italy: Year One, more than any of the director's other films, makes transparent the fact that even Rossellini existed within history. Like his earlier historical films, *Italy: Year One* was built around the life of a famous man, in this case Alcide De Gasperi, the Christian Democratic prime minister who rose to power in Italy from the ashes of the Second World War. Most of the funds for the film were provided by the Italian state film company. Rossellini's son, excusing the willingness of his father to make an essentially Christian Democratic political film, later pointed to the drastic financial situation in which his father found himself at the time the film was made.

It is essential to observe right away that the opening sequences of *Italy: Year One*, depicting both Italian-resistance struggles against fascism and the liberation of the nation, are genuinely harrowing and represent some of the finest filmmaking of Rossellini's long career. But the lionization of De Gasperi—and of the role of the Christian Democratic Party in postwar Italy—was not a view of history universally shared, even among the Italians themselves. The Italian Communist Party, for example, subscribed to a very different account of postwar politics.

The main problem with *Italy: Year One* is its one-sided presentation of its central figure, De Gasperi. "We see De Gasperi defying the Papal authority," says Tag Gallagher, "but not De Gasperi seeking Papal help. We see him as anti-Fascist, but not sending former partisans to prison, letting Fascists out, and keeping Fascists in government posts." Historian Tobias Abse put it in a nutshell: "Neo-fascism has never been a force clearly separable from the structures of the Italian state that emerged—in many respects largely unreconstructed—after the Second World War."

It was this central historical fact that Rossellini managed to exclude from his homage to De Gasperi and postwar Italian unity. It was a unity presided over by the Christian Democrats, a political party that Abse asserts had "always been within brushing distance . . . of black intrigues and conspiracies," and that, appropriately enough, collapsed as a coherent political force once the Cold War and its anticommunist priorities had been replaced by new times.

Rossellini's sister, who helped write the screenplay for *Italy: Year One*, defended the film's anticommunism, according to Peter Brunette, "on the grounds that the Communists of the period were Stalinists, and had to be neutralized so as to prevent a totalitarian revolution." The point here, however, is not that this view of Italian politics is *wrong*, but rather that, right or wrong, it can hardly be considered as nonideological, outside of history, neutral, or value-free. Rossellini's perspective on these events is just that, a perspective, an angle on events, a specific point of view. The film does not convey Rossellini's vaunted direct experience of history, rendered in all its "naked purity." Films of historical reconstruction can "show us people as they are," but *Italy: Year One* does not present people and politics "as they are" but rather as the Christian Democratic Party of Italy wished them to be seen. It is not that Rossellini sold out, his son's comments about his financial situation to the contrary notwithstanding, but rather that it is simply impossible to argue that *Italy: Year One* is the only historical portrait of the period that one could possibly paint. If it is only the contemporary quality of the political and historical issues specific to *Italy: Year One* that brings this fact to our attention, then perhaps we should ask more questions about the perspective Rossellini brought to more remote periods of human history.

Brunette acknowledges that by taking on a contemporary subject, like that of *Italy: Year One*, Rossellini risked revealing the contradictions of his approach to filmmaking. Accuracy in historical reconstruction is necessarily a matter of degree and we should approach warily any filmmaker's claim to have trapped history itself within the camera's gaze.

Historical Sociology: Germany

In spite of their shared commitment to capitalist social institutions, corporate economic policies, and the ideology of anticommunism, the

United States, Britain, Germany, and Japan went to war with each other during the period 1939–45. The single most important reason for this conflict is the existence, up to 1945, of two *different and competing forms of capitalism*, which confronted each other across the globe in the Second World War. The Allied Powers (excluding the Soviet Union) generally had in common a liberal capitalist history of modernization while the Axis Powers had taken an authoritarian capitalist road to industrial development. These forces represented, in a sense, two sides of the same coin.

We elsewhere refer to Harvard historian Stanley Hoffman's observation that capitalism is compatible with both totalitarian societies and liberal ones, comfortable with either democracy or the police state. While Hoffman is a liberal, Francis Fukuyama is a conservative and former Reagan administration official. Yet Fukuyama, extending Hoffman's observation, points out in his controversial *The End of History and the Last Man* that in fact empirical evidence suggests that market-oriented *authoritarian* modernizers may be more successful than their "democratic counterparts." Among the cases Fukuyama cites to support his argument are imperial Germany and Meiji Japan.

A compelling analysis of this particular view of modernization can be found in historical sociologist Barrington Moore, Jr.'s, *Social Origins of Dictatorship and Democracy*. Moore, according to Geoff Eley, sought to provide a coherent explanation for why fascist states generally, and Germany in particular, suffered from errant development and illiberalism—in other words, the absence of democratic constitutionalism and the rule of law. Moore's conclusion, based upon wide-ranging historical evidence, was that authoritarian capitalist societies were a product of a "disjunction between economic modernity and political backwardness, the grand contradiction of a dynamic economy developing within an unreformed political framework, in which preindustrial elites preserved their dominance against the rising forces of a modern society."

Some of the strongest arguments in behalf of this view of modern world history come, ironically, from Eley, who counts himself as one of its critics. He begins with a long list of concessions to Moore's thesis and acknowledges it as the dominant Anglo-American view of German history after 1945. It became the most widely embraced perspective among German historians themselves over the next thirty years, and, even in the more conservative 1980s and 1990s, "remained the preferred approach to their past of most progressive Germans."

In addition to Moore's research, Eley says that earlier work by Alexander Gerschenkron and Hans Rosenberg was essential to full incorporation within the social sciences of this particular view of German history. Having traced its development back to the work of Weber and Marx, Eley nevertheless observes that the "*locus classicus* in the immediate German literature" was to be found in Ralf Dahrendorf's *Society and Democracy in Germany*, published two years after Moore's *Social Origins*. "The key to Germany's vulnerability to Nazism," Dahrendorf had argued, "was taken to be the persistence of pre-industrial and authoritarian traditions at the center of the state." Thus Germany's historical development excluded it from being a part of that European liberalism whose emergence, according to Roberto Unger, had fostered the rule of law as a dominant political principle. Under the Nazis, the authoritarian state would become a law unto itself.

As German historian Fritz Fischer put it bluntly in *From Kaiser-reich to Third Reich*, German politicians in the nineteenth century, especially Bismarck, successfully promoted an "assimilation of the new industrial big bourgeoisie by the agrarian-feudal forces. This alliance of 'steel and rye,' of the manor and blast furnace, persisted as the hard core of reaction within German society" and ultimately precipitated Hitler's rise to power. Eley admits that, taken together, social scientists and historians like Moore, Dahrendorf, and Fischer have constructed "an extraordinarily powerful structural frame for interpreting the history of the Kaiserreich."

Nevertheless, Eley sharply objects to the common equation of liberalism and democracy and claims that the coupling of liberalism and democracy "makes no sense for most of the nineteenth century, because liberals showed themselves consistently attached to highly restrictive and exclusionary systems of political representation." He objects to confining discussion of democracy to "formal juridical terms" and "parliamentary constitutions." The idea of democracy, as far as Eley is concerned, is far more spacious than that of legality.

"The effects of social movements such as trade unions," concludes Eley, "women's movements, moral reform campaigns, and so on, which involve collective action and organization in a wider societal field, [require] the constitutional definition of a democratic polity to be complemented by some developed conception of civil society." The very forces Eley identifies here—such as women's and working-class social movements—have dedicated themselves to a policy agenda (the right of women to vote, the legalization of trade unions and collective bargaining, equal-protection lawsuits, regulation of job discrimination, equal pay for equal work, the living wage, and so forth) which constitutes the backbone of much of the specifically legal development of the liberal state during the past seventy years.

If liberal societies suffer by comparison with models of more egalitarian social organization, liberalism's image certainly improves by comparison with the reality of fascism. In order to accomplish Wigmore's comparative ambition, to see liberal constitutionalism in sharp outline, we need an equally clear image of authoritarian capitalism. But what is the key element identified by historical sociologists that a filmmaker must capture on the screen in order to reveal the actual legal and political framework of the fascist state—its constitution?

Werner Herzog

Explaining the fascist turn in German history, Barrington Moore referred to preindustrial elites; Jürgen Kocka to prebourgeois traditions; Heinrich August Winkler to the legacies of a feudal and absolutist past; Fritz Fischer to the reactionary compromise of industrial bourgeoisie with agrarian-feudal forces, the alliance of "steel and rye"—of the manor and blast furnace. Is there any film about modern Germany that provides us with a visual rendition of these social contradictions? Certainly there are movies like Fassbinder's *Berlin Alexanderplatz* (1979–80), documentaries like Claude Lanzmann's *Shoah* (1985), propaganda films like Leni Riefenstahl's *Triumph of the Will* (1935), and historical reconstructions like Margarethe von Trotta's *Rosa Luxemburg* (1986), without which our understanding of authoritarianism and German politics would clearly be diminished.

But is there a single film that could somehow be described as representing a transposition onto the motion-picture screen of the complex dialectic of Barrington Moore's *Social Origins of Dictatorship and Democracy*? Has any filmmaker visualized the manor and blast furnace in all their ghastly and nightmarish sociological significance for what "went wrong" in German historical development?

To a remarkable extent, Werner Herzog's *Heart of Glass* (1976) fits the bill. The tale that Herzog has to tell, according to Tony Rayns, "is plainly allegorical: a glass factory declines into bankruptcy when its owner dies without divulging the formula for its special ruby glass, and the village that depended on the factory for employment goes down with it." However "plainly allegorical" *Heart of Glass* may be, Rayns does not even take a stab at what the allegory is about, what real-world history or phenomenon Herzog is exploring, however elliptically or metaphorically, in this stunningly beautiful and eerily gothic motion picture.

In *Heart of Glass*, the inventor of the magnificent ruby glass has died without divulging the secret formula for its manufacture, compelling the glass factory's owner to lead a desperate, increasingly frenetic, search for a secret that must somewhere be hidden. He scours old books to no avail. Next, according to Alan Greenberg, who has written a book on the filming of *Heart of Glass*, the factory owner sends for the shepherd Hias, "who is known for his prophetic gifts." While Hias plays a key role in foreseeing the catastrophic consequences of the community's disintegration, he has no clue where the secret to the glass may be found. "Madness speaks out of the factory owner," says Greenberg, and the "people believe him willingly, for among the glassblowers, madness is rampant."

The factory owner turns to prayer, invoking the ruby-colored glass, which "has an easily breakable soul." Asked what a "heart of glass" might represent, Werner Herzog says: "It seems to involve for me the meaning of a fragile state." Herzog's comment can be taken to refer to both a fragile emotional state and, transposed to the social realm, a fragile political state, perhaps the democratic state in authoritarian capitalist society, a state like the Weimar Republic. Fritz Fischer's manor and blast furnace are certainly both there, structuring Herzog's film. In the scene just mentioned, after the factory owner, taking refuge in his country manor, kneels in prayer, he rises grimly and asks out loud: "Will the future feel the downfall of factories a necessity, such as the downfall of castles was a necessity?" The tension between castles and manors, on the one hand, and factories and blast furnaces on the other, is here suggested. Greenberg even puts one translation of this quote from the film, standing by itself, on the back dust jacket of his book.

This scene is shortly followed by one in the glass factory itself where, surrounding the glowing blast furnaces, glassblowers enthusiastically try to replicate the lost formula, only to have revealed before their eyes the worthlessness of their creation and the corresponding hopelessness of their condition. Despair and then panic follow. Later, there is a tavern scene where, as Greenberg puts it, "there is great turmoil. By and by we realize that a kind of strange and collective madness is breaking out." Hias sits at one table in the corner, while "prophecies drag out of him." A stranger asks what will happen next. "Then the Little One starts war," replies Hias, staring straight ahead into space, "and the Big One across the ocean extinguishes it. Then you won't get a loaf of bread for two hundred florins. Then a strict master comes, who will pull people's shirts up over their heads, together with the skin."

No German seeing this film could miss the "allegorical" content of Hias's beer-hall prophecy. This, in a nutshell, is the concluding chapter in the history of authoritarian capitalism in Germany, from Kaiserreich to Third Reich, in Fritz Fischer's appellation. In *Cinema 2: The Time-Image*, Gilles Deleuze refers to both "a German people, in a country which has bungled its revolutions, and was constituted under Bismarck and Hitler," as well as to the tension between "the spirit and the deepest level of reality," in *Heart of Glass*. The contradiction between blast furnace and feudal manor, "steel and rye," in German history is perfectly mirrored in Herzog's film, an allegorical tale of Germany's bungled liberalism and failed revolutions.

Nuremberg

Stanley Kramer's *Judgment at Nuremberg* (1961) deals with a crucial moment in German history separating the periods confronted respectively by Werner Herzog in *Heart of Glass* and by Rainer Werner Fassbinder in *The Marriage of Maria Braun* (1978). Yves Simoneau's TNT Original motion picture *Nuremberg* (2000) deals with the Nuremberg war-crimes trial, which began in Nuremberg, Germany, on November 20, 1945, and concluded on October 1, 1946, with the final reading of verdicts and opinions by the international tribunal's presiding judges. As Michael R. Marrus explains in *The Nuremberg War Crimes Trial, 1945–46*, of the twenty-two defendants prosecuted at Nuremberg (including Martin Bormann, who was tried in absentia), eight were found guilty of conspiracy, twelve were found guilty of crimes against peace, sixteen were found guilty of war crimes, and sixteen were found guilty of crimes against humanity. On October 15, 1946, Hermann Goering managed to commit suicide in prison, and the following day the remaining eleven defendants sentenced to hang were executed.

Kramer's film takes up where Simoneau's leaves off. The tracking shot that opens the film, following along a rubble-strewn avenue of bombed-out buildings, has the caption placed over it: "Nuremberg, Germany, 1948." Spencer Tracy, as Judge Dan Haywood, candidly acknowledges that he has come in at the tail end of things: "Well, let's face it: Hitler is gone, Goebbels is gone, Goering is gone—committed suicide before they could hang him. Now we're down to the business of judging the doctors, businessmen, and judges. Some people think they shouldn't be judged at all. . . . You had to beat the backwoods of Maine to come up with a hick like me." Asked if he is sorry he has come all the way to Germany, Tracy thoughtfully replies, "No, I think the trials should go on, especially the trials of the German judges."

Stanley Kramer says in his autobiography that he was attracted to the project of filming *Judgment at Nuremberg* by Abby Mann's initial teleplay. Mann's subsequent screenplay "did not," according to Kramer, "concentrate on the most famous aspect of the war crimes trials, the calling to account of men like Hermann Goering, Rudolf Hess, Albert Speer, and Joachim von Ribbentrop. Their cases had been hashed over countless times. *Judgment at Nuremberg* concentrated on the trying of four high judges in the Nazi system—a story considered even more significant because it exposed and studied the very core of the corruption of Hitler's system."

Kramer's conversational recounting of his film career is not designed to delve deeply into questions like what, exactly, he means by "the very core" of the Nazi system. Right after the observation quoted above, Kramer launches into a defense of his film about Nuremberg against charges that the picture, which was not successful at the box office, was too "intellectual." But it is interesting to think that Kramer would regard a story about the role of judges in the Nazi legal system as somehow capable of capturing the essence of "the corruption of Hitler's system."

In *Courtroom's Finest Hour in American Cinema*, Thomas J. Harris quotes Donald Spoto's commentary on *Judgment at Nuremberg*, indicating that the "Nuremberg trials were very different from what is here represented. Judges were not defendants in them— politicians were." Harris quotes Spoto's point that in the real Nuremberg trial, the judges were from four different countries while, in Kramer's film, "all three are Americans." He further quotes Spoto's statement that in contrast to what is portrayed in *Judgment at Nuremberg*, "the actual trials convicted twenty-two men, of whom twelve were sentenced to hang." Finally, Harris points to Spoto's skepticism of Kramer's take on how the Cold War shaped the trials. America's growing anticommunism may have been in the background, but "no such political consideration ever weighed in the final sentences," according to Spoto.

One wonders what exactly Harris and Spoto are talking about here. It is obvious that *Judgment at Nuremberg* is *not* based upon the Nuremberg war-crimes trial of 1945–46. The film's introductory title says that the year is 1948. The film's audience is told right up front by Spencer Tracy's character that Goering is dead, having committed suicide before he could be hanged. There are only American judges in this trial because this is not the international war-crimes trial that took place two years earlier. That trial is over. It is easy to get the impression from Spoto's comments that the authors are unaware of war-crimes trials prosecuted *after* 1946.

Contrary to Spoto's apparent belief, Tracy's Judge Dan Haywood is *not* based upon the American representative on the International Military Tribunal, "Francis Biddle of Massachusetts." As Joseph Borkin points out in *The Crime and Punishment of I.G. Farben*, at the conclusion of the international war-crimes trial in 1946, the United States "promptly initiated plans to proceed with a series of war crimes trials against the leading executives of the I.G., Krupp, and Flick concerns. Judges were recruited from the state and federal judiciaries and from the faculties of law schools to preside over the trials."

Dan Haywood was, in fact, a lot like the judges who presided over cases tried by American prosecutors in the American zone of European occupation. War-crimes trials were indeed being carried out in countries around the world. "The victor nations," observes historian Martin Gilbert, "and the former captive peoples, found some small solace in the continuing trials and sentences of the immediate post-war years, although there was no way in which those trials and executions could ever bring back those who had been murdered against all accepted rules and codes of war."

Finally, as to Spoto's claim that anticommunism and cold war ideology did not "weigh in the final sentences" handed out by war-crimes tribunals, one should consult some of the prosecutors in those trials. Joseph Borkin reports that, when the judgment in the IG Farben war-crimes prosecution was announced, the "prosecution staff was outraged by the court's verdict and the sentences of the guilty. Chief prosecutor Josiah DuBois regarded the sentences as 'light enough to please a chicken thief.' " Writing in 1952 in his book *The Devil's Chemists*, DuBois stated candidly: "I believe it fair to say that since 1945 the principal factor behind our foreign policy, like the motivation of the Farben judgment, has been fear of Communism."

But what of the specifically jurisprudential lessons that can be drawn from *Judgment at Nuremberg*? What caused Stanley Kramer to conclude that judges were somehow key players, if not necessarily the backbone, of the Nazi system of authoritarian rule? The answer to this question is not to be found in Kramer's autobiography. But it is found in Abby Mann's script and in lead U.S. prosecutor Colonel Tad Lawson (Richard Widmark)'s direct examination of Dr. Wieck (John Wengraf), a law professor and lawyer, at the beginning of *Judgment at Nuremberg*. As a German university lecturer, Wieck had Ernst Janning (Burt Lancaster), one of the defendants standing trial for war crimes in the film, as one of his students. After 1929, Wieck got to know Janning well in the German Ministry of Justice. "Dr. Wieck," asks prosecutor Lawson (Richard Widmark), "would you tell us, from your own experience, the position of the judge in Germany prior to the advent of Adolf Hitler?" Wieck replies that the "position of the judge was one of complete independence."

"Now would you describe the contrast," continues Lawson, "if any, after the coming to power of National Socialism in 1933?" Again Wieck responds crisply: "Judges became subject to something outside of objective justice. They became subject to what was necessary for

the protection of a country. . . . The first consideration of the judge
became the punishment of acts against the state rather than objective
consideration of the case." At this point, emphasizing the gravity of
the issues at hand, Judge Haywood interrupts from the bench, asking
Lawson if he might put his own question to the witness. "Did the
judiciary," asks Haywood, "protest these laws abridging their independence?" Wieck replies that while a few did, they soon either re-
signed or were forced to resign. "Others," he continues, while
seeming to cast a glance at defendant Janning, "adapted themselves to
the new situation."

The rest of *Judgment at Nuremberg*, it may be said, hopefully
without oversimplifying, is designed to establish that the Nazi crimes
were only made possible by the willingness of German citizens to
conform, to "adapt themselves to the new situation." Janning is especially culpable because he, as jurist and scholar with (according to
Professor Wieck) a brilliant legal mind, should have had a higher
loyalty than simply to expediency and to the Nazi regime. Annette
Insdorf correctly identifies this theme at the heart of *Judgment at
Nuremberg*, arguing that "the film raises central issues of responsibility—individual, national, universal." All that is necessary for evil to
triumph, Stanley Kramer and Abby Mann seem to be saying, is for
good men to do nothing.

If Kramer and Mann, in avoiding any confusion between the international military tribunal conducted in 1945–46 and the one they
portray in their film, proved themselves better historians than Harris
and Spoto, as we have seen, they nevertheless have stumbled in terms
of the central historical and legal argument animating *Judgment at
Nuremberg*. Of course, the general proposition that decent men and
women should never, as Thoreau once put it, lend themselves to the
wrong that they condemn, represents sound advice. But the more
specific historical and legal argument advanced by Kramer and Mann
misfires. It was not the *absence* of judicial independence that marked
the Nazi judge—just the reverse. Hitler came to power partly *because*
of judicial independence.

"More flagrant" even than the way bureaucrats abused their power
in Germany, according to historian Gordon Craig, was the way in
which judges abused their positions. The independence of German
judges under the Weimar Republic "was interpreted by many of them

as giving them license to express their prevalently monarchist sentiments from the bench, both in word and in deed." Attacks upon
liberalism and the Republic were more likely to be rewarded than
punished by the German judiciary, according to Craig. The Reich
minister of justice, in fact, complained "that there existed 'a state of
war between the people and the judiciary,' and [the socialists] who
had . . . felt it necessary in 1918 to insist upon the irremovability of
judges, admitted later that it had been a mistake not to start with a
clean slate." The leniency which right-wing putschists and antidemo-
cratic counterrevolutionaries came to expect from German courts tops
Craig's long list of ways in which an independent German judiciary
helped dig the grave of the Weimar Republic, Germany's great, if brief,
liberal experiment.

How did Kramer and Mann get the legal and historical bit that
wrong? Perhaps they just projected contemporary American legal
politics backward onto German history and thus facilitated the general ethical argument upon which they had already decided. Condemning the failure of judges to stand up and speak out fit perfectly
with the thesis of the film—that evil succeeds when men and women
of conscience fall silent—even if it did not fit at all with what actually
happened in Germany. After all, at the time *Judgment at Nuremberg*
was made and shown in theaters, Americans were reading in their
newspapers and watching on television the great drama of the civil-
rights movement—including the U.S. Supreme Court, which took a
leadership role in desegregating public schools, and heroic southern
federal judges who, boldly exercising the American tradition of judicial independence, stood up to southern governors and racists and
fought for the implementation of federal law.

But what happens when right-wing judges use their independence
to destroy a liberal constitution and bring into power a fascist regime?
Or, closer to home, during the New Deal period, what happens when
a conservative judiciary fights tooth and nail against the democratic
sentiments of legislative and executive branches of government clearly
in tune with the desires and needs of the people? The legal politics of
Stanley Kramer and Abby Mann fit early 1960s America a lot better
than either Germany or the United States in the period between the
two world wars.

Roberto Unger says that separation of powers is a crucial aspect of liberal constitutionalism. And some form of judicial review, including the practical political independence of judges, may be a necessary component of the separation-of-powers doctrine. But just as capitalism can be reconciled with authoritarianism, so can judicial independence. Unconstrained judges freely joined the assault on liberalism in Germany and helped make the barbarism of the Nazi regime possible. That is a point nowhere to be found in *Judgment at Nuremberg*. One wonders if the film could not just as easily have been made in the form of an attack on independent German judges and legal scholars—"judicial activists"—who boldly deviated from liberal constitutional theory. But that might have made the film even harder for American audiences to understand during the Kennedy and King years when, we should not forget, judicial activism became increasingly identified with liberalism, civil rights, and the Warren Court.

Rainer Werner Fassbinder

In *Imagining the Law*, historian Norman F. Cantor expresses a shrill dislike for Harvard law professor Morton Horwitz's "Marxist historiography," yet it is actually rather difficult to distinguish the broad outline of Cantor's legal history from that of the law professor at whom he takes aim. For example, Cantor suggests that Horwitz's approach can be "challenged along economic lines. How could industrialization have proceeded if the old common-law doctrine of strict liability had continued to be applied in the nineteenth-century courts? Strict liability would have severely impeded, possibly prevented industrialization in both England and the United States."

Without quoting Horwitz, and presumably in stark opposition to him, Cantor's own version of why the law changed is rather like what is usually called, with whatever degree of reductionism, "the Horwitz thesis." "The coming of factories," argues Cantor, "with workers on assembly lines in front of dangerous machines, and railroads that were long notorious for inflicting injury on their employees and passengers alike, changed the law of liability in both England and the United States at about the same time, from about 1850 into the first decade of the next century." If you said that Morton Horwitz, Lawrence Friedman, or Willard Hurst had written that paragraph, rather than Cantor himself, no one would doubt you for a moment. What all of these writers, Cantor included, have in common is an implicit base/super-structure model of the relationship between law and society. According to Cantor, because of railroad development an erosion of strict liability "had to occur." The coming of factories "changed the law of liability," not the other way around. Changes in social and economic base produce corresponding and necessary changes in legal super-structure. These are lessons one can learn by reading the classical political economy of Karl Marx, Adam Smith, and David Ricardo. But can these same lessons be learned from motion pictures?

Rainer W. Fassbinder was born in 1945 and died of a drug overdose in Munich, in 1982, at the peak of his filmmaking career. Though still in his thirties, he was nevertheless the most prolific of German film-makers, perhaps making more feature films in a shorter period of time than anyone anywhere except for those working on a cinematic as-sembly line making contract pictures under a studio system.

Following Fassbinder's own practice, film theorist and historian Thomas Elsaesser refers to three films, *The Marriage of Maria Braun*, *Lola*, and *Veronika Voss*, as Fassbinder's "BRD trilogy," or Bundes-republik Deutschland (Federal Republic of Germany) trilogy. He says that *The Marriage of Maria Braun*, in particular, "was clearly received, especially by foreign critics, as an allegory of West Germany." Exactly how a film becomes received as historical/political commentary on a nation and its identity, and whether that necessarily reflects the pri-mary intention of the work's creators, is just one of the themes deftly handled by Elsaesser in his commentary on *Maria Braun*. But *Maria Braun*, as Joyce Rheuban points out, was seen by half a million view-ers and grossed three million marks *within a month* of its release in Germany. It has been perhaps the most widely viewed postwar Ger-man film shown in the United States.

The Marriage of Maria Braun, "BRD 1" (the first installment in the BRD trilogy) features actress Hanna Schygulla, in the role of Maria Braun, who describes herself at one point in the film as "the Mata Hari of the Economic Miracle," an obvious reference to the popular label given to postwar German economic development. During the dark days of World War II, only hours after their marriage, Maria Braun's new husband, Hermann, is sent to fight with the German army on the Eastern Front. He is reported killed in action and Maria, at first, appears lost. But adjusting to the times, she finds ways to survive the U.S. occupation and becomes involved with an American soldier. To her astonishment, Maria's husband suddenly returns and, almost in shock, she kills her lover. But Hermann, to reciprocate his wife's act of loyalty, confesses to the crime and goes to prison. Most of the film gives focus to the slow but inexorable process by which Maria enters the male world of German business, gradually comes to dominate her boss, Oswald, and accumulates a substantial financial savings.

She even negotiates wages with a trade-union official, an old friend, apparently having mastered the arts of industrial policy. "[T]hanks to her bold and unconventional methods," according to Fassbinder friend and biographer Christian Braad Thomsen, "she is soon indispensable to Oswald's textile company. She knows what German women would like, because she is 'so to speak, an expert in the future,' as she says with a fond thought of the future, she has left in pawn in gaol." Maria becomes a workaholic and seems to live for her tightly held dream of the marital happiness she will share with Hermann one day, when he has served his prison sentence. On the one hand, Maria's hard-won success seems admirable and her devotion to Hermann, despite a sexual liaison with her boss, Oswald, more or less above reproach. Nevertheless, as Thomsen notes, Maria's "life is based on the illusion that life can be postponed, as it were, for a happy future, one that one can save up and prepare for, one that will be great and pure no matter what methods have been employed to realize it."

When Hermann does eventually get out of prison, instead of returning to his wife he decides to travel abroad. Several years later, when he finally comes home to the ever patient Maria Braun, both his wife and the film's audience learn simultaneously, during the reading of Oswald's will, that Hermann has been paid by Maria's boss *not* to return home until after Oswald is dead. Moments after the will has been read in the Brauns' living room, with the World Cup soccer match blaring on the radio, Maria goes into the kitchen to light her cigarette from the burner on the stove. "Whether Maria ignites the gas deliberately," says Thomsen, "or by mistake, the result is the same: the house together with Hermann and Maria is blown up. Only the voice on the radio survives and announces triumphantly that at this very moment Germany has won the football world cup."

In what I regard as a quite Brechtian way, however much unre-marked by any of the reviewers mentioned here, Fassbinder confronts his audience with a series of tantalizing yet unanswered questions: Why did Maria think Hermann was worth murdering someone for? Why did Maria wait for Hermann even *after* he left prison and then left Germany? If Maria had saved all that money, why did Hermann need any of Oswald's? Did Maria cause the explosion on purpose? What has any of this to do with German history?

One might well also ask: Why did Germans support Hitler? Why did Germany reconstruct itself after the war as a capitalist state, rather than a democratic socialist one? Why did Germany submerge its self-critique of Nazism during the Cold War? Why are German corporations and Swiss banks only now being held accountable for their conduct during the Holocaust? What good would it do for Germany to become the most economically powerful nation in Europe (which it has) or win the World Cup (which it did) without knowing why winning mattered?

Almost everyone writing about *Maria Braun* observes the fact that the film starts with a picture of *der Führer*, and concludes with jux-taposed images of later German chancellors (Adenauer, Erhard, Kiesinger, Schmidt). But Elsaesser's explanation is the most interest-ing:

> The portrait of Hitler at the beginning ironically or not so ironically is repeated by a framed official portrait of Helmut Schmidt, and the other Chancellors reversed out in negative, suggesting a continuity amid the total change between a dictatorship and a liberal Western democracy. These literal "framings" of the narratives once more encourage a double, i.e., an allegorical reading, while at the same time never quite disambiguating exactly what the film is finally "saying" about the relation between the private and public, the Nazi past and the democratic present.

So what is Fassbinder "saying," then, about his "Mata Hari of the Economic Miracle" and her relationship to postwar German history or, as Elsaesser puts it, about the relation between "the Nazi past and the democratic present"? Another way of posing this question, espe-cially useful in our present context, is to ask: In what sense is *The*

Marriage of Maria Braun a "legal film"—in other words, how can we situate Fassbinder's work within the genre of legal fiction and film?

At one level, *Maria Braun*'s status as a "legal film" was actually confirmed by the German legal system. Although the film was originally released in 1978, it was years before what Juliane Lorenz describes as the "long-term court battle" over Fassbinder's share in profits earned by *Maria Braun* was finally resolved by the Oberlandesgericht in Düsseldorf. At another level, *Maria Braun* includes a fascinating, postwar, U.S.-occupation, formal inquest into the death of Maria's American soldier-boyfriend. While trial sequences are not an essential element of the legal genre, this hearing should nevertheless qualify as one. "You remember this attic with the crazy elevator," asked production manager Harry Baer, "where the trial scene is supposed to take place? Surely the art department must have offered him a variety of scenery. But he dismissed all their suggestions as boring." In this instance, Fassbinder's instinct for set design served him well: the makeshift attic courtroom, as well as rough-and-ready, on-the-spot German/English translations, perfectly capture the haphazard, "do it yourself" aspect of the occupation itself.

At one more level, however, *Maria Braun* can be interpreted as expressing a complex political conception of modern German history, "continuity amid the total change between a dictatorship and a liberal Western democracy," returning to Elsaesser—in short, Fassbinder's jurisprudence. "Perhaps this ambivalent feeling about truth," recalls Hanna Schygulla, "was precisely what bound [Fassbinder and me] together. Rather than this *or* that, it's this *and* that. It's how Rainer made his movies. . . . His movies were about things that don't fit together at all and don't follow any theory. That is why his movies are still valid." Exactly. Truth, including political truth, is contradictory. Hitler and the later, "democratic" leaders of the (West) German nation do *not* fit together, and yet they do. Liberal capitalism is *not* authoritarian capitalism, and yet it remains capitalism. What Germany got, after Hitler, after the Americans, after the economic miracle, was not liberalism *or* capitalism but liberalism *and* capitalism.

Liberalism—"legal liberalism," David Trubek called it—more familiarly, the rule of law: all designate a jurisprudence radically different from that of the Nazis. But that rule of law is always conditioned by the social and economic structure of capitalist society. "How much justice can you afford?" asks a lawyer in a favorite *New Yorker* cartoon. The kind of trial a man gets, U.S. Supreme Court justice Hugo Black asserted, should not depend on the amount of money he has. But everyone knows that it depends more upon *that* than, perhaps, any other single factor. The gap between liberalism's claims and its performance, Harold Laski observed, has always been wide.

"Symmetry and repetition," proposes Elsaesser, "are deemed to symbolize the postwar history of Germany, with the apparent changes from one regime to another, from one Chancellor (Hitler) to the Federal Chancellors . . . provoking a shoulder-shrugging *'plus ça change (plus c'est la même chose).'*" But not quite. Fassbinder himself, asked why Willy Brandt's portrait was missing from those of the other chancellors at the end of *Maria Braun*, replied that the omission was intentional: "[W]e talked this over for a long time. . . . He was still a symbol of the reform movement, and despite his failure—and that's another story—there is still a difference between him and the other chancellors."

Fassbinder's respect for contradiction makes possible the tension which pervades his cinema. Neither liberalism's reform impulse nor German political philosopher Jürgen Habermas's famous theory of noncoercive systems of free communication can be disconnected from the possibilities and constraints implicit in postwar (German) capitalism's economic miracle. Just as Maria Braun's existence is based on the illusion that life can be postponed, liberal legalism and its theoretical construction of the world seem predicated at times on the illusion that economics can be ignored. However allegorically, Fassbinder suggests that such ignorance, like the explosion that finally rocks the Brauns' "happy" home, can be fatal.

Chapter 7

Popular Culture,
Legal Genre, Realism

IN *THE CULTURAL Study of Law*, one of the most remarkable manifestos, of sorts, to hit the law-school world in many years, Yale's Paul W. Kahn argues that the central problem with legal scholarship is not that it is too theoretical, but that it is too practical. In the face of protest from judges and lawyers who regularly complain that law schools seem to have become lost in space, pursuing a kind of "abstract expressionist" legal writing that rarely comes down to earth and solves concrete problems, Kahn replies that the reverse is in fact true. Legal scholarship has been incorporated into the practical project of legal reform to such a degree that law professors no longer even have a sense of the way in which they should function *separately* from the practice and profession of law itself. What legal scholars have failed to do is to see clearly their proper subject: the culture of law.

"There is remarkably little study of the culture of the rule of law itself," says Kahn, "as a way of understanding and perceiving meaning in the events of our political and social life." The more broadly one conceives the phrase "the events of our political and social life," the broader the culture of participation in the construction and interpretation of those events becomes. So what does that mean, specifically, for the study of legal culture? Put candidly, in this instance by Richard K. Sherwin in *When the Law Goes Pop: The Vanishing Line Between Law and Popular Culture*, "Legal reality can no longer be properly understood, or assessed, apart from what appears on the screen."

According to lawyer and best-selling novelist Lisa Scottoline (dubbed "the female John Grisham" by *People* magazine), "the line between the reality of lawyering and its fictional representation on television and in books has gone well beyond blurred" and, she insists, there is an "almost complete merger of fiction and reality when it comes to the law." If we place side by side the observations of commentators like Kahn, Sherwin, and Scottoline, it seems obvious we are short on serious writing about legal culture. And, whether it is high art or low, legal culture counts.

The purpose of this chapter is to conclude our critique of the legal system on the silver screen within a somewhat larger cultural frame of reference. Explored here will be the relationship between intellectuals and popular art, elite and mass culture, radical theory and the entertainment business. First, we will explore the emergence of serious reservations about mass art among radical theorists as well as among cultural mandarins after the Second World War, and how movies in particular have been regarded by opposing sides across the "cultural studies" battlefield. Then we will focus in on the practice of different writers and critics who have analyzed legal films in an effort to conceptualize a comprehensive definition of the legal genre. Finally, the realist orientation to film criticism and evaluation is assessed, specifically in the context of legal films.

While this chapter is somewhat more "theoretical" than those that have preceded it, a number of individual films still receive substantial treatment and the general overview of the cultural field provided here eventually returns to the kind of analysis by which we have been preoccupied throughout: how do particular films work and what representation or image of law and the legal system do they project?

High and Low

In the fall 1939 issue of *Partisan Review*, Clement Greenberg published an essay titled "Avant-Garde and Kitsch." Described by his editors at the time as a "young writer who works in the New York customs house," Greenberg would become, along with Meyer Shapiro, Harold Rosenberg, and very few others, universally recognized as one of America's most significant art critics. His "Avant-Garde and Kitsch" soon became the most influential critical essay ever written within the cultural confines of American art. In his effort to confront the dynamics of cutting-edge artistic production Greenberg drew a sharp contrast between avant-garde painters and the purveyors of popular culture.

The avant-garde, for Greenberg, was a cadre of creative artists engaged in antithetical cultural activity. "It is among the hopeful signs," Greenberg stated, "in the midst of the decay of our present society that we—some of us—have been unwilling to accept this last phase for our own culture," this last phase being equivalent to a "motionless Alexandrianism, an academicism in which the really important issues are left untouched because they involve controversy." At the same time, overwhelming capitulation to what Claes Oldenberg would later call "the B values," the taste and sentiments of the bourgeoisie, was abroad in the land and a "rear guard," according to Greenberg, championed "that thing to which the Germans give the wonderful name of *Kitsch*: popular, commercial art and literature with their chromeotypes, magazine covers, illustrations, ads, slick and pulp fiction, comics, Tin Pan Alley music, tap dancing, Hollywood movies, etc., etc." Along with other forms of popular culture, the movies apparently ranked no higher within Greenberg's aesthetic system than did, for example, jazz or astrology within the critique of the "culture industry" later advanced by members of the Frankfurt School of Social Research.

However much Greenberg's support for abstract painting and his commitment to modernism "with a vengeance" may eventually have marked him as the high priest of formalism, he nevertheless wrote, on the eve of World War II, as a quite political cultural theorist. Perhaps the leading Marxist art critic of a subsequent generation, T. J. Clark quotes at length from Greenberg's characterization of the avant-garde as an aspect of revolutionary thought in Europe. Clark adds that in his analysis of the state of culture, Greenberg referred specifically to "the thought of Marx, to whom the reader is grimly directed at the end of the essay, after a miserable and just description of fascism's skill at providing 'art for the people.'" In advancing his argument that a socialist orientation to the arts is required—not so much in order to imagine a new culture but simply in order to preserve whatever living culture still exists—Greenberg says it is "necessary to quote Marx word for word." Paradoxically, Greenberg added that the avant-garde artist was inescapably "attached by an umbilical cord of gold" to an elite within society's ruling class.

In his history of the twentieth century, Eric Hobsbawm observes that between the world wars modernism "became the badge of those who wanted to prove they were both cultured and up to date." He argues that the modernist avant-garde "rarely reached beyond small minorities" and that it was mass art or popular culture that achieved "undeniable cultural hegemony" during the period. The forces that Hobsbawm identifies as dominating the popular arts were "primarily technological and industrial: press, camera, film, record, and radio." In the period after the Second World War, and especially after the center of the world art market shifted from Europe to the United States, from Paris to New York, he indicates that "the rich still collected—old money, as a rule, preferring old masters, new money going for novelty—but increasingly art-purchasers bought for investment, as once men had bought speculative gold shares."

It was as true after the end of the Cold War as it was during it that people who were willing and able to pay hundreds of thousands of dollars for paintings, figurative or abstract, or for any other kind of art, including that of the "avant-garde," were almost certainly among the very richest members of society and, by definition, part of the ruling elite. For the fine artist challenging the cultural status quo, financial patronage, from either public or private sources, remained an unfortunate necessity. The incorporation of the arts into the modern university, as Hobsbawm points out, solved the problem of economic survival for many contemporary artists. But the radical stylistic experiments carried out in the 1950s by those to whom Harold Rosenberg referred as "action painters" were dependent, in part, upon the wealth of private art collectors and escalating prices made possible by a burgeoning New York art market. On the specific question of "accepting sponsorship from an enlightened patron"—Greenberg's "umbilical cord of gold"—Hobsbawm says only, and rather flatly, that the "relation between money and the arts is always ambiguous."

Social Theory of Culture

Trying to explain Clement Greenberg's "umbilical cord of gold" comment, art historian Thomas Crow suggests that Greenberg may have been making the kind of argument, at the end of the Depression decade, that Herbert Marcuse would later make in *One-Dimensional Man*: the important thing was the great refusal, an absolute unwillingness to give in to what existed, an outright rejection of cooptation. According to Crow, in Greenberg's theory, the genuinely avant-garde artist "could expect no audience outside those cultivated members of the privileged classes who maintain in their patronage a pre-modern independence of taste."

The real opposition in Greenberg's critique was thus between popular culture, or "kitsch," hopelessly enslaved to reproduction of the dominant ideology, on the one hand, and real art, high art, however difficult, however financed, on the other. So it is hardly surprising, from Crow's perspective, that Greenberg should have "posited the relationship between modernism and mass culture as one of relentless refusal." And refusing, in the absence of mass employment by university art departments, could be expensive. Even dangerous artists had to pay the bills.

If avant-garde art was not as dangerous to the status quo as Greenberg claimed, was mass art itself as bad as he believed—did popular culture really threaten to destroy civilized taste? "The alternatives to the institutional museum ruled by those who own everything," says art critic Lucy Lippard in her book *On the Beaten Track* "have ironically emerged from the realm of popular culture." Here, briefly, Lippard points the way to an alternative and more nuanced view of popular culture, the movies, and their relationship to dominant ideas and images, including a socially and politically dominant legal ideology.

Greenberg, of course, was not alone in his hostility toward popular taste and consumer art. Matthew Arnold's influential *Culture and Anarchy* of 1869 was animated by a barely disguised contempt for "the masses." Presumably because of their popularity with the reading public—according to Leslie Fiedler—Fielding, Scott, the Brontës, even Dickens, were excluded from the Great Tradition of English literature by F. R. Leavis, in the "first fury of his superelitism." Was it covert elitism or a Marcusean great refusal that led Adorno and Horkheimer, giants of the Frankfurt School of Social Research, to lump all the products of the "culture industry" together as artifacts of a desultory retreat from enlightenment into mythology?

The myth of the twentieth century, in the view of Horkheimer and Adorno, was nothing other than fascism, or ideology in general—a destructive fraud, according to Peter Brantlinger, "practiced by those rational instruments of ultimate irrationality, the mass media, controlled 'by the wholly enlightened as they steer society toward barbarism.'" After World War II, when abstract expressionism was coming into its own and trends toward cultural conformity seemed to take a quantum leap forward with the spread of television viewing and mass consumption, few cultural critics on the left looked to Chester Riley and his wife, Peg, from the popular TV show *Life with Riley*, or Ralph and Alice Kramden (or even their friends, the Nortons) from *The Honeymooners*, for models of what socialist Americans might one day look or act like.

On the contrary, popular culture was seen by these theorists as part of the baggage of ruling-class ideology, a sophisticated barrage of loaded imagery that reduced people to a life of mindless consumerism and diverted them from an authentic confrontation with the way America really was. And is. From George Orwell's *1984*, to Louis Althusser's theory of the media as a form of ideological state apparatus, through Noam Chomsky's systematic critique of "manufactured consent"—one or another version of this kind of cultural theory, sometimes called "the dominant-ideology thesis," has survived and recruited to its banner articulate proponents.

A long list of objections to this perspective on popular culture has been filed by a range of cultural historians and mass-media theorists. In the 1980s, film historian Robert Sklar complained that the dominant-ideology approach to cinema studies made everything a little too easy. According to the theory, ideology flowed "smoothly from its source (whether this is the state, the bourgeoisie or capitalism, or a compendium of all three, is not often clarified or specified) through the film production and distribution process into the spectator's willing eyes and ears." There was a little more to the writing of cultural history than that, Sklar confided. Following objections like the ones he raised, a backlash set in against the dominant-ideology critique during the 1990s.

"The discovery of pleasure as a respectable research topic" became, according to Anne Karpf, the next wave in media studies, and researchers began "falling over each other to reclaim hitherto derided genres." Not only did pleasure become respectable but popular culture (e.g., Madonna) was institutionalized as a legitimate field of academic teaching and scholarship. In time, and in turn, a fierce reaction against "cultural studies" set in and pop culture in the university was often bracketed with political correctness as evidence of the deterioration of Western cultural values. As the assault on academia's purported legitimization of cultural dreck began to assume a tone similar to that pioneered by right-wing congressmen in their original attacks on abstract art, left-wing hostility to mass culture was itself revived and "the supposed evidence of mass media awash with the rumblings of anti-capitalist discontent and subversion," as Alan Milchman puts it, was sharply questioned. And so it goes.

Thomas Crow concludes his assessment of the debate over abstract expressionism's politics with the comment that discussion of the issue has "suffered from a surplus of verdicts," and he adds that typically "one moment of the series of transformations" is almost randomly "chosen as the definitive one." If a "vast wasteland" moment or instance of mass-media manipulation is given exclusive focus, then ideology critique scores points. The reverse is true, however, if what is emphasized is an aspect of popular culture that seems to unmask the system or undercut its apologies for injustice. In the latter case, popular culture turns the dominant-ideology thesis on its head and reappears as the "weak link" in a global system under attack from Seattle to Genoa.

Perhaps the best reason for questioning both of these approaches is that they tend to cancel each other out. Popular culture, in any event, cannot simply constitute a form of ideological manipulation if film after film about the legal system draws into question the legitimacy and fairness of that system. Films like *Revolution*, in the realm of political and constitutional history; the classic due-process films in criminal-law cinema; legal-conspiracy thrillers and underground films; the master discourse of tort cinema—just to take a few examples—make clear that in its reflection upon the American legal system, popular culture is not of a single piece, a simple prop supporting the facade of blind justice and legalization of the way things are. Motion pictures belong, more often than not, to the universe of low culture. But life itself, says Sean O'Casey, "depends on low reality."

A Legal Genre?

If genre provides the essential entry point for students of high culture's literary pantheon (sorting works into tragedy versus comedy, the novel or poetry as against the essay form, and so forth), it likewise provides a revealing method of inventorying those works that together represent the foundation of popular culture (e.g., science fiction, the Western, mysteries, horror, musicals and melodrama, gangster or detective fiction and film). On the one hand, it has been easy for us to think about films dealing with criminal courts or tort liability or international law as part of a "legal genre." But is there a formal distinction or category—a legal genre—comparable to other genres? What are its rules? What are the specific boundaries, the borderlands, of the legal system on the silver screen?

One response, obviously rejected in this book, has been that such a genre classification requires the presence in film or fiction of an important, perhaps decisive, legal trial. Not only are trials potentially dramatic events, but most people probably associate law and lawyers with trials and trial courts as much as with any other ready image or symbol. In fact, the "Lawyers and the Law" filmography published by *Legal Reference Services Quarterly*, J. L. Breen's pioneering *Novel Verdicts: A Guide to Courtroom Fiction*, and Thomas J. Harris's *Courtroom's Finest Hour in American Cinema*, all published in the 1980s, uniformly regard trials as the key identifying feature of the films and novels they include and annotate within their scope of reference.

Pitched to a different readership and constructed around more difficult concepts, Carol J. Clover's sparkling essay "God Bless Juries!"—included in Nick Browne's *Refiguring American Film Genres*—carves out a niche for the trial film as a genre, or subgenre, on its own. She does not attempt to work out the definition of the legal genre, within which her trial film would no doubt fit. Clover argues that conventional trial narratives usually have a double structure: they include an official legal trial and a second, unofficial, "trial" that is still central to the narrative and which turns on a larger aspect of the legal system. Jonathan Kaplan's *The Accused* (1988), one of the examples Clover provides in support of her thesis, includes an official trial, clearly based upon the New Bedford gang-rape prosecution. The latter, broadcast by public television, was one of the first nationally televised criminal trials in U.S. history.

In addition to this official trial, where Jodie Foster plays a sexual-assault victim, Clover also identifies an unofficial trial, whose "dramatic tension lies as much in whether one female lawyer can buck a male system set in its ways and a male law structurally biased against victims of rape." Clover's official trials are what invariably mark the films she discusses as trial films. But her unofficial trials are especially interesting because they are not really trials at all; while demanding a verdict or judgment, they are not so much "trials" as issues or questions that the system cannot dodge. And they are certainly the kind of thing with which legal films, with or without formal trial proceedings, are likely to be concerned. "Is the system fair across various social differences—class, race, and gender?" she asks. Or can the system be corrupted or diverted from the goal of justice by outside pressures? "Are lawyers human?" These are all questions that any legal film can pose in an acute way.

In two subsequent essays, Clover continues her focus on the trial film. In "Law and the Order of Popular Culture," she claims that "real-life trials become movies (by which I mean both film and television dramas) as easily as they do . . . because trials are already movielike to begin with and movies are already trial-like to begin with." Some trials may be movielike and some movies may be trial-like but generalization here is tricky. Certainly most movies and many trials have in common an attempt to tell a story.

But most complex litigation, trials involving commercial and antitrust law or intellectual property, tax, and bankruptcy statutes, have little to do with any movie ever made, other than perhaps those that seem to go on far too long. Ridley Scott's *Gladiator* (2000) may be "trial-like" in that like many trials, the film includes winners and losers, but most movies fall into genres which are *not* trial-like, or at least into genres that are sufficiently *unlike* trials and trial movies that there appears to be a reason for carving out a separate trial film genre of its own.

Clover returns to this theme in "Judging Audiences: The Case of the Trial Movie," where she argues that the silent film *Falsely Accused* (1907) "is not just a movie about a trial" but, in fact, a "trial movie that spells out the natural fit between trials and movies." Almost every film genre has been described by someone as constituting the essence of cinema. There is an entire branch of film criticism which argues that Clover's natural fit exists—but between the cinema and the dream, not movies and trials. No doubt movies (or more sophisticated computer imagery) are used in flight-simulation training because of the seemingly "natural fit" between motion-picture images and what pilots see when they look out of an airplane.

Clover's argument that movies put audiences in the position of jurors is interesting, and certainly gets to the heart of how *some* trial movies work. But in others, the jury is not only visible within the film but plays an important role. "The reason that juries are largely unseen in trial movies," asserts Clover, "and the jury system largely uncontested within the regime of cinema is surely that we understand the jury to constitute a kind of necessary blank space in the text." But do we think of juries that way? Not in John Grisham's novels, one of which is titled *The Runaway Jury* (1996). Not in television legal dramas, from *L.A. Law* through *Law and Order* and *The Practice*. And not in movies such as Brian Gibson's *The Juror* (1996), Heywood Gould's *Trial by Jury* (1994), or Peter Yates's *Suspect* (1987), in each of which a juror becomes either the leading character or one of two main characters in the film. And Alfred Hitchcock is not the only director whose juries sometimes must make key mistakes for the movie's plot to thicken.

One of the trial movies to which Clover gives primary focus in "Judging Audiences" is Barbet Schroeder's *Reversal of Fortune* (1991), which Clover describes as "Alan Dershowitz's account of Claus von Bülow's second trial for attempting the 'insulin murder' of his heiress wife, Sunny." But the film is not about a trial at all. It begins with a verdict of guilty being read out in von Bülow's first murder trial and then recounts the effort made by Dershowitz and his assistants to prepare the argument in behalf of an appellate reversal of von Bülow's trial conviction.

The film includes a very brief, and extremely rare, scene depicting oral argument by counsel on appeal, and literally ends with a shot of the comatose Sunny von Bülow in bed, her imaginary voice-over saying, "Claus von Bülow *was* given a second trial and acquitted on both counts. This is all you can know, all you can be told." The *only* account of von Bülow's second trial provided in *Reversal of Fortune* is contained in those four words, "acquitted on both counts." While *Reversal of Fortune* may be an important legal film, it is not a trial film, if that genre requires a trial at least somewhere in the film.

In his introduction to a collection of essays titled, *Legal Reelism: Movies as Legal Texts*, John Denvir acknowledges that only a few essays in the book deal with courtroom dramas. This he takes to constitute "additional evidence of the pluralism that has broken law from its narrow institutional bindings," and it is evident that the contributors to *Legal Reelism* believe they are writing about law in film even when they are not writing about trial films, which they rarely are. But what kinds of films are they writing about, then? Denvir says that the films surveyed in the book "cover a wide variety of film genres; westerns, gangster films, foreign classics, contemporary comedies and sex thrillers." Foreign films may have their own section at the video-rental store, but the fact they were made abroad does not say much about their genre. The other categories Denvir lists, however, *are* independent genres and thus he suggests, without saying it in so many words, that *Legal Reelism* deals with legal issues raised in film—*not* with a supposed legal genre, cordoned off from the rest of cinema. Unless, of course, "legal issues raised in film" represents for Denvir and his coauthors a tentative definition of the legal genre.

David A. Black's *Law in Film* is not so much an odd book as it is an oddly titled book. Indicating that he had intended to write a book on "films about law," a project that, the author states with a Clintonesque appreciation for the language, "depending on one's definition of *about*, opens the category up at least to detective films and prison films and possibly to virtually every commercial fiction film ever made." While it is not obvious from the author's introductory comments what compelled him to make the jump from legal films to "virtually every commercial fiction film ever made," it is clear that we are not going to get a new definition of the legal genre itself. And a quick alphabetical inspection of the movies listed in the filmography (such as *All About Eve, Blue Velvet, Casablanca, Day for Night, Flashdance, Gentlemen Prefer Blondes, It's a Wonderful Life*) indicates that the book turns, in significant part, on examination of films which do not have much to do with law, at least as conventionally understood. Black readily acknowledges this fact, saying that "chiefly, this book is not a survey of films about law, nor any significant subset about them." Rather few films discussed in the book, he observes, "are treated in real depth, certainly far fewer than would be if this were a book of essays about individual films." And, indeed, very few films are treated for more than a couple of paragraphs. The only one considered in detail, Nicholas Ray's *In a Lonely Place* (1950), which gets six luxuriant pages, is hard to see as a legal film, certainly without explanation. Black quotes another critic describing *In a Lonely Place* as representing a point of overlap between film noir, screwball comedy, and "woman's Gothic film," three genres presumably distinct from legal films.

Nicholas Ray's *Knock on Any Door* (1949), however, is an important courtroom picture, which Carol Clover, among others, discusses, though she regards it as "generically offbeat." While it would seem a prime candidate for discussion in a book on law in film, Black does not mention *Knock on Any Door*. On the other hand, the reason he devotes as much space as he does to *In a Lonely Place* is because it perfectly illustrates the real subject of his book: reflexivity. "Reflexivity in textual theory," says Black, "is an exponentially more complex matter than reflexivity in grammar," from which, nevertheless, the concept is drawn. "The claim that a text—book, film, television show, and so forth—takes itself as its own object" the author regards as worth investigating, and it may well be. But it remains an odd focus for a book titled *Law in Film*.

In any event, I think a definition of the legal genre should be located somewhere between trial films (too narrow) and every commercial fiction film ever made (too broad). British film critic Tom Ryall, quoted in Stephen Neale's *Genre*, says that "[g]enres may be defined as patterns/forms/styles/structures which transcend individual films, and which supervise both their construction by the film maker, and their reading by the audience." Describing his own research on cinematic genres, Neale observes that "[t]ime and time again, it emerged that generic specificity is extremely difficult to pin down in general statements that are anything other than rudimentary and banal, such as the narrative setting of the western is that of the American frontier; the gangster film involves the depiction of organised crime in the context of industrial capitalism," and so forth.

The depiction of lawyers and clients, officials and citizens, courts or other social institutions (for example: legislatures, corporations, newspapers, police departments) grappling with legal issues and conflicts, cases, and statutes, or the politics of the rule of law itself, provides the sort of rudimentary and banal definition of the legal genre to which Neale refers. The patterns/forms/styles/structures that transcend individual films within the legal genre, following Ryall, have still to be formally theorized but are nevertheless occasionally implicit in the working definition of legal genre employed in this book.

That approach to legal genre has been borrowed more from law and legal practice than aesthetic theory, and has turned informally upon the identification and analysis of discrete fields of legal doctrine and experience: liberal constitutionalism, criminal law and procedure, tort liability, international law, comparative jurisprudence. Specifically within these legal/cinematic fields or subdivisions, individual films have often been provided a close reading or analysis. An eclectic set of ideas about pattern and style, form and structure (visual continuity, historical contrast, adaptation and revision, dialectical tension, cycles and stereotypes, recurrent situations and iconography, alternative models and master discourse) has been employed, while remaining alert to conventions established and then transcended. Rudimentary and banal though this strategy may be, it is a start.

Realism

For most filmgoers, the question of whether a particular motion picture can technically be defined within the parameters of a "legal genre" would almost certainly be a lot less interesting or important than whether a legal picture or courtroom drama is true, or accurate, or "realistic." This concluding section deals with that issue: what does realism mean within the context of legal cinema?

Although Paul Bergman and Michael Asimow's *Reel Justice: The Courtroom Goes to the Movies* deals with trial movies and *Past Imperfect: History According to the Movies*, edited by Mark C. Carnes, surveys historical films, there is some overlap between the two books. Fred Zinnemann's *A Man for All Seasons* (1966) and John Ford's *Young Mr. Lincoln* (1939), for example, are reviewed in both books. It is useful to compare analyses of these two films about lawyers and the law to see where their respective authors come down on the question of realist critique in film.

Bergman and Asimow like *A Man for All Seasons*, a film previously discussed in this book within the context of international-law films. A contributor to *Past Imperfect*, Richard Marius, whose biography of Thomas More was a National Book Award finalist, thinks rather less of the movie than Bergman and Asimow. The authors of *Reel Justice* regard the film as *legally* realistic, believe it "accurately describes" both the conflict between Thomas More and Henry VIII as well as More's trial, and thus award the film four gavels, their highest ranking, for "quality, dramatic power, and authenticity of the trial scenes."

Marius, on the other hand, who is interested in *historical* rather than trial "authenticity," uses *A Man for All Seasons* as a punching bag. After a daunting list of "the film's errors and distortions," Marius adds that "[f]ar more contemptible, however, is the saccharine picture that both play and film present of More's religion and his furious and cascading hatred of the Protestants." To be sure, both Robert Bolt's original play and Zinnemann's film manage to render with accuracy as well as sympathy Thomas More's great faith in the law. "The attitude More adopted towards the primacy and authority of law," writes biographer Peter Ackroyd, "governed all his subsequent actions," and the principles of law were those "by which More's life and career were guided." Anthony Julius, reviewing Ackroyd's biography in the *Manchester Guardian*, goes so far as to suggest that More was "not only a Catholic martyr; he was also, in a certain sense, a lawyer-martyr too."

Bergman and Asimow do not ignore More's alleged bigotry. "Like many pious people of the time," they observe, "he favored the burning of heretics." Nor do they deny that *A Man for All Seasons* would have been a rather different film had it actually included scenes of heretics being burned at the stake, as in Ridley Scott's exemplary, if horrifying, *1492: The Conquest of Paradise* (1992). The point is simply that *historical* accuracy rates no higher in Bergman and Asimow's gavel system than does *legal* or trial authenticity in Marius's canon of cinematic values.

With transparent import for this divergence of critical concern, in an essay on John Ford's Lincoln biopic, British film scholar Ben Brewster observes that "it is obvious that any number of 'readings' could be (and are) given of *Young Mr. Lincoln* which are legitimate, i.e., can justify themselves in relation to their specific ends." What sort of "readings" does Brewster have in mind? The film, he says, "can be read for its historical 'accuracy' (in a certain ideology of history) by a history teacher, for its sexual morality and attitude to crime by a censor, for the likely political effect of showing it in a certain conjuncture by a political activist, etc." Brewster's "etc." might well include, for our purposes here, that films can also be read by law professors for their legal "accuracy" or trial authenticity.

Like the "dominant ideology" and "weak link" approaches to the social theory of culture discussed earlier, competing cinematic realisms tend to cancel each other out. Richard Marius's historical realism cancels out *Reel Justice*'s legal realism. And as soon as some filmmaker manages to satisfy historians and lawyers, along comes the curator of a textile and design museum to complain about costumes and sets. Or a psychiatrist finds the film's psychology simply unbelievable.

A New York lawyer complains that, for him, the ending of Oliver Stone's *Wall Street* (1987) actually ruined the movie. In this scene, a sadder but wiser Bud Fox (Charlie Sheen) hustles up some courthouse steps to help convict Gordon Gekko (Michael Douglas). Fox is entering a New York (state), rather than U.S. (federal), court building. The securities fraud committed by Gekko in the film, lawyers and law professors no doubt suspect, would have been a *federal* offense, since the regulation of the securities market is a federal, not state, responsibility. In other words, Bud Fox is heading straight into the *wrong* building. In its last scene, *Wall Street*'s hard-edged realism, for some legally trained viewers at any rate, collapses. Where does this kind of realist criticism end?

There is a terrific insight, however offhandedly presented, in Bergman and Asimow's essay on Sidney Lumet's *The Verdict* (1982). "Soliciting clients by showing up at funerals," they point out, "would also probably get [Frank] Galvin [Paul Newman] disbarred. That may be a bit surprising to TV viewers who have become used to seeing lawyers drum up business with commercials that make sales pitches for used cars and cubic zirconium diamonds seem sophisticated." Just so. Much of what the authors of *Reel Justice* know from law school, and from their own professional teaching and writing, is totally unknown to most movie viewers, who remain within a shadowy half world of legal knowledge and legal ignorance. Movies are made, exhibited, and experienced by audiences within that half world, a universe of light and dark; to simply illuminate the obscure bits after the fact, as Bergman and Asimow do in the pages of their book, does not tell us much about what movies mean to real audiences or how they are interpreted in practice.

Another contributor to *Past Imperfect*, historian Mark E. Neely, Jr., doesn't think much of *Young Mr. Lincoln*, arguing that "John Ford's film was mostly fiction, and corny fiction at that, and it is redeemed only by the director's eye for landscape, the folk tunes in the musical score, and Henry Fonda's considerable acting ability." He points out, however, that the actor who plays Lincoln's political opponent, Stephen A. Douglas, "does bear a very strong resemblance to the real Douglas as he appeared in early photographs." Now the relationship between how actors cast for parts in *Young Mr. Lincoln* look and the appearance of their real historical counterparts is not Neely's primary angle on John Ford the historian. Ford naturally did not think of himself as an historian; his famous self-description, after all, was "I make Westerns." But Neely's reference to Douglas's actual appearance demonstrates the potential for an entire realm of historical criticism as much beside the point as any commentary on which courthouse is filmed at the end of *Wall Street*. How many audience members have a picture in the back of their mind of *either* the real Stephen A. Douglas or the street layout of downtown New York court buildings?

Like Neely, John E. Walsh does not rate *Young Mr. Lincoln* very highly as history. "The Armstrong case forms a large part of the film's continuing action," reports Walsh in his book *Moonlight: Abraham Lincoln and the Almanac Trial*, "though with all the names changed and most of the circumstances far removed from the reality." Walsh specifically assails the film's culminating scene, where "the exposed culprit with branded brow reels and staggers from the courtroom, now in custody of the sheriff. As an example of Hollywood's famous finagling with fact, the sequence is a gem." Remarkably, however, Walsh does not comment on the fact that the photograph he includes in his book, depicting the Beardstown, Illinois, courtroom where the famous "almanac trial" actually took place, could almost be a still from Ford's film, the movie courtroom is so much like that where Lincoln worked his moonlight magic.

While uninterested in *Young Mr. Lincoln* as history, Bergman and Asimow are quite concerned with the film's distortion of the rules that govern criminal trials. Had the rail-splitting attorney from Illinois actually "conducted his cross-examination of [Jack] Cass [Ward Bond] as argumentatively as depicted in the film," they contend, "Judge Bell might well have disciplined him. The ensuing blemish on his record might have prevented him from being elected president." So this was a major liberty for the director to have taken with the truth. What is wrong with Lincoln's cross-examination of this particular witness is that in the process of eliciting a confession to the murder for which his clients are on trial, Lincoln manages to transgress the Constitution. Like all witnesses, Bergman and Asimow inform us, "Cass has a constitutional right under the Fifth Amendment not to provide evidence that could be used against him in a criminal proceeding. Once it became clear Lincoln was accusing Cass of the murder, Judge Bell should have warned Cass of his right not to incriminate himself, and given Cass an immediate opportunity to consult with an attorney."

The authors of *Reel Justice* are certainly onto something when they emphasize the role played by Henry Fonda's powerful cross-examination within the dramatic structure of *Young Mr. Lincoln*. But the legal critique they provide at this crucial juncture in their review misfires. Harvard law professor Laurence Tribe reminds us that, so long as the answers a witness gives might be used as evidence in a future criminal trial where that witness has become a defendant, then the Fifth Amendment, as applied to the states by the Fourteenth

Amendment, confers the privilege of silence. *Young Mr. Lincoln's* Jack Cass would have a Fifth Amendment right not to incriminate himself, as Bergman and Asimow argue, if that right had been applied to the states, as Tribe adds, by the Fourteenth Amendment.

Whatever one may think of John Ford as historian, his film is clearly set during the early years of Lincoln's law practice, and the criminal trial, which Bergman and Asimow regard as key to understanding the film, is set in an Illinois state court, prior to Lincoln's launching a political career. In other words, before the Civil War. Before the Fourteenth Amendment to the Constitution was adopted. Before the 1908 U.S. Supreme Court decision in *Twining vs. New Jersey*, in which the Court held that protection against self-incrimination, while a significant rule of evidence, did not rise to the level of a fundamental right. Before the Court subsequently decided, in 1964, that maybe the rule against self-incrimination ought to be regarded as a fundamental right after all, and applicable to the states, including Illinois, via the Fourteenth Amendment.

In their introduction, Asimow and Bergman say they "think it's important to know how Hollywood bends the rules to inject drama or humor into trial movies, and we try to alert you to when the filmmakers do so." Their analysis of *Young Mr. Lincoln*, however, seems more a case where *the authors* have bent the rules, or at least their history. Perhaps they have tried to inject a bit of "legal realism" where there is no real need for it, where it just becomes excess legal baggage, in a film that works well enough without our having to know the history of the incorporation doctrine or the evolution of rules governing the art of cross-examination.

Of course, one could at least argue that there is consistency to *Reel Justice*'s realism if all films, regardless of when they are set historically, were treated by the book's authors as if they took place in the present. Movies would thus be subjected to current rules of procedure, evidence, ethics, and so forth, given application across the board, however awkward or inappropriate that might appear with respect to films *not* set in the present. But that is not the uniform practice of Bergman and Asimow. In their discussion of Peter Hyams's *The Star Chamber* (1983), for example, the authors indicate an evidentiary ruling by the film's Judge Hardin "was correct at the time it was issued" (i.e., presumably, when the film is set, rather than today), and then further state that another of his rulings was "probably correct under California law at the time the movie was made" (i.e., when the film itself was released, 1983).

This isn't rule bending, it's mind bending. Legal realism as a form of film criticism quickly threatens to career off into deep theoretical space, leaving deconstruction, virtual reality, and the science of complex systems dead in their tracks. Are trial films to be measured against the actual legal rules and procedures in existence (1) at the time when the film is historically set, (2) at the time when the film is released in theaters, or (3) at the time the critic is reviewing the film? *Reel Justice* questions *Young Mr. Lincoln*'s authenticity as a trial film because it was made in 1939, set a century earlier, and fails to reflect changes in constitutional criminal procedure from the 1960s. Again, "Cass has a constitutional right under the Fifth Amendment," the authors claim, and "Judge Bell should have warned Cass of his right not to incriminate himself." Only if Judge Bell, like James Cole (Bruce Willis) in Terry Gilliam's *12 Monkeys* (1995), was a time traveler returning to the past from a distant future realm with a copy of Tribe's constitutional law treatise tucked under his arm, just as James Cole carries a World War I bullet in his leg across the face of history.

Film writer Andrew Sarris and the authors of *Reel Justice* are miles apart in their approach to *Young Mr. Lincoln*. In his analysis of the confession scene, where Jack Cass has finally given way to Lincoln's relentless cross-examination, Sarris compares "Bond's extremely histrionic breakdown" with a "similar courtroom breakdown in *Sergeant Rutledge* more than two decades later. In both instances Ford encourages the culprits to overact their confessions as if catharsis were a function of the most agonizing atonement, again suggesting a religious quest for absolutes rather than a humanist acceptance of ambiguities."

But is not the adversary system of American justice an embodiment of process values, betraying an inevitably frustrating indifference to absolutes? And is this not a result of its professional commitment to zealous representation of clients and its rhetorical foundation in the ambiguity of language—the art of "doing things with words"? Reflecting back upon our discussion of Justitia blindfolded, to what extent does the contradiction to which Sarris points, between absolutes and ambiguity, mirror Martin Jay's contrast of substance with procedure, the image of justice versus a law dispensed solely through language? What if the American legal profession, like Robert Bolt's (if not history's) Thomas More, sees itself finally as the night watchman, a critical stumbling block to any quest for absolutes, ultimately drawing its moral justification from a profoundly antimajoritarian Constitution? In this sense, Ford's Lincoln is a different kind of lawyer not only from the prosecutor he opposes in a Springfield, Illinois, courtroom, but also, one can argue, from the kind of attorney most secular law schools in the United States have been training for years.

Or consider an observation by British film theorist Peter Wollen, who suggests that in Ford's film "Lincoln's efforts are not directed towards presenting a case or swaying the jury. Like a missile with a homing device, he homes in on the lies he senses and explodes them. Truth, for Lincoln . . . is essentially subjective: honest men speak the truth." But what if truth, *legal* truth, is objective, not subjective? What if the problem of justice cannot be solved the way it is in *Young Mr. Lincoln*? What if justice, to be equal, must necessarily be blind?

Wollen, at any rate, concludes that "Lincoln's virtue resides in his closeness to the natural essence which supposedly is within us all." And, echoing Sarris, "[h]is role in the trial is fundamentally religious—his contact with the truth is on a sacred rather than secular level." This intuitive capacity for seeing that justice is done renders Ford's Lincoln one of the greatest figures in the history of American film. Lincoln is able, as Wollen puts it, "to solve the problem of justice posed in the movie: on the one hand, the popular, direct justice of the mob; on the other hand, the artificial, elitist, mumbo-jumbo of the courts, embodied in the lawyer for the prosecution. Lincoln's victory in the court underscores his victory on the steps of the jail." But Lincoln is not sui generis; he rejects the very same "elitist mumbo-jumbo of the courts" against which William Penn and Robert Rantoul had railed—and Charles Dickens as well. In *Young Mr. Lincoln*, the self-effacing John Ford, modest director of cowboy pictures, has struck a genuinely resonant chord within common-law legal culture.

It is on the basis of his victory "on the steps of the jail," however, where Lincoln stands down a lynch mob, that one can legitimately advance a more secular, liberal reading of Ford's motion picture and, perhaps, find a link between it and Robert Mulligan's benchmark legal film *To Kill a Mockingbird* (1962). "Trouble is when men start takin' the law into their own hands," Lincoln says, with remarkable composure, to the frenzied mob, "they're just as apt, in all the confusion and fun, to start hangin' somebody who's not a murderer as somebody who is. And the next thing you know they're hangin' one another just for fun. Till it gets'a place a man can't pass a tree or look at a rope without feeling uneasy."

Here he pauses, recognizing his words are beginning to take effect. "We seem," he continues, "to lose our heads in times like this. We do things together we'd be mighty ashamed to do by ourselves." Lincoln then singles out an individual in the mob and forces him to think about what he is doing, quotes from the Bible, suggests they could do worse than take the passage to heart, and then asks if the boys might not feel better setting down that heavy log with which they *were* just about to break down the jailhouse door. Like Atticus Finch in *To Kill a Mockingbird*, an attorney who also confronts an angry mob itching to hang an accused man without going through the formality of a trial, Lincoln shames a lynch mob into recalling a different aspect of legal culture: the morality of process.

Historian Norman Rosenberg, one of the contributors to *Legal Reelism*, disagrees with this view of *Young Mr. Lincoln*. He feels Lincoln's jailhouse speech, excerpted here, "is hardly an exposition on the rule of law." Rather than buy the argument that Lincoln is primarily interested in defending the virtue of legal procedure, Rosenberg stresses the fact that "Lincoln reminds the crowd that they will cheat him, a struggling young lawyer, out of a potential legal fee if they hang the Clay boys without a trial." Acknowledging that *Young Mr. Lincoln*'s "hero does defend the social order and the idea of a trial by jury," Rosenberg adds, "but not with elaborate legal arguments."

However one wishes to characterize the script—the specific text spoken by Henry Fonda—the impact of Ford's visual rendering of this scene is overwhelming. Fonda stands in gleaming moonlight, white shirt, black suit and tie, right there in the doorway, framed by the shadow of tree leaves playing against the front wall of the jail. Shots of the mob, carrying torches, are intercut with the serene figure of Lincoln: "Blessed are the merciful, for they shall obtain mercy." Then a brief image fills the screen—the tearful face of Mrs. Clay, mother of the boys about to be lynched. And so back to Lincoln, for the first time with an edge to his voice, "That's all I've got to say, friends. Good night."

There is an even better scene in *Young Mr. Lincoln*, right at the very end of the film, a sequence characterized by the editors of *Cahiers du cinema* as an encore to Lincoln's performance in the criminal trial itself. But this encore "takes place not in the court in front of the spectators of the trial, but on another stage (the street, the town, the country) and in front of a crowd *which is not shown* (which is no longer only the inhabitants of Springfield but of America)." The dramatic conclusion to *Young Mr. Lincoln* demonstrates that the trial itself, including Lincoln's cross-examination of one J. Palmer Cass, was a "simple rehearsal (provincial tour) and what is to follow on the other stage . . . will be the real performance (national tour) and the *encore* is, in fact, the true entrance on the stage of legend." The stage of legend, yes. But also the stage of history.

"Everybody knows," Ford told Peter Bogdanovich, "Lincoln was a great man, but the idea of the picture was to give the feeling that even as a young man you could sense there was going to be something great about this man." The editors of *Cahiers du cinema*, who assert that Lincoln represents Law (a power that is legitimized by its own statement rather than physical force) as well as a prohibition upon the use of unauthorized violence (i.e., the rule of law), make the same link between the lawyer and the legend that Ford himself—as is clear from his comment to Bogdanovich—hoped to forge in this film.

"I think I might go on apiece," says Lincoln, "maybe to the top of that hill," as Ford's camera follows him up the path behind a covered wagon, at dusk, the upper two-thirds of the screen filled with big gray clouds that suddenly burst open in a hard rain. As the thunder rolls and "The Battle Hymn of the Republic" gradually swells in volume and emotion, Ford fades from an ominous dark sky, now streaked with lightning, to the gray stone of the Lincoln Memorial and to Lincoln's monumental and dignified form, also blanketed with cascading rain as the music reaches a crescendo, effectively putting into image and sound the historic commentary, "and now he belongs to the ages . . ."

A legend, perhaps, but one rendered with a cinematic complexity that makes transparent how much more there is to films like *Young Mr. Lincoln* than a one-to-one, "realist" comparison between movie trials and contemporary codes of criminal procedure could ever reveal. "I am not a devotee of the director John Ford," concedes novelist Gore Vidal, "but he and his cameraman achieved a moment at [*Young Mr. Lincoln's*] end which still demonstrates that the right picture can be equal, almost, to the right word." Only almost?

We have seen throughout this book that the right picture can indeed be worth a thousand words. That images are capable of providing as compelling a portrait of law and the legal system as words has been demonstrated by selectively examining the respective cinemas of revolution and constitutional history, criminal law and the law of torts, international and comparative law and politics. But of greater importance still is the way in which pictures, especially moving pictures, provide a different *kind* of narrative, a different impression of the legal system than conventional legal narrative, the language of lawyers and courts.

Just as *Revolution* imagines the birth of a nation from the bottom up in contrast to constitutional documents and standard histories, and *Dirty Harry* visualizes a justice alternative to that of the formal due-process model, *True Believer* uncovers a truth to which official legality can rarely admit and *Traffic* manages to transcend conventional oppositions by viewing illegality as a self-contained system with its own rules. Just as *A Civil Action* tells the story of civil liability and corporate power in a way that the real judicial system tragically failed to match and *Three Kings* zeroes in on the unofficial story of human rights, *Heart of Glass* penetrates the legal mist surrounding authoritarian constitutionalism and achieves a poetic yet intellectually acute juridical vision.

What does it all mean? The evidence, finally, is in conflict. We may regard the visualization of legality—that which Justicia sees and then enables us to see once her blindfold is removed—as more or less true than the authorized version, an alternative and parallel legality or a critique of the existing rules and their application, perhaps shadows cast across the wall of the cave. But it is impossible to argue that movies are simply a mirror held up to a system of blind justice, providing one more authorized account, one more official version.

Movies about law and lawyers can threaten legal legitimacy or sanction it, reveal the persons behind the masks of law as heroes or villains, victims or hoodlums, champions of the little guy or servants of the rich and powerful. But it is hard to believe that the visualization of justice can indefinitely be cordoned off from the sociology of law, from popular discussion of how well legal institutions work, and from the strategies and practices of professionals who operate a system being transformed right before their eyes.

References

Introduction

Bloomfield, Maxwell. *Peaceful Revolution: Constitutional Change and American Culture from Progressivism to the New Deal* (Cambridge: Harvard University Press, 2000).

Castoriadis, Cornelius. *World in Fragments: Writings on Politics, Society, Psychoanalysis, and the Imagination* (Stanford, Calif.: Stanford University Press, Werner Hamacher and David E. Wellbery, eds., 1997).

Curtis, Dennis E., and Judith Resnik. "Images of Justice." 96 *Yale Law Journal* 1727 (1987).

Durgnat, Raymond. *Durgnat on Film* (London: Faber and Faber, 1976).

Garvey, Megan. "Hollywood Back in D.C.'s Woodshed." *Los Angeles Times* (21 July 2001), p. A15.

Grey, Thomas C. "Langdell's Orthodoxy." 45 *University of Pittsburgh Law Review* 1 (1983).

The Movies on Trial: The Views and Opinions of Outstanding Personalities Anent Screen Entertainment Past and Present (New York: Macmillan, William J. Perlman, ed., 1936).

Valenti, Jack. "Valenti Testifies That Industry's Self-Regulation Best Help to Parents, Not Government Intervention." *Jack Valenti Press Releases* (Motion Picture Association of America, 25 July 2001).

Chapter 1: Legal Visibility

Andrew, Geoff. *"Anatomy of a Murder." TimeOut Film Guide* (London: Penguin, John Pym, ed., 9th ed., 2001).

Barnouw, Erik. *Documentary: A History of the Non-Fiction Film* (New York: Oxford University Press, 1993).

Chase, Anthony. *Law and History* (New York: New Press, 1997).

Cohen, Morris L. *Law: The Art of Justice* (New York: Macmillan, 1992).

Connor, Steven. *Charles Dickens* (New York: Basil Blackwell, 1985).

Crary, Jonathan. *Suspensions of Perception: Attention, Spectacle, and Modern Culture* (Cambridge: MIT Press, 1999).

Freedberg, David. *The Power of Images: Studies in the History and Theory of Response* (Chicago: University of Chicago Press, 1989).

Hegel, G. W. F. *Hegel's Philosophy of Right* (New York: Oxford University Press, T. M. Knox, trans., 1967).

Hollander, Anne. *Feeding the Eye: Essays* (New York: Farrar, Straus, and Giroux, 1999).

Jay, Martin. "Must Justice Be Blind? The Challenge of Images to the Law." *Law and the Image: The Authority of Art and the Aesthetics of Law* (Chicago: University of Chicago Press, Costas Douzinas and Lynda Nead, eds., 1999).

Kittler, Friedrich A. *Gramophone, Film, Typewriter* (Stanford, Calif.: Stanford University Press, 1999).

Levy, Leonard W. *The Palladium of Justice: Origins of Trial by Jury* (Chicago: Ivan R. Dee, 1999).

McCloskey, Robert G. *The American Supreme Court* (Chicago: University of Chicago Press, 2nd ed., 1994).

Presser, Stephen B., and Jamil S. Zainaldin. *Law and Jurisprudence in American History* (St. Paul: West Group, 2000).

Seagle, William. *The Quest for Law* (New York: Alfred A. Knopf, 1941).

Searles, Baird. *Epic! History on the Big Screen* (New York: Harry Abrams, 1990).

Stafford, Barbara Maria. *Good Looking: Essays on the Virtue of Images* (Cambridge: MIT Press, 1996).

Stephen, James Fitzjames. *A History of the Criminal Law of England*, vol. I (London: Macmillan, 1883).

Warren, Charles. *History of the Harvard Law School and of Early Legal Conditions in America* (New York: Lewis Publishing Company, 1908).

Chapter 2: Constitutional Foundation

Attie, Jeanie. "Illusions of History: A Review of *The Civil War*." *Radical History Review*, no. 52 (1992), pp. 95–104.

184   *References*

Auerbach, Jerold. *Unequal Justice: Lawyers and Social Change in Modern America* (New York: Oxford University Press, 1976).

Birnbaum's Walt Disney World (New York: Hearst Professional Magazines, Stephen Birnbaum, ed., 1991).

Brown, Joshua. "Into the Minds of Babes: Children's Books and the Past." *Presenting the Past: Essays on History and the Public* (Philadelphia: Temple University Press, Susan Porter Benson, Stephen Brier, and Roy Rosenzweig, eds., 1986).

Chase, Anthony. "Lawyers and Popular Culture: A Review of Mass Media Portrayals of American Attorneys." *Lawyers: A Critical Reader* (New York: New Press, Richard L. Abel, ed., 1997).

Christensen, Terry. *Reel Politics: American Political Movies from Birth of a Nation to Platoon* (New York: Basil Blackwell, 1987).

Davis, Mike. *Prisoners of the American Dream* (New York: Verso, 1986).

Fjellman, Stephen M. *Vinyl Leaves: Walt Disney World and America* (Boulder: Westview Press, 1992).

Fraser, George MacDonald. *The Hollywood History of the World* (New York: William Morrow, 1988).

Howard, Dick. "Why Return to the American Revolution?" *Thesis Eleven*, nos. 18–19 (1987–88), pp. 5–12.

Kammen, Michael G. *A Season of Youth: The American Revolution and the Historical Imagination* (Ithaca: Cornell University Press, 1988).

Kerber, Linda. "Consensus History, with Complications." *Radical History Review*, no. 42 (1988), pp. 18–23.

Klein, Norman M. *Seven Minutes: The Life and Death of the American Animated Cartoon* (New York: Verso, 1993).

Lawson, Robert. *Ben and Me* (Boston: Little, Brown, 1988).

Legal Papers of John Adams, vols. 2–3 (Cambridge: Harvard University Press, L. Kinvin Wroth and Hiller B. Zobel, eds., 1965).

Maltin, Leonard. *The Disney Films* (New York: Hyperion, 2000).

McGilligan, Patrick. "Thomas Jefferson Still Survives." *Velvet Light Trap*, no. 17 (Winter 1977) 57–63.

Moore, Barrington. *The Social Origins of Dictatorship and Democracy: Lord and Peasant in the Making of the Modern World.* (Boston: Beacon, 1966).

Mosley, Leonard. *Disney's World: A Biography* (New York: Stein and Day, 1985).

Parenti, Michael. *Make-Believe Media: The Politics of Entertainment* (New York: St. Martin's, 1991).

Schickel, Richard. *D. W. Griffith: An American Life* (New York: Simon and Schuster, 1975).

Searles, Baird. *Epic! History on the Big Screen* (New York: Harry Abrams, 1990).

Selway, Jennifer. "First Monday in October." *TimeOut Film Guide* (London: Penguin, John Pym, ed., 9th ed., 2001).

Smoodin, Eric. *Animating Culture: Hollywood Cartoons from the Sound Era* (New Brunswick: Rutgers University Press, 1993).

Therborn, Goran. "Reconsidering Revolutions." *New Left Review* (March–April 2000), pp. 148–53.

Thomas, Bob. *Walt Disney: An American Original* (New York: Hyperion, 1994).

Thomas, Evan. "Founders Chic: Live from Philadelphia." *Newsweek* (9 July 2001), pp. 48–51.

Unger, Roberto Mangabeira. *Knowledge and Politics* (New York: Free Press, 1985).

Wallace, Michael. "Visiting the Past: History Museums in the United States." *Presenting the Past: Essays on History and the Public* (Philadelphia: Temple University Press, Susan Porter Benson, Stephen Brier, and Roy Rosenzweig, eds., 1986).

Wallerstein, Immanuel. "The USA in the World Today." *The Politics of the World Economy* (New York: Cambridge University Press, 1984).

Watts, Steven. *The Magic Kingdom: Walt Disney and the American Way of Life* (Boston: Houghton Mifflin, 1997).

Young, Alfred E. "The Framers of the Constitution and the 'Genius' of the People." *Radical History Review*, no. 42 (1988), pp. 9–18.

Chapter 3: Criminal-Law Films

Bobbio, Norberto. *The Future of Democracy: A Defence of the Rules of the Game* (Minneapolis: University of Minnesota Press, 1987).

Cawelti, John. "*Chinatown* and Generic Transformation in Recent American Films." *Film Theory and Criticism: Introductory Readings* (New York: Oxford University Press, Gerald Mast and Marshall Cohen, eds., 3rd ed., 1985).

Chase, Anthony. "Popular Culture / Popular Justice." *Legal Reelism: Movies as Legal Texts* (Urbana: University of Illinois Press, John Denvir, ed., 1996).

Clarens, Carlos. *Crime Movies: An Illustrated History of the Gangster Genre from D. W. Griffith to Pulp Fiction* (New York: Da Capo, 1997).

Denning, Michael. *The Cultural Front: The Laboring of American Culture in the Twentieth Century* (London: Verso, 1996).

Estrich, Susan. *Getting Away with Murder: How Politics Is Destroying the Criminal Justice System* (Cambridge: Harvard University Press, 1998).

Fenster, Mark. *Conspiracy Theories: Secrecy and Power in American Culture* (Minneapolis: University of Minnesota Press, 1999).

Forbes, Jill. "*Germinal*: Keeping It in the Family." *Sight and Sound* (May 1994).

Goldberg, Harvey. Lecture at University of Wisconsin (8 December 1975).

Gomery, Douglas. *Movie History: A Survey* (Belmont, Mass.: Wadsworth, 1991).

Griffiths, John. "Ideology in Criminal Procedure; or, A Third 'Model' of the Criminal Process." 79 *Yale Law Journal* 359 (1970).

Haacke, Hans. *Framing and Being Framed: 7 Works 1970–75* (New York: New York University Press, 1975).

Hoberman, J. "Film: Blood Sports," *Village Voice*, January 2, 2001.

Jameson, Fredric. *The Geopolitical Aesthetic: Cinema and Space in the World System* (Bloomington: Indiana University Press, 1995).

———. "Reading Hitchcock." *October* (Winter 1982), pp. 15–24.

Kael, Pauline. "The Current Cinema: Marriages." *The New Yorker* (20 February 1989), pp. 95–96.

Masterpiece Theatre: A Celebration of 25 Years of Outstanding Television (San Francisco: KQED Books, Terrence O'Flaherty and Karen Sharpe, eds., 1996).

McGilligan, Patrick. *Clint: The Life and the Legend* (London: HarperCollins, 1999).

———, and Paul Buhle. *Tender Comrades: A Backstory of the Hollywood Blacklist* (New York: St. Martin's, 1997).

Oglesby, Carl. *The Yankee and Cowboy War: Conspiracies from Dallas to Watergate and Beyond* (New York: Berkley Medallion, 1977).

Parenti, Michael. *Make-Believe Media: The Politics of Entertainment* (New York: St. Martin's, 1991).

Petrey, Sandy. "Nature, Society, and the Discourse of Class." *A New History of French Literature* (Cambridge: Harvard University Press, Dennis Hollier, ed., 1989).

Rafter, Nicole. *Shots in the Mirror: Crime Films and Society* (New York: Oxford University Press, 2000).

Reeves, Richard. *President Kennedy: Profile of Power* (New York: Touchstone, 1994).

Rorty, Richard. *Achieving Our Country* (Cambridge: Harvard University Press, 1998).

Ryan, Michael, and Douglas Kellner. *Camera Politica: The Politics and Ideology of Contemporary Hollywood Film* (Bloomington: Indiana University Press, 1990).

Scheck, Barry, Peter Neufeld, and Jim Dwyer. *Actual Innocence* (New York: Doubleday, 2000).

TimeOut Film Guide (London: Penguin, John Pym, ed., 9th ed., 2001).

Tindall, George Brown, and David E. Shi. *America: A Narrative History* (New York: W. W. Norton, 4th ed., 1996).

Wallerstein, Immanuel. "The Agonies of Liberalism: What Hope Progress?" *New Left Review* (March–April 1994), pp. 3–15.

Williams, Rosalind. *Notes on the Underground: An Essay on Technology, Society, and the Imagination* (Cambridge: MIT Press, 1990).

Chapter 4: Civil-Law Films

Abramson, Jeffrey. "The Jury and Popular Culture." 50 *De Paul Law Review* 497 (2000).

Alloway, Lawrence. *Violent America: The Movies, 1946–1964* (New York: Museum of Modern Art, 1971).

Ewick, Patricia, and Susan Silbey. *The Common Place of Law: Stories from Everyday Life* (Chicago: University of Chicago Press, 1998).

Galanter, Marc. "Real World Torts." 55 *Maryland Law Review* 1093 (1996).

Grossman, Lewis A., and Robert G. Vaughn. *A Documentary Companion to "A Civil Action"* (New York: Foundation Press, 1999).

Haddad, Tonja. "Silver Tongues on the Silver Screen: Legal Ethics in the Movies." 24 *Nova Law Review* 673 (2000).

Mandel, Ernest. *The Formation of the Economic Thought of Karl Marx* (New York: Monthly Review Press, 1971).

McNair, James. "Company Pans Its Role in Movie: 'A Civil Action' Dredges up Boca Firm's Past." *Miami Herald* (30 December 1998), p. 1.

Rashke, Richard. *The Killing of Karen Silkwood: The Story Behind the Kerr-McGee Plutonium Case* (Boston: Houghton Mifflin, 1981).

Rustad, Michael. "Nationalizing Tort Law: The Republican Attack on Women, Blue Collar Workers, and Consumers." 48 *Rutgers Law Review* 673 (1996).

Sarat, Austin. "Exploring the Hidden Domains of Civil Justice: 'Naming, Blaming, and Claiming' in Popular Culture." 50 *De Paul Law Review* 425 (2000).

Schickel, Richard. "The Arts/Cinema: Conditional Knockout." *Time* (11 October 1999).

Shadoian, Jack. *Dreams and Dead Ends: The American Gangster/Crime Film* (Cambridge: MIT Press, 1977).

Solomon, Andrew. *The Noonday Demon: An Atlas of Depression* (New York: Scribner, 2001).

Spence, Gerry. *Give Me Liberty!* (New York: St. Martin's, 1998).

Chapter 5: International-Law Films

Arend, Anthony Clark, and Robert J. Beck. *International Law and the Use of Force* (London: Routledge, 1993).

Atkinson, Rick. *Crusade: The Untold Story of the Persian Gulf War* (Boston: Houghton Mifflin, 1993).

Brunette, Peter. *Roberto Rossellini* (New York: Oxford University Press, 1987).

Christensen, Terry. *Reel Politics* (New York: Basil Blackwell, 1987).

Frakes, Michael. "Film Review: *Three Kings*." *The Tech* (MIT) (13 October 1999).

Furst, Alan. *Dark Star* (Boston: Houghton Mifflin, 1991).

Gregg, Robert W. *International Relations on Film* (Boulder: Lynne Rienner, 1998).

Masterpiece Theatre: A Celebration of 25 Years of Outstanding Television (San Francisco: KQED Books, Terrence O'Flaherty and Karen Sharpe, eds., 1996).

Moore, Barrington, Jr. *The Social Origins of Dictatorship and Democracy: Lord and Peasant in the Making of the Modern World* (Boston: Beacon, 1966).

Rossellini, Roberto. *My Method: Writings and Interviews* (New York: Marsilio Publishers, 1992).

Steiner, Henry J., Detlev F. Vagts, and Harold Hongju Koh. *Transnational Legal Problems* (Westbury: Foundation Press, 1994).

Unger, Roberto Mangabeira. *Law in Modern Society: Toward a Criticism of Social Theory* (New York: Free Press, 1976).

Wallerstein, Immanuel. "The USA in the World Today." *The Politics of the World Economy* (New York: Cambridge University Press, 1984).

Westbrook, David A. "Law Through War." 48 *Buffalo Law Review* 299 (2000).

Chapter 6: Comparative Law

Abse, Tobias. "Judging the PCI." *New Left Review* (September–October 1985), pp. 5–40.

Anderson, Perry. *The Origins of Postmodernity* (London: Verso, 1998).

Borkin, Joseph. *The Crime and Punishment of I.G. Farben* (New York: Barnes and Noble, 1997).

Brunette, Peter. *Roberto Rossellini* (New York: Oxford University Press, 1987).

Cantor, Norman F. *Imagining the Law: Common Law and the Foundations of the American Legal System* (New York: HarperCollins, 1997).

Craig, Gordon A. *Germany: 1866–1945* (New York: Oxford University Press, 1978).

Deleuze, Gilles. *Cinema 2: The Time-Image* (Minneapolis: University of Minnesota Press, 1989).

DuBois, Josiah E., Jr. *The Devil's Chemists* (Boston: Beacon, 1952).

Eley, Geoff. "The Social Construction of Democracy in Germany, 1871–1933." *The Social Construction of Democracy, 1870–1990* (New York: New York University Press, George Reid Andrews and Herrick Chapman, eds., 1995).

Elsaesser, Thomas. *Fassbinder's Germany: History, Identity, Subject* (Amsterdam: Amsterdam University Press, 1996).

Erlanger, Philippe. *Louis XIV* (New York: Praeger, 1970).

Fischer, Fritz. *From Kaiserreich to Third Reich: Elements of Continuity in German History, 1871–1945* (London: Allen and Unwin, 1986).

Gallagher, Tag. *The Adventures of Roberto Rossellini* (New York: Da Capo, 1998).

———. "Roberto Rossellini and Historical Neorealism." *Artforum* (Summer 1975), pp. 40–49.

Gilbert, Martin. *The Second World War: A Complete History* (New York: Henry Holt, 1989).

Greenberg, Alan. *Heart of Glass* (Munich: Skellig Edition, 1976).

Harris, Thomas J. *Courtroom's Finest Hour in American Cinema* (Metuchen, N.J.: Scarecrow Press, 1987).

Insdorf, Annette. *Indelible Shadows: Film and the Holocaust* (New York: Random House, 1983).

Kramer, Stanley. *A Mad, Mad, Mad, Mad World: A Life in Hollywood* (New York: Harcourt Brace, 1997).

Lorenz, Juliane, ed. *Chaos as Usual: Conversations About Rainer Werner Fassbinder* (New York: Applause Theatre Books, 1999).

Marrus, Michael R. *The Nuremberg War Crimes Trial, 1945–46* (New York: St. Martin's, 1997).

Moore, Barrington, Jr. *The Social Origins of Dictatorship and Democracy: Lord and Peasant in the Making of the Modern World* (Boston: Beacon, 1966).

Palmer, R. R. *The Age of Democratic Revolutions: The Challenge* (Princeton: Princeton University Press, 1959).

Rayns, Tony. "*Heart of Glass*." *TimeOut Film Guide* (London: Penguin, John Pym, ed., 9th edition, 2001).

Rheuban, Joyce, ed. *The Marriage of Maria Braun.* (New Brunswick: Rutgers University Press, 1986).

Rude, George. *Europe in the Eighteenth Century: Aristocracy and the Bourgeois Challenge* (New York: Praeger, 1972).

Thomsen, Christian Braad. *Fassbinder: The Life and Work of a Provocative Genius* (London: Faber and Faber, 1997).

Unger, Roberto Mangabeira. *Law in Modern Society: Toward a Criticism of Social Theory* (New York: Free Press, 1976).

Wigmore, John Henry. *A Panorama of the World's Legal Systems*, 3 vols. (St. Paul: West Publications, 1928).

Woloch, Isser. *The New Regime: Transformations of the French Civic Order, 1780–1820s* (New York: W. W. Norton, 1994).

Womack, John, Jr. *Zapata and the Mexican Revolution.* (New York: Random House, 1970).

Chapter 7: Popular Culture and Realism

Ackroyd, Peter. *The Life of Thomas More* (New York: Anchor Books, 1999).

Ashton, Dore. *The New York School: A Cultural Reckoning* (Berkeley: University of California Press, 1992).

Bergman, Paul, and Michael Asimow. *Reel Justice: The Courtroom Goes to the Movies* (Kansas City: Andrews and McMeel, 1996).

Black, David A. *Law in Film: Resonance and Representation* (Urbana: University of Illinois Press, 1999).

Bogdanovich, Peter. *John Ford* (Berkeley: University of California Press, 1968).

Brantlinger, Peter. *Bread and Circuses: Theories of Mass Culture as Social Decay* (Ithaca: Cornell University Press, 1985).

Brewster, Ben. "Notes on the Text 'John Ford's *Young Mr. Lincoln*' by the Editors of *Cahiers du Cinema.*" *Screen Reader 1: Cinema/Ideology/Politics* (London: Society for Education in Film and Television, 1977).

Burger, Peter. *The Institutions of Art* (Lincoln: University of Nebraska Press, 1992).

———. *Theory of the Avant Garde* (Minneapolis: University of Minnesota Press, 1984).

Carnes, Mark C., ed. *Past Imperfect: History According to the Movies* (New York: Henry Holt, 1995).

Clarke, T. J. "Clement Greenberg's Theory of Art." *Pollock and After: The Critical Debate* (London: Routledge, Francis Frascina, ed., 2001).

———. *Farewell to an Idea: Episodes from a History of Modernism* (New Haven: Yale University Press, 1999).

Clover, Carol J. "God Bless Juries!" *Refiguring American Film Genres: History and Theory* (Berkeley: University of California Press, Nick Brown, ed., 1998).

———. "Judging Audiences: The Case of the Trial Movie." *Reinventing Film Studies* (New York: Oxford University Press, Christine Gledhill and Linda Williams, eds., 2000).

———. "Law and the Order of Popular Culture." *Law in the Domains of Culture* (Ann Arbor: University of Michigan Press, Austin Sarat and Thomas R. Kearns, eds., 2000).

Crow, Thomas. *Modern Art in the Common Culture* (New Haven: Yale University Press, 1996).

Denvir, John. *Legal Reelism: Movies as Legal Texts* (Urbana: University of Illinois Press, 1996).

Fiedler, Leslie. *What Was Literature? Class Culture and Mass Society* (New York: Simon and Schuster, 1982).

Greenberg, Clement. "Avant-Garde and Kitsch." *Collected Essays and Criticism: Perceptions and Judgments, 1939–1944*, vol. 1 (Chicago: University of Chicago Press, John O'Brian, ed., 1986).

Hobsbawm, Eric. *The Age of Extremes: A History of the World, 1914–1991* (New York: Pantheon, 1994).

Jameson, Fredric. *Signatures of the Visible* (New York: Routledge, Chapman, and Hall, 1992).

Kahn, Paul W. *The Cultural Study of Law* (Chicago: University of Chicago Press, 1999).

Karpf, Anne. Book review. *Media Culture and Society* (January 1987).

Lippard, Lucy R. *On the Beaten Track: Tourism, Art, and Place* (New York: New Press, 1999).

Milchman, Alan. Book review. *Socialism and Democracy* (Spring–Summer 1988), pp. 198, 203.

Neale, Stephen. *Genre* (London: British Film Institute Books, 1983).

Neve, Brian. *Film and Politics in America: A Social Tradition* (New York: Routledge, 1992).

Nochlin, Linda. *Realism* (London: Penguin, 1971).

Rosenberg, Norman. "*Young Mr. Lincoln*: The Lawyer as Super-hero." *Legal Studies Forum* 15, no. 3 (1991), pp. 215–31.

Rosenstone, Robert A. *Visions of the Past: The Challenge of Film to Our Idea of History* (Cambridge: Harvard University Press, 1995).

Ryan, Michael, and Douglas Kellner. *Camera Politica: The Politics and Ideology of Contemporary Hollywood Film* (Bloomington: Indiana University Press, 1988).

Sarris, Andrew. *The John Ford Movie Mystery* (Bloomington: Indiana University Press, 1975).

Scottoline, Lisa. "Get Off the Screen." 24 *Nova Law Review* 653 (Winter 2000).

Sklar, Robert. "Oh Althusser! Historiography and the Rise of Cinema Studies." *Radical History Review*, no. 41 (April 1988).

Sherwin, Richard K. *When Law Goes Pop: The Vanishing Line Between Law and Popular Culture* (Chicago: University of Chicago Press, 2000).

Vidal, Gore. *Screening History* (Cambridge: Harvard University Press, 1992).

Walsh, John E. *Moonlight: Abraham Lincoln and the Almanac Trial* (New York: St. Martin's, 2000).

Wollen, Peter. Afterword to *Screen Reader 1: Cinema/Ideology/Politics* (London: Society for Education in Film and Television, 1977).

Index